Amazing Grace for Mothers

Amazing Grace
for Mothers

101 Stories of Faith, Hope, Inspiration, and Humor

Edited by
Emily Cavins and Patti Maguire Armstrong
with Jeff Cavins and Matthew Pinto

ASCENSION PRESS

West Chester, Pennsylvania

Ascension Press
Post Office Box 1990
West Chester, PA 19380
Orders: 1-800-376-0520
www.AscensionPress.com

Cover design: Kinsey Caruth

Printed in the United States of America
11 12 13 7 6 5 4

ISBN 978-1-932645-26-2

To each of our mothers:

Alice Tobler
Julie Maguire
Trish Cavins
and
Barbara Pinto

Thank you for giving us life, for all the sacrifices you made, for the guidance you shared, and for the love you provided.

—Emily Cavins, Patti Maguire Armstrong,
Jeff Cavins, and Matthew Pinto

Contents

Introduction *1*

Chapter 1 – **A Mother's Love**

My Son the Matchmaker
Regina Rico Ferreira *3*

The Miracle of Theresa Rose
Elise McKeown Skolnick *8*

The Most Beautiful Word
Angilee Wallis *12*

The Mother
Joseph Cardinal Mindszenty *19*

Grit, Grace, and Goofy Grins
Patrick Coffin *20*

Three's the Charm
Jacque Tucker *26*

Just For Today
Anonymous *30*

Faith, Hope, and Love
Roxanne Reese *32*

The Gift of Dallas
Connie Gross *38*

A Halloween Angel
Debbie Farmer *42*

Duffy's Rose
Sean Patrick *45*

Chapter 2 – A Mother's Wisdom

Mother's Day
Daria Sockey. 51

Ballet Lessons
Elizabeth Foss. 54

When Jeff Met Mom
Emily Cavins. 57

Somebody Said
Anonymous. 60

Necessity Is the Mother of Invention – *cartoon*
Glenn Bernhardt. 62

Just Love Me
Gayle Bell. 63

Optimistic Antidotes
Patti Maguire Armstrong 65

A Lover of Frail Humanity
Fr. John Klockeman 68

Words to Live By
Various 73

Church Antics
Daria Sockey. 75

When Opportunity Calls
Phyllis Edgerly Ring 79

Chapter 3 – A Mother's Strength

The Healing Power of Love
Cindy Speltz 83

The Strength to Trust Again
Madonna Silvernagel 90

Help Is On The Way!
Eileen Braden *96*

Total Sacrifice
Joe Cunningham *100*

Mom's Faithfulness Until the End
Lynn Klika *105*

Bedtime
Anonymous *111*

No Rest For The Weary – *cartoon*
Glenn Bernhardt *113*

My Angel, Brianne
Stacey Carter *114*

We All Have Special Needs
Wendy Haefliger *119*

This Too Shall Pass
Jeanette E. Akin *123*

Motherhood Gave Me the Will to Live
Denise LeBlanc *127*

Chapter 4 – A Mother's Tears

For Just A Short Time
Brenda Vogsland *135*

No Longer a Child
Emily Cavins *139*

Cold News
Mary Lou Smith *142*

Thirty Minutes
Peggy Stoks *147*

The Long Road
Sharon Lee Wagner *152*

A New Saint in Heaven
Kathleen Miller. *158*

In Search of My Mother
Susan Handle Terbay *165*

The Freedom to Love All My Babies
Charnette Messe *168*

Please Hold Him for Me
Christine Trollinger. *174*

Tiny Handprint
Gretchen Thibault *177*

Chapter 5 – A Mother's Lighter Side

Planet Magazine
Daria Sockey. *183*

Dear Santa
Debbie Farmer *187*

Just Like Mother Used to Say
Patti Maguire Armstrong *189*

Holy Humor *191*

New and Natural Barbie
Debbie Farmer *193*

My Favorite
Barbara Winters Pinto *196*

A Grimy Greeting – *cartoon*
George B. Abbott *198*

Baby Gauge
Anonymous. *199*

Relish the Moment
Emily Cavins. *201*

Mother's Day Breakfast
Patti Maguire Armstrong 203

The Many Faces of Mom
Debbie Farmer 206

Test For Mothers
Patti Maguire Armstrong 208

Mom's Vacation – *cartoon*
George B. Abbott 212

A Mother's Prayer
Anonymous 213

The Mom Olympics
Danielle Bean 214

Chapter 6 – A Mother's Epiphany

What Adorable Children You Have
Kristin McGuire 217

Sunny Above the Clouds
Katrina J. Zeno 220

Coming to Sunday Dinner
Jean McGinty 222

The Most Important Job
Jeanne Gilbert 224

The Blessings I Almost Missed
Patti Maguire Armstrong 225

Words from Mother
Blessed Teresa of Calcutta 229

Lasting Legacy
Deb Kalmbach 230

A Mom's Workout – *cartoon*
George B. Abbott 233

Learning Patience in the Pews
Jackie Zimmerer 234

Jewels in My Crown
Anna Wind 236

Modern Mom - *cartoon*
George B. Abbott 241

For Mothers Who Stay
Kathleen R. Fitzgerald 242

A Luxury I Took for Granted
Marybeth Hicks 245

Surrendering to a Better Plan
Elizabeth Foss 248

Chapter 7 – **A Mother's Prayer**

A Cana Wedding
Christine Trollinger 251

A Modern-Day Monica
LaChita Calloway 255

Two Gifts
Maureen (Mo) Merritt Bergman 261

God's Answer
Cathy Tressider 265

I Know He Hears Me
Celia Sattler 267

The 21-Year Wait
Carrie Olson 271

Mary's Magnificat
Luke 1:46-55 276

Angel to the Rescue
Paulie Ruby 277

A Good Friday Blessing
Christine Trollinger. 279

Parent's Prayer
Mary L. Robbins 281

The Angel's Nudge
Elizabeth Matthews 282

Thank You For My Little Ones
Elizabeth Matthews 285

Witness to a Miracle
Rita Pastal. 287

Chapter 8 – A Mother's Blessing

Meeting My Daughter
Marsha Stocker 291

Miracles Can Happen
Brian J. Gail 296

Ten Minutes
Theresa Thomas 300

Keep On Giving
Deborah Harding 305

An Easter Miracle
Margie Doran 307

A Blessing, No Matter What
Kathy Smith 309

Hug of Faith
Mary Frovarp 314

What I Want to Be
Carly Cavins 316

Incomparable Joy
Emily Cavins. 317

For Love of Mom
Jay Copp 322

A Christmas Delivery
Bridget Robinson 328

Billy: A Family Story
Jay Copp 330

Casting My Cares on the Lord
Adrian McKee. 334

Five Miracles in One Day
Jody Murphy 338

Acknowledgments. 343
Editor and Contributor Contact Information 345
About the Editors 347

Introduction

Motherhood is a line of demarcation like no other. Regardless of all other aspects of a woman's life, this reality alone speaks volumes of her life and her heart. Motherhood also contains a coming of age factor—"before children" and "after children." Motherhood changes everything. And it does so forever.

Before motherhood, a good day was good and a bad day was bad. But now, even on a bad day, there is love deeper than the deepest ocean. Even if a day is hard to get through, there is always a reason to keep trying. On a good day, that means the richness of your world overflows with blessings. The love, the hugs, the precious one that calls you mommy... are gifts beyond measure.

This book is a treasure of mothers' stories. It is the sister laughing over a cup of coffee about the latest childhood antic. It is the friend revealing a miracle or the amazing grace that has gotten her through a struggle. It is a fellow mother sharing her joys, her sorrows, and her awe at the life children have created for her. And it is about God: His blessings, His guidance, His gift of grace.

Although the stories in this book cover a wide spectrum of motherhood, God's amazing grace is in each one. For He is the one who gives us the incredible gift of motherhood, and He is the one who can best lead us through its challenges.

When you get a moment...no, wait, what mother ever gets a moment? Rather, please take a moment from the tasks of your day to relish your motherhood. It is who you are and what you are, right down to your soul. It is your crowning glory. You are a mother because God deigned it to be so. He entrusted you with His precious treasures. So, enjoy these stories that will lift you up, strengthen you, sometimes make you cry, but always share the wonder and richness of who you are—a mother.

—Emily Cavins, Patti Maguire Armstrong,
Jeff Cavins, and Matthew Pinto

Chapter 1

A Mother's Love

My Son, the Matchmaker

"Mommy, where's my daddy?" my four-year-old son Jacob asked me. The question was a jolt to our leisurely Sunday afternoon walk together. I always knew the question would come one day, but I was not expecting it so soon.

"Dear God," I prayed, "help me find the words." How could I possibly explain to my young son the mistakes of my foolhardy past? His father, Carlos, and I had been dating only a month when I became pregnant. Since I had ignored the symptoms for at least three months, there was doubt as to whom the father was when I finally took a pregnancy test. I had gotten together with an old boyfriend for a one-night fling just before I began seeing Carlos.

Carlos was the first person that I told about the pregnancy. Although he understood that a paternity test would be needed to determine fatherhood, he was willing to stand by me. Unfortunately, as my pregnancy advanced, I realized that he was not willing to abandon the partying lifestyle we had previously both enjoyed. "You cannot keep doing this if you want to be a parent," I told him.

Yet Carlos continued with his wild lifestyle. I realized he was not ready to take on the responsibility of fatherhood. Carlos was present at Jacob's birth. "I don't care whose baby this is," he told me. "I will stay with you."

When the DNA test came back from the lab, I held the slip of paper tightly in my hand. Carlos *was* the father. But I wondered, "What kind of a father would he be?" Believing I had the best interest of my innocent newborn son at heart, I made a decision. "Carlos, you're not the father," I lied. "I think it will be best if we go our separate ways."

Life as a single mother was difficult, but my wonderful parents and two sisters stood by me. And thankfully, I had a loving, devout, Hispanic grandmother, who recognized the great spiritual void in my life. When Jacob was three, she finally succeeded in convincing my sisters and me to attend a parish mission and then a "Life in the Spirit" seminar. The Holy Spirit began working on us. By Pentecost Sunday— June 3, 2001—I was firmly on the path that led toward God. I had returned to the sacraments and fully embraced my Catholic faith. Although on the surface it seemed nothing in my life had changed, on the inside everything had changed. Prayer and my relationship with God became my guiding force.

So when Jacob asked about his dad, I had a newfound source of strength. I prayed for God to give me the words. "Honey," I began, "Your daddy is really a great guy, but when you were born I couldn't see that. I didn't used to pray to God for answers or go to church much, so I made a bad decision. I told your daddy to go away." Jacob stood motionless, carefully listening to my every word. "He doesn't really know about us, but if he did, I know he would be here for you all the time. I'm so sorry."

Jacob looked stunned. "Why didn't you let me meet him first?" he demanded to know.

"I made a huge mistake," I said. "I didn't understand what I was doing back then." I looked into his thoughtful little face. "Do you want to meet your daddy?" I asked.

After his quick nod, we put our hands together and prayed to God to help us find Jacob's daddy and make things right.

Now what? I asked myself. *How am I going to get myself out of this situation?*

It took four months and countless rosaries before I mustered up the courage to contact Carlos. One of my sisters joined me on the three-hour drive from Fort Lauderdale to Orlando. The entire drive was spent in prayer.

In Orlando, Carlos and I sat across from each other at a restaurant, my sister at my side. We did the usual small talk: "It's been a long time. What have you been up to?"

I shared my faith journey so Carlos would understand that I had become a very different person. "It's one of the reasons I'm here now," I explained.

There was a pause in the conversation. The thought flashed through my mind that I didn't have to go through with it. He didn't have to know. I looked at my sister. She nodded her head as if to say, "It's time."

I took a deep breath. "He *is* your son." I blurted out.

The blood drained from Carlos' face and he slumped back in his chair. He took a moment to collect himself and then said, "Gina, this is a huge bomb to lay on me. Why did you tell me he wasn't mine back then?"

"I'm sorry. I was an idiot and I wish I could take it back, but I can't." The lump in my throat ached. "You had every right to know and Jacob has every right to a father. I'm here to try to fix that relationship and I'm willing to do whatever you need me to do." I handed him a picture of his son. His shaking hands clutched the photo as he studied it in disbelief.

We agreed that I would bring Jacob to meet him the following weekend. When I returned home, I sat down with Jacob. I told him that I had found his dad and we would go together to meet him in five more days. Jacob gave me a nervous smile and said he thought he was going to cry. Carlos called me that same evening. I expected that by then he probably had worked himself up into anger with me. Instead, he asked me what cartoons Jacob liked and whether he had health insurance.

The following weekend we met at a park. As Jacob came down the slide, I pointed to a distant figure walking toward us. "There's your dad," I announced. I could see both Jacob and Carlos were nervous. "Let's go sit at a table," I suggested.

Jacob carefully studied his father and then blurted out, "Where have you been?"

"Remember, I explained to you that it wasn't his fault," I quickly intervened. We took a walk around the park. Carlos and I did most the talking while Jacob kept staring at his dad. Then we had dinner together at a friend's house and said good-bye. By evening, the strain was evident when Jacob had an uncharacteristic, wild tantrum. Luckily, Carlos was not there to witness it. I understood. Jacob and I held each other tightly, cried and prayed for strength.

By the next day, the awkwardness faded and we became more comfortable. The weekend visits continued and eventually included holidays. My heart warmed to see the joy my son experienced in the company of his dad. As Christmas approached the first year, I asked Jacob what we should get for his dad. His answer brought tears to my eyes: "A picture of me on top of a heart that was broken but now is fixed."

One day Jacob asked me to marry his daddy. "People don't just get married," I explained. "It's something that starts with friendship and grows into love until the two people decide they want to stay together forever." My explanation did not seem to register. I realized I could not expect a boy his age to understand all of this.

Shortly after this conversation, I informed Jacob that his daddy was going to move closer to our city. Jacob's reply was: "Good. The mistake in your heart is almost fixed."

Carlos and I began having long conversations on the phone. Soon, his visits were not just exciting for Jacob but for me as well. I began seeing what a brilliant gem Carlos was. He admitted to me that even though he had dated other women during the five years we were apart, he had never gotten me out of his mind. "I really don't want to marry anyone else," he told me one day.

So thanks to our son, the matchmaker, and his obvious cohort, the Holy Spirit, Carlos and I became man and wife on May 11, 2003. God surely heard the prayers of a child and healed our adult mistakes. We are now a loving family. And God's blessings just keep coming. We had the joy of welcoming a beautiful baby girl, Tess Abigail Ferreira, on January 20, 2004. We are so blessed.

—Regina Rico Ferreira

Regina Rico Ferreira lives in Ft. Lauderdale, Florida. She loves God, Mary, St. Paul, her family, and her CCD class. When not thanking God for the turn of events in her life, Regina tends to her new family and aspires to write children's books.

The Miracle of Theresa Rose

"She's alive!" the doctor announced, his voice filled with the same relief that Kathryn Rossi felt. But no first cry echoed through the delivery room. "I need a breathing tube!" the doctor shouted.

As her baby disappeared behind a wall of doctors and nurses, Kathryn and her husband, Robert, clasped hands. *Please*, the couple prayed, *our baby needs a miracle.*

Kathryn and Robert had been overjoyed when they learned they were expecting their fourth child. Their three older children were just as thrilled. "I feel like I've won a million dollars!" nine-year-old Anna exclaimed as Maria, six, and Thomas, four, beamed.

Yet, as blessed as she felt, Kathryn also felt achy and exhausted. Then, at twenty weeks, a routine blood test to check for chromosomal defects came back abnormal. Her doctor ordered an amniocentesis. Helpless and scared, Kathryn turned to prayer. "Watch over my baby," she prayed. Then, calling upon the saint noted for her love of children, she pleaded, "St. Therese, I need your help..."

Immediately, Kathryn felt calm. And the night before the test, Kathryn felt reassured that St. Therese had sent roses as a sign that her prayers would be answered. To Robert, it was just a fluke. The case of entirely white paper towels they had bought did not have entirely white rolls after all. The roll Kathryn opened had roses on it. Tears sprang to her eyes. "They say when St. Therese hears a prayer, she sends a rose to let you know," she said.

Yet, the amnio results were not what they had hoped for. "There is a problem with the placenta," the doctor began, explaining that it was not delivering the proper nutrients to the baby. There was no way Kathryn could carry the baby to term. They would wait as long as possible, but the doctor cautioned that most babies with this condition were born too small to survive.

"No!" Kathryn sobbed. She longed to believe it would turn out all right, but there was nobody to tell her so. Between ultrasounds, Kathryn would lie in bed, searching for some sign that her baby was still OK. Meanwhile, family and friends began sending flowers and cards. And though Kathryn had not told the story of St. Therese and the roses to anyone but Robert, in every bouquet, on every card, there was a rose. Even the ceramic angel her mother-in-law gave her was holding a rose—a surprise to even Robert's mom since the box had showed the angel's hands empty.

Could it be? Kathryn dared to wonder. Is God sending a message through St. Therese, letting us know our baby will live? But as Kathryn lay in the delivery room while doctors fought to save her baby, it looked doubtful. Any infant born at just 25 weeks would be dangerously tiny. But at fourteen ounces, Kathryn's baby was even worse off. She was only half the size she should be at that stage. And her lungs were so underdeveloped, she could not even cry, much less breathe.

"She's here," the doctor said. "That's a miracle in itself."

"Yes," Kathryn said. "We've come this far." Then she announced: "I'd like to name her Theresa Rose."

"It's perfect," Robert agreed.

But the doctor had grim news. "She's got a tough fight ahead," he said, ticking off a myriad of serious medical problems. Her chances of surviving were a mere five percent, and that was assuming she survived surgery.

"Surgery?" Kathryn asked. She learned that as soon as little Theresa Rose was stable, they would need to close a major vessel in her heart.

Just thinking about them opening her baby's tiny chest was unbearable. Kathryn placed a statue of St. Therese beside her. "You've brought her this far," Kathryn prayed, "Please, see her through the rest of the way."

On the day of the surgery, Kathryn tucked a picture of the saint in a nurse's pocket. "Her guardian angel," she explained to the nurse.

At two weeks old, Theresa Rose was the smallest baby the surgeon had ever performed this procedure on. It seemed impossible. But after the surgery, he announced, "She did great!"

There would be more surgeries to remove fluid from Theresa Rose's brain and to prevent her retinas from detaching. Looking at her daughter, Kathryn worried, "How much more can her little body take?" But then her eyes fell on the statue of St. Therese. "I really believe in my heart that you're hearing my prayers," Kathryn wept. "All the roses I've gotten...it's no coincidence. Please, God," Kathryn begged, "let me know I'm right."

The next morning, the doctor was shaking his head in astonishment. "I don't believe it!" he cried. "All of Theresa Rose's vital signs show marked improvement. There's just no explanation," he marveled. But there *was* one, Kathryn knew. Looking at the statue of St. Therese, she closed her eyes and breathed: "Thank you."

With every day, Theresa Rose grew stronger. Finally, after four and a half months the doctor announced, "You can take your daughter home."

"Here's your million dollars," Kathryn cried, handing Anna, Maria, and Thomas their baby sister.

Over the coming months, Theresa Rose bloomed just like her name. Today, about to turn four, she's a happy, healthy little girl. Watching Theresa Rose giggle and play with her big sisters and brother, Kathryn's eyes fill with tears. "Her name says it all," she sighs. "Theresa Rose is a miracle."

—Elise McKeown Skolnick

Elise McKeown Skolnick lives in Youngstown, Ohio, with her husband and two daughters. She is a reporter for The Business Journal *and has written for* Woman's World *magazine,* Hard Hat News, Female Forum, *and several newspapers. She enjoys reading, photography, and spending time with her family.*

The Most Beautiful Word

"Please God, let my son live," I pleaded during the hour-long drive to the hospital. All I knew was that Terry and his friend, Lowell "Chubs," had been in a terrible car accident early that Saturday morning in July of 1984. My son was just eighteen with a wife and beautiful six-week old baby girl, Amber.

Since we had no phone at that time, a neighbor had come over to tell me the hospital was trying to contact us. There had been a bad accident. My husband Jerry was out on errands with our other two sons, Perry and George, ages seventeen and ten. Terry's place was about a mile away, so I drove over to break the news to his wife, Sandy. Chub's wife was there also. With a car full of various family members, we sped off to the hospital in a panic.

A cloud of fear and disbelief hung over us all. We prayed unceasingly, pleading for the lives of Terry and Chubs. My shock prevented any tears.

I could not believe this was happening to us. We lived a simple but happy life in a modest, two-bedroom house in Marshall, Arkansas. The two youngest boys lived at home while my daughter, Tammy, and Terry both lived close by with their spouses. At the time, my husband Jerry worked as a mechanic. I had been employed at a shirt factory for eight years.

When we reached the hospital, we were told the boys had both been taken by helicopter to Springfield Hospital, a trauma center that was three hours away. We got back into the car for the longest drive of our lives.

At the trauma center, we were taken aside so medical personnel could prepare us. Terry had a brain stem injury.

This meant paralysis was a possibility. He had been given medication to reduce his brain swelling, but the swelling still continued.

"There will be machines and a lot of tubes," the nurse explained. "Terry has been given medication for pain and is not awake. It is possible he might be able to hear you, so it is very important that you remain calm. We do not want to upset him further in any way."

As I walked into the room and saw all the tubes and machines, my emotions spilled out. I quickly turned around and stepped back out. Shaking, crying, and gasping for air, I tried hard to get myself under control so I could go back in.

Taking deep breaths to calm myself, I walked over to Terry's bedside. Love and fear overwhelmed me as I looked at my son lying unconscious. Yet, seeing him gave me hope. The only physical sign of the accident was a cut over his eye that required three stitches. Terry's arms were twisting back and forth. "Isn't that good?" I asked the nurse when I saw his arms moving. "He can't be paralyzed if his arms are moving."

The nurse explained to me that twitching arms were a reaction to his brain swelling and it was not a good sign. I swallowed hard but could not stop my tears from flowing. I touched his hand and struggled to keep my voice steady. "Terry, hang in there. I love you and I'm going to be here for you," I whispered.

His wife also touched his hand and talked to him reassuringly. I looked at my boy who had always been so healthy and energetic, lying there with tubes going into him. *This can't be*, I thought. But I could not change reality. I could only pray that Terry would recover.

Chubs did not make it. It was still possible that Terry could die also. For several days the doctors tried in vain to stop his brain from swelling. And day after day the only word was: "We don't know what the extent of his injuries will be."

But whatever kind of life Terry would have, as his mother—the one who gave him life—I would be there for him. For weeks I slept on a couch in a waiting room. Jerry came often with the other kids. Together, we kept praying and reassuring Terry to hang in there.

After a few weeks, Sandy and I worked out a routine where we took turns being with Terry. Although visiting hours were over at 8 p.m., the nurses let us stay much later. After a couple months, they also let us sleep in the nurses' dorm next to the hospital.

Towards the end of October, the doctor told us that there was no longer any reason to keep Terry in the hospital. He was still in a coma, so he needed to be moved to a nursing home. I had not given up hope, but the doctors could do no more for him.

Terry was placed in a nursing home two hours away from our house. At this point, people started losing hope. Some questioned if perhaps it would have been better for Terry to have died in the accident. If he never came out of the coma, was my desire to keep him alive selfish? I did not want to let him go, and yet, what did Terry want?

I began asking God what He wanted. "Lord, I love Terry and I want You to heal him, but Your will be done," I started praying. "I trust in you, God." In the midst of my pain, I began to feel some peace. If Terry continued to live, it would be because God wanted Him to.

I returned to work, where I had been given a leave of absence, but I spent every other weekend at the nursing home. My mother and sister lived near by, so I often stayed with them or simply slept in a recliner in Terry's room.

As Christmas neared that first year after the accident, I could not imagine a family celebration without Terry. I wanted him home. Since he was still in a coma, there was great concern that this would be too difficult. I was scared but I was also determined; Terry needed to be home during Christmas.

Terry's feeding tube was removed shortly after Thanksgiving. I had watched the nurses feed him with a syringe and decided I could manage. Staff from the nursing home helped us carry Terry into the car. Family and friends helped us carry him into the house once we got him home.

In the familiar setting of home and surrounded by family and friends, loved ones came by to wish Terry a Merry Christmas. Everyone talked to him as if he were the old Terry. He was still in a coma, but I believed he had to know the difference between being in the nursing home and being at home. I could not prove it, but I felt it with my whole heart.

From that time on, we started bringing Terry home every other weekend. By the end of the next year, Terry was moved into a nursing home in Mountain View, which is the town where I work. I frequently stopped by to see him after work and we brought him home every weekend.

The months turned into years—five, ten, fifteen—and people saw no improvement. Terry's young wife had gotten on with her life. His daughter, Amber, only occasionally saw her father as she grew up. A few people questioned the wisdom of bringing him home every weekend but most of our family and friends supported us. It was a strain, but Jerry and I were united in our unwavering love for Terry.

Like a bud that blooms so slowly that its movement is imperceptible, Jerry and I felt that our son *was* opening up. It was so gradual, it escaped others. There were little things like a blink or a wink. One day, Terry laughed. And once Terry did something, he could continue to do it.

Driving with Terry in the car one morning, his head bobbed up and down after I asked him a question. I paid no attention, thinking it was the bouncing of the car that caused it. But Jerry cried out: "Look, he's answering you. He's shaking his head yes!" From that moment on, Terry was able to shake his head when asked a question. Later on, he started making the sound: "uh-huh."

Nineteen years after the accident, on Wednesday, June 11, 2003, I walked into Terry's room and said "Hi, Terry," as I always did. One of the nursing home aides asked him, "Who is that, Terry?"

"Mom," he answered clearly. I almost fell over I was so shocked. The aid and I looked at each other with the same astonished expressions on our faces. Tears of joy rolled down our laughing cheeks as we ran over and hugged Terry.

"Did you hear that?" I cried. "He said 'Mom!' Terry say that again!"

Terry laughed and again said the most beautiful word I had ever heard: "Mom."

Terry did not say another word that day, but after nineteen years, he had spoken! His one word was music to my ears, more incredible than his first "mamma" so many years before. We brought him home for a weekend visit that Friday. I kept asking him questions that he could answer with "Mom." Later that day, I got him to say "Pepsi."

On Saturday morning, I awoke to turn him over at 4 a.m., which was a necessary task. This was always a time when I would talk with him. Terry was mumbling.

"I know you are trying to tell me something," I said. "Just keep trying and I'll catch it," I told him. He kept struggling until "Mom and Dad" tumbled out.

"Say it again," I pleaded excitedly through my tears.

Terry repeated: "Mom and Dad."

"Terry, tomorrow is Father's Day," I cried. "When Dad gets up, we'll tell him what you can say. It will be his Father's Day present from you."

When Jerry got up, I could not contain my excitement. "Jerry, Terry has a Father's Day present for you," I said, escorting him to Terry's bedside. Then, very clearly, Terry spoke: "Mom and Dad."

Jerry is not one given to emotions, but tears glistened in his eyes. "That's the best Father's Day present I could have," he said.

For breakfast, I expected Terry to ask for Pepsi—his new word—when I asked him what he wanted to drink. Instead, he said: "Milk."

When a nurse at the nursing home learned of all Terry's words, she arranged for a speech therapist to visit Terry. "Angilee, I believe he will be speaking in full sentences within a week," she announced.

The next week, when I walked into his room, he was telling the people around him that his birthday was April 7, 1964. I laughed and hugged him then asked: "Terry, what else can you say?"

"Anything I want," he answered, laughing.

By the end of August we brought Terry home to stay. I quit my job to care for him full-time. His daughter Amber is nineteen now. She comes every day to spend time with her dad. She loves Terry just because he is her dad.

Terry is a quadriplegic as a result of the accident. Yet, many times he has told me, "I'm so happy." God wanted Terry to live and now I know Terry also wanted to survive. My family is still the center of my life, but God is also there with us.

My son's life is a miracle. I keep praying and trusting that God will continue to see us all through.

—Angilee Wallis

Angilee Wallis is home full-time to care for Terry and Jerry ranches to support the family. In spite of much media attention to this story, the Wallis family carefully guards their privacy. Their main concern is to provide good medical care and therapy for Terry's continued recovery, which is expensive and hard to come by. Donations to help Terry's recovery are greatly appreciated and can be sent to the Terry Wallis Trust at: www.terrywallisfund.org. *In the fall of 2004, a book about Terry Wallis' story,* Miracle at Mountain View *by Damon DiMarco, will be available in hardcover from Revolution Publishing.*

The Mother

The most important person on earth is a mother. She cannot claim the honor of having built Notre Dame Cathedral. She need not. She has built something more magnificent than any cathedral—a dwelling place for an immortal soul, the tiny perfection of her baby's body. The angels have not been blessed with such a grace. They cannot share in God's creative miracle to bring new saints to heaven. Only a human mother can. Mothers are closer to God the Creator than any other creature. God joins forces with mothers in performing this act of creation. What on God's good earth is more glorious than this: to be a mother.

—Joseph Cardinal Mindszenty
from the book The Mother

Grit, Grace, and Goofy Grins

I should have suspected something. In retrospect, the clues were absurdly obvious: the goofy grin; the sashay as she handed over the envelope; the fact that she'd just come from the doctor. The blare of Los Angeles traffic and talk radio still rang in my ears and I was even less "centered" than my usual distracted self as I opened the envelope. I asked my wife, Mariella, absently how her doctor appointment went. No, they don't call it masculine intuition.

She just nodded for me to open and read. "I'm only little right now," started the note, written in baby script. "But I can't wait to meet you, Daddy." That's all I could get out. Though I'd longed for the news with all my heart, for some reason I wasn't prepared for it. My eyes filled up, my throat grew a melon-sized lump, and the dining room began a surreal counter-clockwise spin.

I was going to be a father.

By God's ingenious design of marriage as a two-in-one bond, news of maternity is also news of paternity. We had lost our first pregnancy to a miscarriage some months before, a sad event that only intensified our desire for another baby. We knew Mariella had two physical abnormalities that indicated premature delivery: uterine fibroids or myomas (benign cysts in the wall of the womb) and a bicornate uterus (shaped like a bird in flight instead of a pear.) Just one of these conditions is a premature delivery risk; having both is a five-bell alarm. We didn't know that she also suffered from endometriosis and a rare hormonal dysfunction.

The pregnancy went swimmingly. At first. Then one Sunday, we took a walk in downtown L.A. to window shop. Returning to the car, Mariella suddenly went white and doubled over in pain. We rushed back to the car. I eased her into the passenger seat and inserted the key into the ignition. Nothing. The engine would not turn over. Mariella was now softly keening, rocking back and forth the way you do when you're trying to escape a pain that you know is inescapable.

A nearby gas station happened to have a mechanic there on a Sunday. We finally got home and called Mariella's ob-gyn, who told us to come in immediately. His diagnosis was terse and swift. "Mariella, you've started contracting," he said. "For the rest of your term you must quit your job, stay in bed 24/7, and be waited on hand and foot." I gulped.

She was only twenty-one weeks into her pregnancy. We were scared—fear injected with a thick dose of numbness. We tried home bedrest for a month. But things got worse— so much worse that our doctor handed over her medical care to his mentor, Dr. Khalil Tabsh, chief of perinatal medicine at UCLA-Santa Monica Medical Center and a specialist in high-risk pregnancies. Dr. Tabsh's specialty has earned him the nickname "Dr. Amnio." After doing an ultrasound, Dr. Amnio peered over his glasses and gave us a look that made us brace for the worst. "Mariella, starting this minute, you must begin full-time hospitalization," he intoned. "Get packed and meet me at UCLA-Santa Monica. Your cervix has already effaced by 80 percent." Near the end of a pregnancy, this would be great news; near the beginning, it's catastrophic.

So began our new relationship with dread. We drove straight from his San Fernando Valley office to the Santa Monica hospital room that would be my wife's address for God-only-knew how long. The dark cloud of miscarriage hung pall-like over us as we said our rosary beads, trying to absorb the concept of full-time hospitalization.

Hospitals are studies in acute ambiguity. They somehow instill simultaneous feelings of security and insecurity, of community and isolation. They are places of entry onto and exit from life's stage. If one's stay is simply for the sake of continuous observation, they can be more like a bad motel with no checkout time. Mariella's hospital routine was quickly set: unremitting boredom punctuated by emotional jolts, all within four unchanging walls.

Her early contractions returned in full force, and the hospital bed had to be locked in a reverse incline position to counteract gravity. Good-bye to the cross-stitching to bide the time. Adios to the window view of sunny Santa Monica. Farewell to reading in bed. Fetal monitoring sessions meant abrupt wake-up calls at 2 a.m. and 5 a.m., thus Mariella's last luxury—restful sleep—was taken from her. Well-meaning nurses dropped little comments, hinting at worst-case preemie scenarios, perhaps to provide motivation to hang in there. "Your baby could be born blind." "Your baby could have kidney failure/dysfunctional lungs/severe brain damage." "Your baby could die."

With each new bad turn, Mariella gained a level of courage and patience I can only call heroic. Amid mounting deprivations she endured the agonizing work of doing precisely nothing. How did she do it? I've asked myself a hundred times. Whereas I would have been loud and self-pitying—"Look at me! I'm stuck here! I'm lonely! Oh, the tragedy!"—she never complained. If I'd been sentenced to her circumstances, I would have flung myself out the window inside of a week. Not including the four-week home rest, Mariella took it for 70 days in the hospital.

Later, she told me that what kept her going was the interpretive choice to see the anguished waiting as a sacrifice for the hidden wee one. That decision changed the meaning of her suffering altogether. Looking back, I see that she was already in possession of a great secret: love without sacrifice is sentimentality and sacrifice without love is masochism. Not prone to being talkative about her faith, she seemed to embrace each new deprivation in light of Christ's suffering. And she did it in a distinctly Marian way: hidden and humble, though far from passive. Early on she had bonded with our hidden treasure and was prepared to undergo whatever it took to bring him or her to light. When she crossed the 25-week gestational mark, we prayed for 26 weeks; at 29, we prayed for 30. When we crossed the 30-week line, we prepared ourselves for the inevitable premature delivery that could come at any minute.

It did not come. Upon passing 35 weeks, Mariella was released from the hospital. Three more weeks went by. A lot of medical heads were scratched. Finally, on September 23rd, 2002, at 10 p.m. sharp, tears of pain became tears of joy. Our hidden treasure had arrived.

After all my wife had already been through, complete with atrophied muscles due to months of immobilization, Mariella declined all pain medication during labor; she wanted to stay as alert and present to the baby as possible. Mariclare Sarah Coffin drew her first breath—at full term—missing a perfect APGAR score by just a tick. Dr. Tabsh pronounced the baby a miracle, and the mother a prizefighter. She was named Mariclare in honor of our Blessed Mother and St. Clare of Assisi, and Sarah as a grateful nod to the wife of Abraham, the Old Testament patroness of implausible pregnancies. Today, Mariclare is an unusually happy, secure little girl whose entry into life was the fruit of her mother's prayer-soaked, sacrificial waiting.

Witnessing her mother's sacrifice has made me think hard about mothers and motherhood, and Scripture's references to them. In Isaiah 49:15, for instance, the prophet asks, "Can a woman forget her sucking child, that she should have no compassion on the son of her womb? Even these may forget, yet I will not forget you." The Lord contrasts His care here not with a father's love but with a mother's. Our Heavenly Father tells us that His divine grace "out loves" even the intense earthly bond of mother and child.

There are exceptions, but in the suffering department men are the microwaves, women the slow-cookers. Male nature seems to incline toward quick heroism, often daring and dramatic. One thinks of taking a bullet in battle, breaking an athletic record, or getting speared by pygmies. But female nature seems to favor a more sustained form of heroism, a capacity to bear what Blessed Mother Teresa of Calcutta called the "white martyrdom" of loving service. Mariella's 70-day white martyrdom was a vivid reminder that the term "deadbeat mom" does not exist.

The co-redemptive work, so to speak, of the Blessed Mother at Calvary also came to mind. She, who was prophesied in Genesis 3:15 to usher in Christ's new life through the "enmity" between herself and Satan, consented in her heart to her Son's suffering and death during a cataclysmic moment of maternal pain. But her pain, and His, was our gain. All mothers are extended a unique share in this mysterious redemptive pattern. Fathers can only stand by and marvel, and, if they're smart, they are grateful for the example of selflessness they witness.

Mariella was recently operated on by Dr. Thomas Hilgers, M.D., director of the Pope Paul VI Institute in Omaha, Nebraska. As a result, the fibroids are gone and the endometriosis is gone, leaving only our hope for more diaper-clad treasures. Pope John Paul II, from whose hand we received the newlywed blessing in Rome, wrote that the greatest possible gift for a child is a new brother or sister. Buoyed daily by Mariclare's goofy grin, we're on the case.

—Patrick Coffin

Patrick Coffin was born in Nova Scotia and educated at Mount Saint Vincent University in Halifax, McGill University in Montreal, and earned a master's degree in theology at Franciscan University of Steubenville in Ohio. He has been writing and speaking about the impact of the Catholic faith on culture for twelve years. The Coffins live in Los Angeles.

Three's the Charm

"I can't…I'm sorry," I sputtered, fumbling for the words to explain why I could not attend a baby shower. As I hung up the phone, I burst into tears. "I should go," I thought, "but if I see one more pretty bib or a mobile of teddy bears, my heart will break."

For years, my husband, Mike, and I had been trying to have a baby. As our dream seemed to fade from reach, I sank into despair. As a teenager, I did not worry that I never got a period. Doctors found nothing wrong with me and, at that time in my life, having a family was not on my mind. But in my twenties, after I fell in love and married Mike, I began consulting fertility specialists. Mike and I were so happy together, we yearned for a baby to complete our family.

This time, doctors found out why I never menstruated. My ovaries did not produce follicles, which meant my eggs failed to ripen and were never released. Once I had a diagnosis, the doctor worked on a treatment. I began a program of hormone pills and shots. Each day I went for a sonogram to see if follicles were growing. I also took my temperature daily to see if I was ovulating.

One morning, I excitedly dialed Mike at work on a commercial fishing boat. "My temperature is high," I announced. It looked very possible that I could be fertile.

"I'll be there," Mike promised. It was three hours to shore and one more by plane, but Mike made it home. Still, I did not get pregnant—not that month, or the next, or the next. The ache I felt each time the doctor said, "I'm sorry," soon became as familiar as my tears.

Every birth announcement, every mom with a stroller, every diaper ad was a painful reminder. It was as if everyone in the world was having a baby except me.

Finally in 1984, after three years of heartbreak, Mike said, "You've gone through enough. Let's adopt."

"He's right," I thought sadly. "Maybe it's just not meant to be. Besides, I do not have to give birth to a baby to love it." Before long an agency called to announce they had a baby for us. Mike and I refinished an old cradle and started studying baby-name books. We waited anxiously for the call that could come "any day."

But the call that came was not what we had prayed for. The birth mom had changed her mind. Mike comforted me as I sobbed with disappointment. "We just have to be patient," he said.

Then, in 1986, we brought home a baby at last—a nine-month-old baby girl named Robin. Born with a heart defect, Robin would need surgery and plenty of care. I did not mind. I was a mom at last! I would give my new angel all the love and care she needed to get better. But one night, just a month after I became Robin's mommy, I had to rush her to the hospital. She would die there of cardiac arrest.

"There was nothing you could have done," the doctor insisted. His words were useless to me; I was beyond consolation. I wanted so much to be a mother but I failed at every turn. Mike and I turned to counseling and to God. Slowly, I let go of my grief and put my life in God's hands. I grew stronger. I told Mike I wanted to try adoption again. At first he was leery of all the emotional ups and downs of waiting, but I assured him I was strong enough now to handle whatever God allowed to happen. Within a few months we welcomed a healthy, five-month-old baby boy into our home—Kyle.

Now, I looked no further than my own backyard for joy. God had blessed us and our family was complete. Our love now encompassed a precious little boy—a child of our own! Four years later my love doubled. A friend who was single and pregnant told me she wanted us to adopt her baby. She told us she thought we were wonderful parents and hoped we would give her baby a home. Tears welled in my eyes to think that she thought I was a good enough mother to give me another child—her very own—to raise.

With my two boys, Kyle and Curtis, to fill my days and heart, my dreams had come true beyond my wildest imagination. "I feel so honored to have my family," I wrote in my diary.

Then, in 1994, I came home from a vacation in Hawaii feeling queasy and tired. When I could not shake it after a couple weeks, I went to my doctor who ordered some blood work done.

"You are pregnant," he told me.

"Yeah, right," I responded, refusing to take his words seriously. I knew he was wrong on this one. I was almost 41 years old now. Yet somehow his words touched me deep in my heart. It was what I had longed to hear for so long, but had finally accepted it would never be. The doctor insisted on scheduling an ultrasound. My heart started pounding so loud, I thought he could hear it. "OK," I agreed. "But there is no way I am pregnant."

I insisted to Mike that evening, "They will see it's a mistake." Mike just kept telling me to wait and see. After all we had been through, neither one of us dared even imagine this could be possible.

The next day, Mike and I gasped as the ultrasound screen lit up. There was a tiny form with a tiny heart beating away. Mike and I looked at each other and cried tears of joy. A baby after all these years! I never imagined it in my wildest dreams.

On October 3, 1995, our little girl entered the world. We named her Kalani Faye, Hawaiian for "little princess" and "trust in God."

Today, my once empty home could not be busier—and I love it. I never stop thanking God for trusting me enough to send me three such beautiful blessings.

—Jacque Tucker

Jacque and Mike Tucker have been married for twenty years. They live in Anchorage, Alaska, and are very active in their church. Jacque is a stay-at-home mom, teaches a swim aerobics class, and works part-time at her kids' school. Kyle is now 17, Curtis is 12, and Kalani is 8.

Just For Today

Just for this morning, I am going to step over the laundry, and pick you up and take you to the park to play.

Just for this morning, I will leave the dishes in the sink, and let you teach me how to put that puzzle of yours together.

Just for this afternoon, I will unplug the telephone and keep the computer off, and sit with you in the back yard and blow bubbles.

Just for this afternoon, I will not yell once, not even a tiny grumble when you scream and whine for the ice cream truck, and I will buy you a treat if he comes by.

Just for this afternoon, I won't worry about what you are going to be when you grow up, or second-guess every decision I have made where you are concerned.

Just for this afternoon, I will let you help me bake cookies, and I won't stand over you trying to fix them.

Just for this afternoon, I will take us to McDonald's and buy us both a Happy Meal so you can have both toys.

Just for this evening, I will hold you in my arms and tell you a story about how you were born and how much I love you.

Just for this evening, I will let you splash in the tub and not get angry.

Just for this evening, I will let you stay up late while we sit on the porch and count all the stars.

Just for this evening, I will snuggle beside you for hours, and miss my favorite TV shows.

Just for this evening when I run my finger through your hair as you pray, I will simply be grateful that God has given me the greatest gift ever given.

I will think about the mothers and fathers who are searching for their missing children, the mothers and fathers who are visiting their children's graves instead of their bedrooms, and mothers and fathers who are in hospital rooms watching their children suffer, and screaming inside that they can't handle it anymore.

And when I kiss you good night I will hold you a little tighter, a little longer. It is then that I will thank God for you, and ask Him for nothing, except one more day.

Faith, Hope, and Love

The altar server genuflected, snuffed out the candles, and returned to the sacristy after the funeral Mass of my father-in-law. Outside the church, small orange flags tied to each of the vehicles of the funeral procession crackled back and forth in the cold spring wind.

My husband stood with our four sons at the back of the church, along with his sisters and brothers gathered by their mother's side. Seizing a moment of quiet, I slipped into a back pew with the weights of anxiety and sorrow pulling my knees down to the kneeler.

Silently I prayed to my husband's deceased father, "OK, Frank. I am not going to let you rest on your laurels. I need you to pray for me. You see, twenty-five years ago, before I married your son Tom, I gave birth to a baby boy. I never had the privilege of raising him, because I gave him up for adoption." I had never told my father-in-law about this because society and those around me had told me to get on with my life and to forget. The truth is that I never forgot. A mother does not forget. "Pray for me, Frank, and for my firstborn child. We have started corresponding through the adoption agency and I want it to turn out okay."

I hurried after my family as they exited, grabbing a few of Grandpa Frank's funeral prayer cards on the table by the door. I intended to place one in our family Bible, a tradition that I learned from my Irish grandmother.

My husband had been supportive of me contacting my first son. My initial call to the agency felt like a kick in my stomach when the social worker reported that my file contained no letters or updates. But finally after four years the agency informed me that my son had written of his intent to contact me. My emotions spun me around. For so many years I had tried to push the memory of losing him under the surface of my conscious awareness. Now the idea of contact with him brought a thrill and terror all together. When I received his first letter, it contained a photo of him. He looked more like me than did my other boys. He definitely had my hair.

Since the day I had last seen my son, I began the habit of searching the face of every boy near the age my son would have been at the time. Having no idea where my son had been placed, he could have been the lad on the swings, the boy in the car next to me, the teen grocery carryout, or the lector at church. Now that I knew how he looked, I still found myself studying each young man's features. I had to remind myself, "You have found him! You know what he looks like!"

As summer vacation arrived, I found myself checking daily for a second letter from my son. It was like waiting for labor to begin. I wrote him a purposefully short note just to let him know that I was thinking of him, but I did not want to place any pressure upon him to respond until he might be ready.

While writing I glanced at my hand and realized I hadn't worn my Claddaugh ring for a while. The ring, a gift from my husband, bears a crown, heart, and a pair of hands, which for me symbolized faith, hope, and love. I would have to search for the ring later.

On July 5, I received my second letter from my son, and I was ecstatic. He stated that he wanted to exchange identifying information. I would finally know his full name and where he lived and vice versa. I hoped that he would want to know me.

Christmas came three months early for me when on September 25th my son released his identifying information to me. We corresponded though email and decided to phone one another. When we spoke for the first time on the phone I listened intently to his adult voice, trying to memorize it; I was finally able to let it sink down into the atrophied part of my brain where once his baby voice sang.

My birthday falls about a week before Halloween. My husband brought home a cake for me. As I blew out the candles, my wish was really a prayer: if it's God's will, let me see my son before the close of the year. Smoke from the cake candles twirled up to the kitchen ceiling as the phone rang. It was my son calling to wish me a Happy Birthday and to invite me to see him in three weeks!

Three weeks had to pass before I flew out to see my son "again for the first time." My skin did not feel like it would contain my being. I literally had trouble breathing at times. There were too many emotions to identify, but I counted each day until I could see my son's face. Merging the face of my infant with the photo I had of this grown man was a difficult task.

I was planning to bring my son a gift, my Claddaugh ring. I had worn it on my hand for most of his life, and it represented my Irish heritage and that of his father's. Panicking that I would not find my ring, I ransacked every spot where I might have stashed the ring on the day I had caught my four-year-old playing inside the closet. In my frenzy I opened a silver gift box with the word's "love, love, love" on the top. There it was! With a sigh of relief, I placed the ring into a gift box and pressed an embossed golden Claddaugh seal onto its top.

Two days before my flight, I received a lovely email from my son stating that he was looking forward to my visit. He closed with part of 1 Corinthians—love is patient, love is kind—I held tight to the words about patience because I found myself insanely impatient to see his face again.

Also, I was having doubts about giving my son such a personal gift at our first meeting. I worried that he might be offended. I didn't want him to feel any obligation to accept a gift from me.

The day before my flight, I was still undecided and anxious about the gift of the ring. I opened my Bible to 1 Corinthians to find the last part of that verse about faith, hope, and love in order to copy it into a gift enclosure note. I was instantly relieved of my doubts about giving him this particular gift when I found Grandpa Frank's obituary tucked right between the pages containing 1 Corinthians 13: 13, "So faith, hope, love abide, these three; but the greatest of these is love." At that moment, I knew Grandpa Frank was praying for us.

My husband drove me to the airport for my three-day trip. "Go hug your son," he said with an encouraging smile as he dropped me off. With a hug and kiss from Tom, I hurried on my way. As the plane lifted up over a large military cemetery, I looked down at the rows of white markers. My son's biological grandparents were both buried there and I asked them to pray for me, to. I kept my composure through the flight, but tears began to pour as we landed. I headed for the baggage area to meet him.

My son! There he was! I approached him slowly and deliberately to hug him. "You do look like me!" I gasped, looking as closely as I dared. I clasped his hands and gazed at them. His fingers were long just as they had been the last time I had held the then tiny hands. I pressed my lips to his hands with his consent.

"I need to sit down," I said, overcome with emotion. The moment was here I had always wished for but for which I had never really dared to dream over all those years. No longer did I have to live in denial. I could now take a baby step over the grief and fear of rejection from my son to try to build a relationship.

I spent three amazing—and to me, miraculous—days with my son. I was in shock most of the time. Just before I boarded the plane to return to Minnesota, I gave my son the ring along with the little note to explain to him its history and symbolism. He appeared pleased with this gift.

Since then my son and I have been able to spend several other times together. Always, the trips involve much preplanning and travel because of the 2,000 miles between us.

During one of my visits to see him, we went to one of his favorite beaches. It seemed strange to me that for our first trip to the beach together, my grown son was the one to drive us there, and he was the one to show me the pathway to the shoreline and to tell me where to put my shoes down next to his much larger ones.

While standing with him on the beach, I believe that for one moment I experienced a little bit of heaven. For just one moment, time became totally irrelevant. We were simply together, my son and I, standing in silence and awe of the Creator's beauty around us. For one moment, the separation of years and miles between us burned away until the beat of the waves brought me back to this everyday, earthly sense of time.

My son, a musician and sometime surfer, told me that ocean waves rush to the shore in rhythms of three. Since the reconnection with my son, at times emotional waves crash into me and knock me completely prostrate. There are no phases of the moon to observe and warn me of these rising tides not only of joy, amazement, and peace but also of grief, pain, and fear. I like to think that in some mysterious way, the undercurrents which drive forward such waves of grief, pain, and fear can be overcome with three much more powerful forces: faith, hope, and the greatest of these, love.

—Roxanne Reese

Roxanne Reese lives in Minneapolis, Minnesota. She is married and the mother of five sons. She is employed by the public school system and continues to write during the off hours. Some of her essays and poems have been published locally.

The fruit of Silence is prayer.
The fruit of Prayer is faith.
The fruit of Faith is love.
The fruit of Love is service.
The fruit of Service is peace.

—Blessed Teresa of Calcutta

The Gift of Dallas

"He has cystic fibrosis," the doctor solemnly told my husband, Jeff, and me. "There is no cure."

Even though Dallas had been big and healthy at birth, we always knew there was something not quite right with our first-born son. He had struggled to gain weight from the start. Even at eight months, Dallas still weighed less than thirteen pounds. Yet, he always had a good appetite. He was pale looking, but I blamed his blondish hair and fair complexion for that.

Jeff and I listened in shock. He needed four treatments a day to loosen up his phlegm and clear his lungs. His eleven different medications would be expensive. It was December 11, 1973, when the expected lifespan of a child with CF was just sixteen years.

As the oldest of twelve children, caring for babies had always come naturally to me. I had married right out of high school, but Jeff and I agreed that we wanted as many children as God would send us. But now I wondered: "Can I even take care of my own baby anymore?"

Since CF was genetic, the doctor told us there was a twenty-five percent chance per pregnancy that any future child would have it. Now we wondered if a large family still made sense. Our prayer life and faith in God was strong. We agreed to trust in Him. Jeff and I practiced Natural Family Planning as a way to space our children, knowing that each one might need extra care. The realization that any child born to us might not reach adulthood had no bearing on our decision to be open to life. The souls of our children were destined for eternity. Yes, early separation from them would be painful, but it would not diminish their eternal value. When Dallas was three, we welcomed our daughter, Taunia, into our family. Her robust health reassured us that she had not inherited the disease.

Caring for Dallas was a labor of love, but his slow physical development brought additional worries. He did not walk until he was almost two and he fell a lot. The doctor suggested it could be a Vitamin A deficiency causing weak muscles. His coordination remained poor for years. When Dallas was five, our doctor referred us to a neurologist. A muscle biopsy revealed he had a Duchennes muscular dystrophy—the worst kind.

Sitting across from the doctor's grave face, my mind felt numb. "Didn't my poor son have a big enough cross to carry? Why this, too?" I thought. But as I listened to the doctor's grim prognosis, I felt God giving me strength. I had to be strong for my son's sake.

The more negative the doctors were, the more stubborn I felt inside. "We are going to take good care of him," I said determinedly. "And maybe there will be a cure one day." Jeff and I believed that all children were valued in God's eyes. We would remain open to His blessings.

Later on, when our doctor became angry with us upon learning we were expecting our third child, she told us the baby could be tested and aborted if found to have CF or MD. Jeff got upset. "We are going to have this baby and take care of it no matter what," he said.

We were not always so strong, however. Sometimes holding my fragile son in my arms, I cried knowing that we would lose him in a few short years. We wanted a cure or a miracle, but at no point did we refuse to accept God's will.

Taunia was nine years old when our third child was born. "It's a boy," the doctor announced. Our hearts sank. We had been told there were 100 percent odds that any of our boys would inherit MD and die before the age of sixteen. Matthew, however, fooled everyone. He was completely healthy. Three years later, Katie joined our family and tested positive for CF. To me, fifteen years after the first diagnosis, CF no longer seemed so bad. Treatments had improved and life expectancy was now into the forties.

Dallas grew into a loving, bright child with many friends. In spite of his hardships, he was always cheerful. My other children adored their big brother and spent many hours going for walks alongside him, playing, joking and just talking with him. When Dallas began to fall a lot at school, other kids readily helped him up. He was never teased. By the age of ten, Dallas's increased muscle weakness forced him into a wheelchair.

By the time Dallas was thirteen, he needed help lifting his books and going to the bathroom. This period of his life was often very difficult. I watched kids his age running around with their friends, while Dallas returned home, did physical therapy with me and lay on the couch until dinner. Toward the end, friends often came by to play games with him, but I sometimes felt that life was not fair. When Dallas was a child, age sixteen seemed so far away. While his CF had been kept under control, the MD was quickly taking him away from us.

One weekend, we both knew the end was close. Jeff had often talked with Dallas about death not being something to fear. "We will all be together again eventually," he had explained. "And in heaven, with God, you will always be happy."

His doctor came by on Sunday morning and confirmed that it would not be long. That afternoon the other kids were at their grandparents while Jeff and Dallas watched the Minnesota Vikings play the Chicago Bears on TV. Jeff was rooting for the Vikings and Dallas was cheering for the Bears. Suddenly, Dallas could not breathe. Jeff held Dallas in his arms. "Don't be scared," Jeff said softly. "Just ask Jesus to take you home. Don't fight it. Don't hold back."

I sat near Dallas and prayed. I was scared that this was it, but I did not want my son to suffer anymore. "Jesus, take him and take care of him," I cried.

Dallas passed away on September 17, 1989, shortly before the game ended. We wrapped him in a blanket, held him and cried. I called a priest who came to give him last rites. Then we realized that the TV was still on and the Bears had won. "Oh, you stinker," Jeff laughed through his tears. "You're in heaven now and your team won."

It was hard when the undertaker came and took him from our arms. When the other children came home and discovered their brother was gone, they all grieved in different ways. It was Matthew who said, "He is in heaven now, we should be happy for him, not sad for ourselves."

Fourteen years have passed. My other children appreciate the value of all life. They would have absolutely chosen life with their brother, who was destined to die early, rather than to have lived without him. He made us all better people than we would have been if he had never been born. And now, we know someone in heaven who is praying for us and will be there to greet us one day.

—Connie Gross

Connie Gross and her husband, Jeff, have four children: Dallas (their angel in heaven); Taunia, who is married to Sheldon Welch and has two children; Matthew, married to Michelle; and Katie. Connie runs her own home daycare business.

A Halloween Angel

Halloween is the scariest holiday of the year, especially at my house. From the first week of October, I live in sheer terror of my young daughter asking for a homemade costume. Ghosts, ghouls, and goblins don't strike fear into my heart as much as the electric torture device known as "The Sewing Machine." The last time I saw mine, it was holding up the back end of my husband's car while he changed the tire.

"I want you to make me into Cinderella at the ball," my daughter announced on schedule.

"How about a ghost, or something else with one seam?" I pleaded.

"Cinderella," she insisted, "with lace, puffy sleeves, and lots of jewels!"

I envied the other mothers on the block who diligently sewed their children's costumes each year. They could make ten Cinderellas and a fairy godmother in the time it took me to load the dishwasher. Throughout October, the street was filled with the hum of sewing machines coming from every direction but mine.

"Why go to all of the trouble," my husband asked, "when you can buy her a nice costume at the mall?"

"All the other mothers in the neighborhood make them," I said. "It's like having a homemade cake at your birthday party instead of a grocery store special."

"Remember last year, when you used the stapler and her halo kept poking the back of her head and her angel wings blew off into the gutter?" he asked.

"She looked very cute while it lasted," I said, "and I enjoyed making the costume." I paused, "But the last time I turned the sewing machine on, it trapped my sleeves under the bobbin and stitched a seam up my right arm before I could pull the cord out of the wall with my foot."

I drummed my fingers on the counter and bit my lower lip. Then I realized the angel gown was still hanging upstairs in my daughter's closet.

The next day I found it and dyed the white cloth pink and closed the wing holes with masking tape. I added lace to the front with a glue gun and stuffed the shoulders with tissue, then expanded last year's halo into a tiara and sprinkled a stick from the backyard with glitter for a magic wand. I carefully hung my creation back in my daughter's closet and hoped everything would stick together until next week.

On Halloween it took twenty minutes to seal my daughter into her costume.

"I'm beautiful!" She twirled in front of the hall mirror.

"Just like Cinderella?" I asked.

"No," she said, "just like you." She kissed me on the cheek.

I was going to hand out candy this year while my husband chaperoned the trick-or-treating, so I stood in the doorway and watched them walk down the front steps. They only got to the end of the driveway before I saw two strips of masking tape flapping in the wind, the lace beginning to peel, and a wad of tissue working its way out of the right sleeve, but my daughter was laughing and happily waving her wand.

"I love you, Mommy!" She turned and blew me a kiss. Underneath all of the tape and glue Cinderella was still my angel. "See!" I wanted to shout to my husband, "This is the reason I go to all the trouble!" But, I just blew two kisses back and hoped my labor of love would hold together through the night, or at least until she got the first bar of chocolate.

—Debbie Farmer

Debbie Farmer is an internationally syndicated newspaper columnist and author of Don't Put Lipstick on the Cat! *(Windriver Publishing, 2003). Her essays have been published in* Reader's Digest, Family Circle, The Washington Post, Family Fun Magazine, *and hundreds of regional parenting magazines. Visit her website to sign up for her free e-column:* www.familydaze.com

Duffy's Rose

Mama never forgot her "other" son.

Mama kept the items that meant something special in a box labeled "Fanny Farmer Choice Candies." Among them, placed there long ago, were the mummified remains of a single rose, now as hard as a rock and showing only the barest hint of color on the top of one tight petal.

The rose had been a gift to Mama from a special boy named Duffy shortly before he went off to war. Duffy was my brother Kevin's best friend, whom we all had sort of "adopted."

His real name was Dorian Fitzhugh. Duffy's mother, Megan Fitzhugh, died in the labor that gave him life. Consequently, Duffy's dad, Red Hugh, drifted in a world of grief and eventually sent the boy to live with an aunt in Pennsylvania. But when the aunt became ill during his eighth-grade year, young Dorian returned to our city.

At that point, Kevin sought to make his newfound, silent, and somewhat morose friend a part of our life. Giving him the nickname "Duffy" was one step in that direction.

As the two grew in friendship, sharing unparalleled skills as athletes, their kindred spirits drew them even closer. In no time, Duffy became a part of the fabric of our lives. And considering Duffy's difficult upbringing, it was evident he appreciated the acceptance he found in our crowded home.

Over the years, I often heard nuns and priests at St. Columbkille comment on the friendship between Kevin and Duffy. On the athletic field or the basketball court, they were the ones to watch. They truly complemented one another: Kevin's outgoing and genuine laughter never quite overshadowing Duffy's more timid yet radiant smile.

One Sunday in May, though, as we Patricks remembered the day's primary occasion and hustled off to fetch Mama's gift, Duffy disappeared. His only good-bye was a comment that indicated he would be returning shortly.

"Happy Mother's Day, Mama!" we were soon calling while we carried our small gifts out to the oilcloth-covered table. "Happy Mother's Day!"

As she usually did, Mama feigned surprise and wiped her hands on her apron. "Oh my!" What's all this? You'd think it was a birthday or something!" The ritual was the same, year after year. But we liked it, and Mama never seemed to tire of it either.

Carefully, Mama unwrapped the gifts: a lace-bordered handkerchief and a pair of tickets to "Bank Night" at the Pearl Theatre. Now she and Mrs. O'Malley could go without worrying over money. And here was a jar of quince jelly, too — her favorite — with a promise it would be safe in the icebox, left for only her consumption. One by one, the gifts were opened and the homemade cards read. Tommy had sent a card and long letter which Mama counted as precious as any other gifts.

Just as we were leaving the table, Duffy returned, walking through the door without needing to do any knocking. In one hand, he carried his baseball cleats for our weekly Sunday ritual, and in the other, a still-moist American Beauty rose.

"Here, Mrs. Patrick!" he beamed. "Happy Mother's Day!"

Mama took the rose and studied its subtle beauty. Though the flower was still in a fairly tight bud, dew glistened on one velvet petal. Its stem was long and green, with sparkling leaves touched with traces of moisture. Even in the crowded room, the rose's potent fragrance danced sweetly among us.

A pause in our boisterous conversation ensued as we watched Kevin's best friend standing there, his hand still outstretched toward Mama. Thinking back, remembering, I can still see her face. First she gazed on the rose, and then she turned her eyes to the boy who had brought it to her.

"Thank you, Dorian!" Mama said with obvious affection. "Thank you, indeed!"

She motioned for Duffy to lean toward her, and she kissed him as she would one of us.

"Just thought you should have it," Duffy said, blushing self-consciously.

But the drama of the moment was fleeting. With the first good sun of the season and a balmy breeze tempting us, we soon hurried out to offer up our first ball game to the waiting spring. When we returned home that night, Duffy's rose sat beneath the picture of the Sacred Heart in Mama's treasured bud vase, which had once belonged to her own mother in Ireland.

"Lettin' Jesus share your rose, Mama?" Kevin laughed.

Mama just nodded and smiled.

Gradually, in the days that followed, the rose opened to its full glory. For a long time, we thought Mama had simply thrown it away when its beauty had begun to wane. But three years later, we were to learn differently.

Shortly after graduation from Holy Redeemer, Duffy died in combat in the rice paddies of North Korea. The news struck all of us, especially Kevin, with a blow from which we never really recovered. To be sure, in spite of the passage of more than forty years, Kevin will even now sit alone from time to time and remember his friend. But one aspect of our caring for Duffy nearly escaped us in our grief over his untimely death.

Following Duffy's military funeral and interment in the little cemetery behind the church, a get-together was held in the parish hall. When we later returned to the stillness of our apartment to mourn our loss in silence, Tommy, who was home on a furlough, cautioned Danny and me to respect Kevin's inner grief and let him work it out for himself.

Though we all suffered that evening, we learned Kevin was not the only one affected so greatly. As we sat there, David turned on the radio, keeping the sound low. John, Mama's pet canary, chirped hesitantly before lapsing into a respectful silence as if he, too, felt the sense of loss pervading our home.

As the rest of us shared stories of Duffy's life, Mama got up from her chair and disappeared into her bedroom. Moments later, she returned carrying the white candy-box repository containing her earthly treasures.

Then, carefully lifting the rose out of the box, Mama held up the blackened remains of that long-ago Mother's Day. She had cut the stem short so it would fit in the box, but a few leaves remained along with a wealth of dried thorns that had steadfastly weathered the years.

"I pricked my finger," she said softly, "the day Dorian gave this to me. Pricked it on this very thorn when I went to put it in the vase for Jesus to share."

Tapping lightly on the still sharp thorn, she quietly continued. "Dorian had so little in the way of joy when he came among us," she sighed. "Ah! I often wished I could take away that boy's sorrows."

I studied Mama. It was not like her to talk this way. Nor had I ever seen her talk on while tears rolled down her cheeks.

"He gave me this rose," Mama said, "and I kissed his cheek. Then, when you boys were getting ready for your ball game, he sat down beside me to wait. He gently put his hand in mine and he thanked me for being his mother."

Until that moment, we had never known of the touching exchange.

"Ah!" she uttered from the depths of her own grief. "He's got his own mother as well as Mother Mary with him now. But, for awhile, he was like another of my own, and I'll miss him so much!" With that, Mama put the rose back in the box, carried it back to her room, and shut the door. We knew she would grieve in her own privacy, so we let her be.

—Sean Patrick

Editors' Note: You may recognize this story from the previous book in the series, Amazing Grace for the Catholic Heart. *Although we received many more entries for this book than we needed, we believed it was important to include this story in the book because of its beauty and celebration of motherhood.*

Sean Patrick is a professional writer, retired from a lifetime in law enforcement. For the past sixteen years, Sean has been a columnist for Catholic Digest. *His work has also appeared in such publications as* The Family, Our Family, the Ligourian, *and* The Priest. *Sean is the author of three books:* Patrick's Corner, Kingdom of the Flies, *and* The Best of Sean Patrick. *He and his wife live in rural Ohio in the midst of the Old Order Amish.*

Chapter 2

A Mother's Wisdom

Mother's Day

I'll never forget a Mother's Day that went from the sublime to the ridiculous in the course of the morning. The girls were four and two years old, and I was expecting our third. We were all done up in our Sunday best and actually got to church early enough to get a seat near the front. The girls were unusually well behaved, sedately leafing through their picture prayer books. The elder occasionally looked up to whisper what seemed to me to be remarkably astute theological comments about the illustrations—for a four-year-old, that is.

Father's sermon extolled the glories and virtues of motherhood. I basked in it. After Mass, little old ladies stopped to compliment my picture-perfect family. I felt positively radiant in my white linen dress. Now we were off to a restaurant for a delicious Mother's Day breakfast. What a lovely day it was! Nothing more troubling was on my mind than the problem of whether to choose strawberries or blueberries with whipped cream on my pancakes.

But restaurants are crowded on Mother's Day, and as we waited for service my children's haloes began to slip. They became restless and cranky. My relief at the arrival of our food was short-lived, for just at that moment the two-year-old began dancing on her chair with a rapidity that indicated a very swift trip to the restroom was required. An appeal to my usually helpful husband was useless. Mother's Day or not, he would not take a little girl into a men's room. At calmer moments his reluctance seemed understandable, but as I dodged waiters and tables in a frantic race against time, I silently beseeched heaven to give me male triplets next time around, just to get back at him.

Unfortunately the race was lost, and with spectacular results. For the cleanup I had to struggle with tissue when a fire hose would have been more appropriate. I returned to my cold breakfast—with somewhat fragrant daughter in hand—and sitting down, I noticed that my white dress was no longer white in several places. Needless to say we did not linger over a second cup of coffee.

Which half of my Mother's Day was more illustrative of what motherhood is all about? Sentimental idealists would vote for my Hallmark moments in church, while a cynical feminist would choose the restaurant horror as a cruel metaphor for a mother's life. But neither would be correct. One can't judge a career, let alone a vocation, by weighing highs against lows. Most of our time on this earth is spent neither on the summit nor in the pits, but somewhere in between. Nearly everyone's day is filled with much that is routine, repetitive, and even tedious. This is true for corporate climbers and Hollywood actors as well as mothers.

But what is the *point* of the routine tasks a mother performs? It's not to please a boss, or achieve fame, or make money. Everything a mother does, however commonplace, is done to make a difference for the good in someone else's life. That's what makes a mother's work beautiful. But so many seem to forget this.

Some years ago a women's magazine ran a questionnaire for the at-home mother to determine which attractions of home life kept them out of the workforce. It asked them to rate on a scale of 1 to 10 their liking for doing laundry, ironing, cooking, and housecleaning. As if these things in themselves made us want to stay at home! It would have been far better if the poll had asked women to rate "making home a welcoming, comfortable place for my family," which is precisely what gives meaning and value to all the chores. Even still, laundry and dusting are still not the essence of motherhood. One could be an indifferent cook and a slapdash housekeeper, yet still succeed admirably as a mother. The essence of motherhood is love, and household chores are only one way this love is expressed. Far more important is the sympathetic ear when the kids get home from school, full of the day's triumphs and defeats. Far more important are the strong arms a toddler runs to for reassurance before wiggling back down to the floor and running off to play again. And far more important are the bent knees and praying lips that intercede for the eternal salvation of those teenagers.

We're here to love. Life may hand us cards and flowers one minute and a potty-training disaster the next. The joy of teaching a baby her first words or the terror of teaching a sixteen-year-old to drive—it doesn't matter. We'll take it all. We're here to love.

May Mary, Mother of all mothers, keep us from losing sight of that, all the days of our lives.

—Daria Sockey

Daria Sockey is a mother of seven who lives in the wilds of northwest Pennsylvania. She has been writing since her marriage to Bill Sockey in 1980. Credits include several grades of the Faith and Life *catechetical series, plus numerous articles in* Faith & Family, National Catholic Register, *and* New Covenant. *When not engaged in mothering, homemaking, writing, or home schooling, she can be found curled up in an armchair with a soothing novel.*

Ballet Lessons

I was in the dressing room of the ballet school with my daughter, Mary Beth, and two other five-year-olds. Mary Beth was dressed in the school uniform, a plain blue leotard. The other girls were dressed in fancier, prettier leotards.

"We'll be the princesses," said the first little girl. "The princesses are very beautiful."

"Yes," agreed the second, "and Mary Beth will be the queen."

That's nice, I thought. They're including her.

"Oh yes!" continued the first, "Mary Beth can be the queen. Queens aren't very pretty at all."

"That's right," said the second. "We're the pretty ones."

My heart sank. I watched Mary Beth's eyes fill with tears. Every mean-spirited elementary school trio came rushing from the archives of my memory. Every petty, catty high school clique taunted me with the hard-won knowledge that girls can be very cruel.

And then one more memory came to me. It was Mary Beth, just a few weeks old, sitting in an infant seat at my friend Alice's house. There were a dozen or more children there that day and I had crept away to nurse her in a quiet corner. When she was finished, she drifted to sleep in my arms. I put her in her seat and sat back to look at her. Her beauty literally took my breath away. She was my princess, my queen, my lovely little girl.

Drawing myself back to the present, I put the finishing touches on her requisite bun and whispered, "I think you look so very lovely today." She smiled at me and went off to the studio to dance. As I gathered the hairbrush and bobby pins, I glanced around. The place was full of feminine accoutrements. Leotards and ballet shoes, leggings and lovely dresses hung waiting for the girls who would wear them with the grace of a dancer. Mary Beth loved this place, this haven from our male-dominated home. Looking around more closely, I also noticed mirrors everywhere, two scales, and several diet soda cans. I began to wonder about what we tell girls about beauty.

Still stung by the cattiness of little girls, I returned home to tell the tale to a friend who is a former dancer. She remembered well the emphasis that even the best studios placed on body image and appearance. She remembered the inevitable comparisons that occur when girls stare at themselves and other girls in the mirror for long periods of time. She also remembered how much she loved the studio, the culture, and the valuable lessons in movement and carriage she learned there. Sighing, she said, "This is only beginning. Here is where you have to set the tone."

"Oh, I know. I told her she is beautiful, and I plan to tell her again when she returns home. Mike is on board to mention it as well. And maybe we'll find a really pretty leotard for next week…" I rambled on.

"Well, that's fine," responded my friend. "But then you are echoing the idea that beauty is an outward attribute. What you want to affirm is that beauty is from within. Beauty is virtue. Grace is God within her. It's all very nice to dance beautifully and to look lovely, but you want her to *be* lovely."

I thought back to my daughter as a newborn baby. Chances are she was wearing a pretty pink outfit—when you have a little girl after three boys, pink is all you put her in for the first three years. But, truth be told, I don't really remember her clothing that day. I remember the fresh-from-God luminous beauty of a newborn. I remember the tangible feeling of grace that enveloped me as I sat there watching her. I remember marveling at the artistry of her Creator. I remember being glad that I had named this lovely creature after the Blessed Mother. I wanted her then and I want her now to live a life filled with grace and beauty. And that has very little to do with ballet school.

—Elizabeth Foss

Elizabeth Foss is a wife and the home schooling mother of seven. She is an award-winning Catholic family life columnist and the author of Real Learning: Education in the Heart of the Home.

When Jeff Met Mom

Standing in front of the bathroom mirror one evening, I wondered how I had gotten myself into this date with a long-haired boy I had just met that day at school. He wasn't exactly the type that fit into my religious family. Running late for our bowling date, I zipped up my new jeans and began working on my makeup. He would be here any minute. I had one more eye to go when he rang the bell. My mother answered the door.

"Hello, Mrs. Tobler, I'm Jeff," my date announced. He towered over my mother wearing his Elton John platform shoes. His outfit was complete with white bell-bottoms and a yellow silk shirt. Before my mother could invite him up the stairs, Jeff pulled photos from his pocket and proudly showed them to Mother.

"I work as a reporter and here is the latest rock group I interviewed. It's KISS. Do you know them?" I could hear him from the bathroom, and I nearly poked out my eye with my mascara wand. Of all the things to ask *my* mother! It was like asking her if she were friends with the devil.

I imagined the look of horror that crossed my mother's face as she gazed at the photos of Gene Simmons' painted face and blood-covered tongue dangling out with Jeff standing arm-in-arm with him, beer in hand. *This boy is definitely not going to date my daughter!* she must have thought, determined to march up the stairs and stop me.

"Emily," I heard my mother say in her warning tone. Prepared to ward her off, I met her in the hallway with my own look of warning as if to say, "Don't make a scene!" but her demeanor seemed to have changed. Instead of forbidding me to go out with Jeff, she calmly said, "Just be careful."

"Don't worry, Mom. I'll be fine. He's not what you think," I whispered quietly so Jeff wouldn't overhear our conversation. She still wore a worried look as I scurried out of the house with Jeff.

Naturally, she continued to worry the entire time I was gone. When I returned around midnight, a car screeched down the street. Mother figured it was Jeff and she met me at the door. "Did everything go okay?" she asked.

"Yes, Mom, we had a great time. He's really nice. We talked about God the whole time," I replied. Her eyebrows arched in surprise.

"He's interested in God?" she asked hopefully. My mother's whole life revolved around God—Bible reading, church meetings, prayer groups, and discipling others. "I wasn't going to let you go out with him after he showed me those pictures of KISS," she began. "But something stopped me, and it was as if God spoke these words to me: 'Let him go, someday he's going to preach the gospel.'"

Now it was my turn to be surprised. "Maybe he will, Mom."

After that date, Jeff was a frequent visitor to our home, always welcomed by my mother. In fact, I think he spent more time conversing with her than with me while he was over. He and my mom struck up a great friendship and they would sit at the kitchen table to discuss the Bible. Jeff asked her so many questions and as always, she was eager to tell him all about what she knew of the love of Jesus. It wasn't long before Jeff had purchased a Bible like hers so he could study on his own. I sat and listened a lot, but even if I wasn't at home, Jeff would come over just so he could talk to Mom.

"Jeff's eyes remind me of a picture of the Christ child that hung on our wall when I was a girl," my mother said thoughtfully one day after Jeff had gone home. "He is so eager to learn about Jesus. I really do think Jeff is going to be a preacher."

I wasn't terribly interested in being a piano-playing pastor's wife, so I kept my options open and dated a few other boys at the same time. Jeff was ready to throw in the towel on our relationship one day when he was visiting my mother.

"I don't think I can keep competing with these other guys," Jeff confided to my mother.

"Jeff, just hang in there. She'll come around," my mother said encouragingly. I didn't know she was conspiring with God behind my back, but it worked, because the other boys disappeared and Jeff and I got engaged shortly after.

I appreciate how my mother listened to the voice of the Holy Spirit and not to her first impression when it came to a spouse for me. To think that one horrific image of Gene Simmons could have ruined it all. Instead, Mom's prayers, love, and counsel have led both Jeff and me closer to Christ.

—Emily Cavins

A mother laughs our laughter,
Sheds our tears,
Returns our love,
Fears our fears.
She lives our joys,
Cares our cares,
And all our hopes and
dreams she shares.

—Julia Summers

Somebody Said

Somebody said it takes about six weeks to get back to normal after you've had a baby...

Somebody doesn't know that once you're a mother, "normal" is history.

Somebody said you learn how to be a mother by instinct...

Somebody never took a three-year-old shopping.

Somebody said being a mother is boring...

Somebody never rode in a car driven by a teenager with a driver's permit.

Somebody said if you're a "good" mother, your child will "turn out good"...

Somebody thinks a child comes with directions and a guarantee.

Somebody said "good" mothers never raise their voices...

Somebody never came out the back door just in time to see her child walking on top of the swing set.

Somebody said you can't love the fifth child as much as you love the first...

Somebody doesn't have five children.

Somebody said a mother can find all the answers to her child-rearing questions in books...

Somebody never had a child stuff beans up his nose.

Somebody said the hardest part of being a mother is labor and delivery...

Somebody never watched her "baby" get on the bus for the first day of kindergarten.

Somebody said a mother can do her job with her eyes closed and one hand tied behind her back...

Somebody never organized seven giggling Brownies to sell cookies.

Somebody said a mother can stop worrying after her child gets married...

Somebody doesn't know that marriage adds a new son- or daughter-in-law to a mother's heartstrings.

Somebody said a mother's job is done when her last child leaves home...

Somebody never had grandchildren.

Somebody said your mother knows you love her, so you don't need to tell her...

Somebody isn't a mother.

—Anonymous

Necessity in the Mother of Invention

Just Love Me

After arriving home from school one afternoon, my son dumped his backpack on the floor, helped himself to a mammoth bowl of ice cream, and asked me to take him somewhere to buy him something. The behavior was not out of the realm of normal for him, but that day it was the impetus for a mama meltdown. For a full five minutes (I'm sure he would say fifteen) I harangued him about seeing me as little more than a credit-card-bearing taxi driver.

"If I'm not taking you somewhere or buying you something," I nagged, "you have little use for me." I went on about his showing no appreciation for all I did for him on a daily basis. He never acknowledged the clean clothes, healthy meals and well-run household. I ranted about never hearing a compliment or a note of concern about how I might feel. I whined about how seldom he voluntarily spent time with me or seemed to enjoy my company when he did.

"You don't give me a thought unless you're in trouble or need something," I pouted. When my fury subsided and he trudged away, I was left feeling that I had taught him nothing and had done little to further his spiritual growth.

A few days later, the confrontation still burdened me. As I knelt to pray before daily Mass, my mind reviewed all my petitions. But before I settled on a specific intention, I heard a voice speak these words to my soul: "Just love me."

"Just love me." That was the message I had tried to convey to my son. Do not hit me with a list of gimmes. Just love me awhile. Show some appreciation for all I do for you in the normal course of the day. Acknowledge my presence. Voluntarily spend time with me. Take joy in me.

How often do I brush God aside until I want or need something? How often do I sincerely thank Him and acknowledge Him for even the bread I eat and the air I breathe? When do I ever show appreciation for the beauty of a glorious, sunny afternoon created for my enjoyment?

God, in His amazing way, opened my eyes. There was a lesson in my confrontation with my son about my own relationship with the Lord. Our children can teach us about our Heavenly Father. Just as they are dependent on us, we are dependent on God. And when we give so much to our children, we wait and hope for some recognition and the return of our love—just as our Heavenly Father does with us.

—Gayle Bell

Gayle Bell is a former high school English teacher, now a stay-at-home mother with two sons, ages fifteen and eleven. A convert to the Catholic faith, Gayle is a frequent school and church volunteer. She lives with her husband and sons in Charlotte, North Carolina.

Optimistic Antidotes

Warning: Motherhood lends itself to pessimism. Once the euphoria of holding your precious newborn bundle evaporates, you will find infinite reasons to fret and complain. "She never sleeps. It seems like she wants to eat every hour," can give way to, "Her room is always such a mess," and "How many times does she need to be reminded to turn off lights?" Then, of course, there are so many things to worry about now: germs, colic, discipline issues, balanced diets, an unsafe world, and college tuition—just to name a few.

We all agree that snuggling a newborn, hearing a baby's giggles, and a child's "I love you" are priceless treasures; but face it, we are human. The grunt work of parenting and the worries of the world get to us sometimes. I know; I have eight children. Each one of them provides a combination of joy and drudgery. I began to realize early on, however, that if I did not actively work at enjoying the good, the bad would cloud family life for me. So, I have developed a habit of coming up with antidotes—positive thoughts to counteract the poison of pessimism.

Here are some examples to give you the idea of what I am talking about:

Bad: The bathroom I just finished cleaning ten minutes ago now looks like the bathroom before it was cleaned.

Antidote: The rule of Benedictine monks centers on God and work. Surely I'm earning graces here—at least some time off for good behavior from purgatory. St. Joseph the Worker, pray for me!

Bad: Woe is me. My favorite pair of pants is the one I wore when I was five months pregnant and I cannot even afford a pair from the thrift store.

Antidote: God used my body to co-create human beings with everlasting souls. Now how's that for making pants seem insignificant?

Bad: My sick child did not make it to the bathroom in time...again.

Antidote: I've got indoor plumbing and many people around the world do not. It is easier to clean with a bucket of hot water when you do not have dirt floors. Well, maybe not, but I'll take my own flooring anyway. If all else fails, consider that you are performing one of the chief corporal acts of mercy—visiting the sick.

Bad: Your baby keeps you up all night.

Antidote: And who says there's never any time for prayer?

Bad: Pick any of the following.

1) You just discovered your child was playing ball in the house and broke something valuable.

2) Your child stained the carpeting with a brightly colored drink that should not have been drunk in the living room.

3) You cannot find something that your child borrowed without asking.

Antidote: After applying appropriate discipline to the guilty party, remember that Jesus, although God, was born in a manger and collected no worldly wealth. Then, give thanks to God that your child is helping you not become too attached to material possessions. Keep the latter step secret from your child lest he or she feel compelled to give you more to be thankful for.

Bad: Keeping a clean home is no longer possible.
Antidote: You have a home.

Bad: Your children are driving you nuts.
Antidote: Many childless couples would love to trade places with you.

Bad: Your child does not listen and obey you.
Antidote: Neither did God's first children.

Bad: Your child was born with some imperfection.
Antidote: Your child is perfect for what God has planned for him or her.

Bad: I am not prepared for this job.
Antidote: God doesn't call the equipped; He equips those He calls. Pray for the equipment, then trust.

Bad: I have failed. My children have not turned out very well.
Antidote: St. Augustine did not turn out very well—at first. His mother, St. Monica, prayed and prayed and prayed. She never quit. St. Augustine converted and became a Doctor of the Church. Remember, it ain't over 'til it's over.

I think you get the idea now. You may suspect me of being the Pollyanna type that sugar coats everything. I'm not. Just ask my husband. I can fall apart and fret with the best of them. But then I collect my thoughts and emotions, pray, and try to put it all in perspective.

I truly love being a mother even though I definitely do not always find it easy. If I do not come up with antidotes for my negative thinking, I will blow this whole thing called motherhood. Then, in a blink of an eye, it will all be over and I really will have something to be negative about—missing all the blessings and joy that having children had to offer.

—Patti Maguire Armstrong

A Lover of Frail Humanity

It was a deafening silence they both now shared as my mother held my older brother close. The cold of November had come early that morning and the gray of the skies could not match the cloak of gray that covered mother's heart. Tears fell from her eyes as she held my brother, who then was only seven months of age. "Why?" she asked, her mind too fatigued from its troubled wonderings.

Days earlier her entrance into my brother's room was routine. "Jimmy, Mommy's here for breakfast!" There was no response as he lay with his back toward her. She left the room and came in again, repeating her greeting all the louder. Once again there was no response. She approached her son and touched his shoulder. It was then that Jimmy turned and brightly smiled.

She knew something was wrong. Days later her instincts would be confirmed: her son's world was one of silence. He was deaf. His quiet fussing, his rare cries made all the more sense now.

Was it the German measles I contracted? she wondered, holding him tight in a mother's pieta of sorrow. For three days she wept, grieving over his future, and helplessly searching to answer the "whys" of it all. And through that sorrow my mother entered in and united herself to the deafening silence of my brother's world.

"It was your father who saved me," she would often say. Later that month, on Thanksgiving Day, he touched her hand and spoke one line that pierced the heavy clouds of her paralysis, "You know, Pinky, we have an awful lot to be thankful for."

With a new home, a growing family, a good job, and a strong marriage, my father's comment roused her. Her faith and courage were renewed as the shroud of pity gradually lifted like fog before the sun. And so my parents set out, initiated and yet untrained, feeling handicapped themselves against the silence of my brother's world.

Searching for direction, my parents wrote to the Spencer Tracey Foundation. *Surely they would have an answer for us,* they thought. *After all, they have at their disposal the experience of parents in our situation.*

Weeks later my parents received a letter, which essentially advised: "Above all you must develop patience with your child." It was 1959 and the developments and resources of later decades were not yet available. *That's not the answer I wanted, Lord,* Mother prayed. But it was the answer they received, and one that would prove foundational.

In the years ahead my parents would teach their deaf son to speak, to live, and to communicate in a world of sound, they would raise their six children (three girls and three boys), and would continue to fulfill their vows to love and honor one another within the sacrament of marriage.

Our entire family learned sign language, but it was my mother who would spend countless hours with Jimmy, speaking to him as she signed, teaching him how to form his mouth and feel the vibrations of his vocal chords so he could speak the words he was learning to sign. She was stubborn in her attempts with him! All this at a time when the experts definitively told parents of the deaf *not* to speak to their children when using sign language, but my mother's instincts told her differently—years later she would be proven right.

My mother's real name is Eileen, but everyone calls her Pinky—a name given her at the age of three because of her red hair. Throughout her life my mother has been known as a woman with a large heart, a quick wit, a lover of humor and good conversation, and one with a modest, yet permeating faith.

My mother came from a gregarious German family, while my father was from one more stoic. Yet together, even with the special needs of my older brother, they made time for every child and for every activity with which we were involved! Ours was a home of sibling fights, and of laughter, pranks, and discipline, of love and prayer and the importance of church and religious faith. But most of all, ours was a secure home.

As an adult I can better appreciate the sacrifice of time and attention they gave to us. Their example of generosity alone, daily and imperfect, yet motivated by a vocation to love, has contributed much to my character as a man and as a Roman Catholic priest.

Over the years, as my brother Jim grew, he would often ask why God permitted him to be born deaf. The answers given were never fully satisfactory. And, as a family, we often found him contentious and understandably unsettled with his state in life.

When Jim was twenty-four he died suddenly in a car accident on the way to work. Perhaps more difficult than losing him so unexpectedly was the unknown state of his soul at death. *Is my son in heaven? Is he happy? Please give me a sign to let me know if my son is in heaven and if he is happy,* my mother would beg of the Lord in the silence of her prayers.

She believed that God the Father, whose only Son died for our sake, would have compassion on her grief and have mercy on her son, who in moments of frustration proclaimed that he hated God for allowing him to be deaf! In her grief she petitioned Our Lady who knew the rending sorrow of losing a child. And so, in her daily rosary, my mother would repeatedly approach the Father like the persistent woman before the judge in the gospel parable. She privately prayed that God would grant her an unmistakable sign that her son was in heaven and if he was happy.

In January of 1984, three months after we buried Jim, I phoned home from my dorm room in Arizona to relay some good news. I had just been healed from a host of allergies that I had suffered from since my early teens. My mother's "hello" sounded distressed, and her voice cracked with emotion. She had been crying.

"Mom what's wrong?" I asked.

My older sister Lynn was handed the line. "John," Lynn said, "last night I had a vivid dream of Jimmy!"

She told me how, in her dream, she entered the front doors of our local parish church. While walking down the center aisle she saw my brother standing before her. "I know it sounds like a cliché," she said, "but he was dressed all in white. He was so radiant!" A conversation between the two of them ensued.

"Hi Lynn, how are you?" my brother Jim asked.

"You can talk!" Lynn replied amazed.

"Yes, I can hear also."

"Jimmy, you look so beautiful and so happy that I could just stare at you!"

It was then that he got to the heart of the matter and instructed her, "I want you to go to Mom and Dad and tell them that I am in heaven and I am very happy." After speaking the same words Mother had prayed daily to God *alone*, my brother disappeared and Lynn awoke.

Thus the reasons for my mother's tears were ones of joy, consolation, and gratitude to God! The Lord had given my mother, who throughout her lifetime has been a lover of frail humanity, an extraordinary outpouring of His steadfast love. She who has lived a noble life of caring—first for her children and strangers alike, and now over many years for my father following his stroke—has found a lasting comfort in the Father's attentiveness to her grief.

A picture of my brother Jim sits, as it has since his death, in my parent's living room. Positioned in the frame is a line from a poem by Susan Erling: "When I lost you, I lost a lifetime of hopes, plans, dreams, and aspirations. A slice of my future simply vanished overnight." But now in faith we know those hopes, plans, and dreams are eternal, caught up within the aspirations of God.

My mother has a saying, taken from a calendar that states, "I am not putting my nose into your business, I am putting my heart into your troubles." She has used that phrase often, even when it appears that the first portion is given more emphasis, and yet through it all my family thanks God for creating such a heart of compassion within her. We also thank the Lord for the amazing grace He has granted our family through her constant prayers. From our mother's example, I pray that in our daily lives, all will be inspired to make ordinary the doing of the extraordinary, in imitation of Christ's ways of love.

—Fr. John Klockeman

After a career in business, Fr. John Klockeman was ordained a priest on May 27, 2000. He currently serves as formation and spiritual director at St. John Vianney College Seminary in St. Paul, Minnesota.

Words to Live By

∽ The game of life is the game of boomerangs. Our thoughts, deeds, and words return to us sooner or later, with astounding accuracy.
—Florence Scovel Shinn (1871-1940), author

∽ Anger is the only thing to put off till tomorrow.
—Slovakian Proverb

∽ No matter what you've done for yourself or for humanity, if you can't look back on having given love and attention to your own family, what have you really accomplished?
—Lee Iacocca, automobile executive

∽ There's nothing like a newborn baby to renew your spirit—and to buttress your resolve to make the world a better place.
—Virginia Kelley (1923-1994), nurse

∽ There is no greater joy, nor greater reward, than to make a fundamental difference in someone's life.
—Sister Mary Rose McGeady, children's advocate

∽ Parents can tell but never teach, unless they practice what they preach.
—Arnold Glasow, author

∽ Some think it's holding on that makes one strong; sometimes it's letting go.
—Sylvia Robinson

∽ Write your plans in pencil, but give God the eraser.

—Anonymous

∽ A woman will always sacrifice herself if you give her the opportunity. It is her favorite form of self-indulgence.

—W. Somerset Maugham (1874-1965), author

Church Antics

Sometimes a little child's antics in church are kind of cute. Like the toddler running down the aisle to retrieve the rolling coin that just wouldn't stay put in his hand until collection time. Or the time our first baby gave hints one Sunday of her future in the theater. The priest was reading the passage from Matthew where Jesus walks on water: "...and they, seeing Him walking upon the sea, were greatly alarmed, and exclaimed 'It is a ghost!'" At that precise moment Theresa let out an eerie wail that would have done credit to either a ghost or a frightened disciple.

But some episodes are not so cute. There was the time when one of our newborns managed to spit up into the pew in front of us during the Gospel. The occupants, standing and attentive, hadn't noticed. We frantically searched our pockets for Kleenex and bent over to clean up the pew before they sat down again, but we weren't fast enough. As the Gospel ended we had to physically restrain them from landing in the mess, trying to explain with whispers and gestures what had happened. We succeeded in so startling them that they bolted for the far end of the pew and cast furtive glances at us throughout the remainder of Mass.

Then there was the time my husband approached the altar for communion, holding a two-and-a-half-year-old, and felt a sudden rush of warmth. Within milliseconds he knew that this was not due to a spiritual experience, but a lapse in potty-training skills. Now clutching her closer to hide a soaked shirt-front, he headed out for the restroom.

Yuck! How humiliating! Why does God let these things happen in church? Probably because it's so humiliating. It's good for us. Maybe God allows such incidents to illustrate the mystery of what we humans are: body as well as soul, both of which participate in the sacramental life. Or maybe these events serve as graphic reminders that the parental vocation calls us to both exalted tasks and lowly ones, all of which we should be ready to perform, even when it means interrupting our devotions.

It gets more interesting when babies become toddlers. More discouraging, too, because now one might reasonably expect the first blossom of obedience, but at the same time, the effects of original sin are springing up like weeds. I thought our almost three-year-old would enjoy the pageantry of a First Communion and May Crowning. But when she realized that she was *not* in the limelight, vanity made an appearance. "I wanna white dress!" she yelled. "I wanna put a crown on Mary. Gimme the crown for Mary!"

Even more memorable was a Good Friday service when my four-year-old son was increasingly ill-behaved. Finally it was time for that long walk up the aisle and out the door for a richly deserved thump on the bottom. William knew his last hope was to work the audience in the pews. "Don't spank me, Mommy! Please don't spank me!" he wailed piteously. Naturally, I was stifled from action knowing that everyone was listening for the smack, and no doubt preparing to report me to social services.

As each new baby hit this stage we endured it: the crying rooms, the strolls in back during the sermon, the coloring books and toys lugged along to placate them. We lived through untold head-bumpings on pews and mad dashes to the bathroom. Miraculously, it all gets better between four and five years of age. I'd like to say it's because of our diligent efforts at child-training, or because they are beginning to acquire piety. But in reality it's because by this age they have come to grasp the implications of that first principle of the spiritual life: "If you're not good, you won't get a donut after Mass."

A helpful mantra for parents during this time of their lives is, "This, too, shall pass." New parents should take courage from our experience. The boy of the infamous "Don't spank me" episode is today an altar boy who tells us he is thinking about the priesthood. The girl who screamed for a white dress and a crown not only behaves decorously every Sunday, she volunteers to attend weekday Mass with me now and then.

But why bother even bringing small children to Mass (if one has a choice)? Wouldn't it simply be better to wait until they reach a tractable age and then start taking them?

It probably would be easier on parents in the short run, but if life were all about ease, we wouldn't be parents in the first place. Our Lord didn't say, "Let the children age five and up come to me." He wants them all. Tiny children, for all of their non-conforming behavior, are still clothed in their baptismal innocence, and as such belong in God's house. When the sacrifice of Calvary is being re-presented, I'm sure some of the grace pouring forth from the altar overshadows my little monster, and does him good in a way I'll only understand fully in the next life.

Besides, keeping little ones away from Church not only saves you from horror stories, but it deprives you of the lovely ones: a toddler's attempts at genuflecting, or the off-key pre-schooler joining in on the hymns while proudly holding the hymnal upside-down; the sweet enthusiasm for the Sign of Peace, or waving "Bye-bye Jesus" when it's time to go.

There's one more meditation we can make on pre-schoolers' church manners. Little ones demonstrate their short attention spans with their wiggly, noisy bodies. But do our adult attention spans fare much better, even though our physical restraint has improved? Sometimes an antsy toddler is the perfect image of my distracted mind at Mass. Yet do I doubt for a minute that God wants me there despite my restless spirit? No, I'm sure He's glad to see me there. And I'm sure He delights in all of His children, with all their antics and messes.

—Daria Sockey

Previously published in Faith & Family *magazine.*

Daria Sockey's biography appears after Mother's Day *at the beginning of this chapter.*

When Opportunity Calls

One day many years ago, I was waiting to hear from the editor of a major magazine about whether he would publish an article I had submitted a while before.

Our five-year-old son, who was home with me at the time, was terrified of the telephone. Even loving grandparents he adored couldn't coax him to speak on the phone. Nothing we tried seemed to change the situation, so we didn't press it.

I was pretty terrified about the phone myself that day, wondering what this editor was going to say in his impending call. Surely, if he were actually *calling* me, he'd have some news about my manuscript other than "No thanks." But I was trembling with nervous anticipation, nonetheless.

While I tried to keep my mind and attention busy preparing dinner, I listened for the phone and suddenly, in disbelief, saw my son race *toward* it when it rang. Stunned, I watched him pick up the receiver and say cheerily, "Hang up, will ya?" Then he also did exactly that.

Our eyes met in frozen silence before it rang again. "You will sit over there and wait for me until I'm finished," I told him, struggling to restrain a number of things in my voice.

I'll never forget the uncertain fear in his eyes, the way he looked alone and confused. He would later tell me, "I wanted to help because you were busy."

With time and distance from the myopia of being a young mother, I recognize today that his incredible intuitive nature and sensitivity, even—or perhaps especially—as a young child, had picked up on my own nervous "vibe" that afternoon, and he truly was just trying to help.

I never expected humor from the caller when he called back. "After hanging up your manuscript so long, I probably deserved that," he joked. He asked whether my son's reaction was common behavior in small children, or simply a customary greeting at our house. He also told me the magazine was buying my story.

I wanted to call six friends to share this hoped-for news, but I had more important business at the table where my son sat waiting for me, looking miserable. I joined him and asked, more gently than I might have minutes before, why he'd done what he had.

It became obvious that this hadn't been an act of malice toward anyone. From his small perspective, it was his first brave attempt to use the phone and he appeared to have failed dismally.

That editor had provided an opening for a different kind of conversation with my son. "The man was sorry you didn't stay on the phone so he could say 'hello' to you," I told him. Then we talked a little about why telephone courtesy helps everyone feel welcomed and respected.

He then said that he was sorry, too.

I asked whether he'd like to tell the caller that he was sorry. He looked uneasy, but agreed to my suggestion that he find paper and pencil. "Crayons, too?" the young opportunist asked, no doubt hoping to add illustrations to the mix. I nodded, smiling.

He then sat hunched at the kitchen table, oversized, unwieldy crayons in his small hands, pouring every ounce of his attention into filling one side of a sheet of stationery with small drawings and a sentence of letters an inch tall that read: "Dear Mr. _____, I am sorry I hung up and I will be more polite next time. Your Friend," and added his name.

A week later, he received a postcard with a photo of the magazine's headquarters and a very kind message in reply to his letter. At the time, my son *loved* getting mail—and, eventually, came to feel better about phone calls, too. Too many times, I let preoccupation distract me from being present for my child first. But at least once, when life offered the chance, I not only seized it, but managed to see it in the first place.

—Phyllis Edgerly Ring

Phyllis Edgerly Ring, mother of two, writes on issues of family, health, and spirituality from her New Hampshire home. Her work has appeared in Catholic Digest, Christian Science Monitor, Hope, Ligourian, *and* Mamm. *More information about Phyllis and her writings is available at www.phyllisring.com*

Chapter 3
A Mother's Strength

The Healing Power of Love

It seemed impossible that the vast emptiness I had known all my life could grow deeper, but when I was abandoned to a Catholic orphanage at the age of six it grew to a bottomless chasm. In 1963, my father had my mother committed to a state mental institution. He then made me and my five younger siblings wards of the state of Tennessee. We were loaded into a station wagon and dropped off with no good-bye or explanation. Each of us was immediately separated to various floors of the orphanage according to age and gender.

Ironically, it looked to the world like I had been born into a life of privilege. My mother's family were Catholic and multimillionaires. My grandparents owned a popular nightclub in Wisconsin where my glamorous Irish grandmother often performed in her younger years. There was a dark side to all that wealth, however. My grandfather—nicknamed Spider—did side jobs for Al Capone, the well-known Chicago Mafia gangster. Grandfather eventually committed suicide, as did my grandmother and several other relatives. Alcohol, gambling, and extramarital affairs were deadly combinations.

My own mother was a remarkably beautiful woman. She was a Rose Bowl princess in 1955 and screen tested for

motion pictures in Hollywood. Instead of becoming a film
star, she returned home and married my father. He was a
Lutheran and from a poor German/Norwegian family.
I believe he married my mother for the money. My only
memories of him are of an abusive, violent man.

From my earliest memories I believed I was of little
value to my parents. As a girl, I often stood in my mother's
closet and touched her beautiful dresses to my cheek. Her
dresses were as close to her as I could get. When I was
about four, I announced I was going to run away. My father
swung open the front door and said, "Good, I'll help you."
Only after becoming tired, hungry, and scared did I return
home. No one seemed to notice or care.

My father eventually moved us all to Tennessee. He and
my mother grew to bitterly despise each other. When I was
six, I saw my father hold a butcher knife to his throat. "I'm
going to do it, Sheila," he shouted. "I'm going to do it!"

"No, Daddy, no!" I screamed, while my mother
encouraged him with her applause. At that moment I
realized that they did not love each other and could not
possibly love me.

Shortly thereafter, my father had my mother committed
to a mental hospital in Memphis. Eventually, she gave birth
to her seventh child by my father, who was also abandoned
to the orphanage. According to regulations, we were not
allowed regular contact with our siblings. However, on baby
Timmy's first birthday, I sneaked away to catch a glimpse of
him. As I peered through the nursery window at the babies
lined up in high chairs during lunch hour, I was devastated
to realize I could not identify my own baby brother. With
tears of a profound sense of loss streaming down my face, I
whispered, "Happy first Birthday Timmy, whichever one
you are."

When Timmy was ten months old, my mother committed suicide. A volunteer at the orphanage handed me a newspaper clipping about the horrifying incident. I was mostly emotionally numb at the orphanage, but just below the surface was anger. One day, I felt drawn into a schoolyard flower garden that featured a life-sized cement statue of the Blessed Mother. I looked at her with a combination of awe and anger. "You are Mary and you are perfect," I jealously chided her. "You have never sinned and your son is Jesus and you are in heaven. How could you even know what pain is?" I accused.

In spite of my childish envy, I returned regularly. One afternoon, when I was nine years old, I became aware of an unfamiliar sensation. It was peace. Instead of venting, I began sharing my life with the Blessed Mother. A desire grew in me to pick some of the garden flowers and place them in the statue's hand, but it was against the rules. This temptation lasted a whole week. Finally, I looked up at the stone image of Mary and said out loud, "I just can't pick those flowers for you."

Suddenly I heard a sweet, unearthly voice that penetrated the depths of my soul: "I am more honored by your obedience than by having the flowers in my hand." I was delightfully stunned. It was Mary's voice; she understood the intentions of my heart. Although this experience would remain my own special secret, the hardship that was still to come would bury it deeply.

By the time I was fourteen, my father was granted custody of all seven children by a Tennessee juvenile court judge if he agreed to leave the state for good. My father moved us to the outskirts of a Wisconsin town to a home in deplorable condition. He kept his own selected foods chained up in a refrigerator while we survived mostly on lard, bread, cereal, and powdered milk. We were beaten, bullied, and tormented daily when he was home.

I ran away back to the orphanage when I was sixteen. While volunteering to help out with the younger children there, guilt at the fate of my own siblings left with "the monster" pulled at my heartstrings. I reluctantly returned home. My father's only reaction was to say, "What are you doing back here?"

Shortly after I graduated from high school, an acquaintance from a nearby farm had his way with me against my will one night. Having hidden in my closet, he had waited until I was asleep. I told no one out of shame. Years of victimization had left me completely helpless. Three months later, a doctor confirmed I was pregnant. Before my father learned of the news, he had kicked me out onto the streets one night.

Two girls I knew from high school with an apartment agreed to let me sleep on their couch. When the biological father of my unborn baby learned I was expecting, he called to threaten and then bribe me with money to have an abortion. I hung up the phone. Although my life could not have seemed more desperate, the memory of all the abandoned babies that were occasionally dropped off at the orphanage came to my mind. We had all loved them.

When my daughter, Jennifer was born in June of 1975, I was struck with awe as I gazed upon my blue-eyed, dark-haired beauty. Even the delivery room nurse told me that in her twenty years of nursing, Jenni was one of the most beautiful babies she had ever seen. I immediately recognized her as a true gift from God. Even though I had no plans for the future, I stubbornly refused to give in to the heavy pressure to release her for adoption.

A relative reluctantly took me in from the hospital. Very shortly afterwards, a great uncle and his wife approached me to offer me a place in their home. They showed me a dainty, yellow room of lace and ruffles and a canopied crib. I agreed to move in. However, I never saw that yellow room again. I was treated like a slave, banished to their basement. Rarely did I even get a chance to hold my own baby. When Jenni was three months old, my great uncle's wife let on that they planned to have me declared an unfit mother and gain custody of my daughter. The thought of losing Jenni filled me with a lion's courage. I literally pulled her away from my uncle's grasp and fled with just the clothes on our backs.

I stayed with a friend for six months until I went on welfare and found an apartment in another town. Unfortunately, my life continued to spiral out of control. I allowed myself to be pressured into a loveless marriage to an abusive, adulterous man. Abuse was all I had ever known, so I believed that there was no way out. I had a son, Jason, by him. One day, after another episode of physical abuse where my children were endangered, something in me snapped. I told him to leave and never come back. Jenni was around five years old and Jason was nearly three.

The following month I was hospitalized with toxic shock syndrome seemingly only hours from death. As I lay helpless and in pain, I readily accepted leaving this world. It was then that I experienced a familiar, motherly presence and heard a voice: "You shall not die and I will be with you on your journey."

It was the sweet, heavenly voice of Our Blessed Mother whom I had heard so many years ago. Peace filled every part of my being. I realized I was not spiritually prepared to die. So on that day, July 2, 1981, my spiritual journey began. From that point on I craved a personal and intimate relationship with God and desired to fully embrace my Catholic faith.

Shortly after I was released from the hospital, I was still extremely fragile, both physically and emotionally. I also felt profoundly alone. As I shakily climbed the stairs in my townhouse, I glanced up at a crucifix that hung in the hallway. I said to Jesus on the cross, "See how alone I am, there is no one to love me."

I distinctly heard His gentle voice in reply: "I know how you feel, for you have abandoned Me." I broke down and cried. I took the crucifix off the wall. Sinking to the floor, I cradled it in my arms and rocked back and forth.

"I am sorry Jesus I never turned to you," I sobbed. "You are my best friend now, Jesus."

My life was never the same again. I returned to the sacraments and started taking my children with me to confession and daily Mass. I soaked up everything I could read on my faith and worked on instilling its richness in my children. I also went through five years of intense counseling and therapy to deal with my personal issues. I learned that not all men abuse women and children.

Then, on October 1, 1987, I felt an urging, surely from the Holy Spirit, to attend Mass at a church in another town. That is where I first laid eyes on my future husband, Tom. He was nearing the end of a 54-day rosary novena, asking God to lead him to find a good Catholic wife. The Church had granted me an annulment several years earlier. Our courtship proceeded slowly but was surely grounded in our relationship with God. On September 30, 1989, we were joined in holy matrimony. Tom later adopted both of my children.

In spite of my past, I have a heart filled with gratitude and joy. A friend from church once stopped me in the hallway and said, "To look at you, one would think you never had a bad day in your whole life." Her comment was an affirmation of my healing though God's love. By the grace of God, I have experienced the joy and love of motherhood and became part of a family I never knew as a child.

Jesus once said, in John 14:18, "I will not leave you [orphans]; I will come to you." I believe that this verse was meant for me.

— Cindy Speltz

Cindy Speltz has been married to Tom for fifteen years. Jennifer and Cindy often speak together to pro-life groups with the message that children conceived through sexual assault are God's children. Jenni, 28, has recently married, and Jason, 26, works for a finance company.

The Strength to Trust Again

My two little sons Corey, age four, and James, age one, hovered around to see their new sister when I brought her home from the hospital. It was as if she was an adorable little doll. After all the blue around our farmhouse in Braddock, North Dakota, now we could not get enough of pinks, ruffles, and ribbons.

From the start, Theresa was an easy-going baby. But, at three-weeks old, she awoke in the wee hours one morning and would not go back to sleep. I fed her and rocked her, but she refused to settle down. Even though her skin felt cool, I took her temperature. It was 102. I wrapped her up in a warm blanket, and rocked her some more. By 6 a.m. her temperature had reached 103. I told my husband Pat that he had better feed the cattle right away so we could take her to the clinic when it opened. During our frantic one-hour drive to Bismarck, as we fervently prayed the rosary, Theresa's lips began to turn blue. "Dear God, take care of her," we prayed.

Once at the clinic, we sat impatiently in a waiting room full of sick children. I knew something was terribly wrong and I could not stand to wait any longer. "Either we see a doctor or you are going to have a dead baby on your hands," I demanded to the receptionist. We were brought in immediately.

"We are going to do a spinal tap," the doctor announced. "It will be better if you sit in the waiting room." Within the hour, Theresa was transferred to the adjoining hospital. Throughout the day, Pat and I prayed continuous rosaries. No one seemed particularly worried as they kept us updated on the tests that were being administered. At 7 p.m. a nurse came out with unimaginable news: "I am sorry but your little girl died. Would you like to come in and hold her one last time?"

It was if time stopped and none of this was real. My ears must have deceived me. "No, it couldn't be!" I cried. I knew my baby was sick, but never once had I imagined she would die.

I held her limp little body which was wrapped snuggly in a blanket and sobbed. "You can't be dead," I cried. "You can't be gone." Pat also held her and cried. We were devastated. When we buried her on December 23, 1976, we buried a part of ourselves. It seemed Christmas did not come that year.

Our boys were still babies themselves. Our grief had to take a backseat to the here and now of caring for them. They were sometimes confused to see Mommy crying and they wondered where the baby went, but they were too young to understand the immensity of what we had lost.

No one was really sure why Theresa had died. Her death certificate read Reyes Syndrome for lack of any better clues. Two years later the blessing of another baby girl helped fill our loss. Sarah was beautiful, and perfectly healthy. Her sunny disposition brought us great joy and her intelligence amazed us. When Sarah was eleven months-old, and developed flu-like symptoms, I could not help but worry. Once you lose a child, that possibility seems to hang over every illness. Several doctors gave various diagnoses: "She's teething...It's just a virus." It bothered me that they were brushing me off. I took her to an intern in Linton, a smaller town. He listened to my gut feeling and ran some x-rays. One of Sarah's kidneys was shutting down and the other would soon follow. We were sent to the Mayo Clinic in Rochester, Minnesota. Although I was scared, there was an element of relief at being sent to one of the finest, most medically advanced clinics in the country. If anyone could help Sarah, they could. I also believed God would not take another one of our children. Surely, we had already been through enough.

Once we got there, Sarah's health deteriorated quickly. That evening a priest and nun came to our room. The priest offered to give Sarah the final blessing of the sick. At that point, Sarah was suddenly animated and cheerful, as if she was not even sick. It almost seemed inappropriate to be giving the final sacrament to a child who appeared so healthy.

When the priest took out the holy oils, Sarah quickly dipped her hand into the bottle then reached over to Pat and me and made the sign of the cross on our foreheads. We were in awe. Sarah was only fourteen months and had never done anything like that before. That evening she slipped into a coma. The priest came back later and said: "That blessing was for you, not her. I believe she knew what you would have to endure in the days ahead." Twelve days later, Sarah died.

Our grief was overwhelming. A year with an angel had given us such joy. Without her, the world was a darker place. There were no words to describe the loss to her two big brothers when we returned home without their cherished little sister. Life went on, but it was so much harder this time. Why did God allow this to happen? I knew of handicapped children in other families, but God chose to take our healthy, perfect little daughter. So many children suffered child abuse. Why had God not taken one of them and let us keep Sarah?

It was determined that Sarah had died of idiopathic infantile arterial calcification. Her vital organs had shut down and began to calcify. It had to be what caused Theresa's death two years earlier. We were informed that any future children would carry a 75 percent chance of inheriting this genetic disorder.

The following year our drought-starved crops left no harvest in which to support our family. We drove to Oregon and stayed with one of my sisters that summer to earn money painting houses. Life was just so burdensome. I often visited Sarah's grave and collapsed in tears. "Why, Lord, why?" I cried. I wanted to trust God but it was hard.

The following year, rains again renewed the earth. But I wondered, what of our own renewal? Did we dare have more children? Pat and I prayed the rosary every night. After two years of praying without any clear answers, we attended a Marriage Encounter weekend. During this time, I learned that Pat resented me. He believed our losses had not hurt me as much as it did him. I strove to be strong for the family and maintain a level of normalcy. I had talked about our losses in attempt to heal. Pat felt it hurt too much to talk. For the first time we uncovered pain and resentment that still lay buried. We cried and hugged and relived the pain we had experienced together. Then, just as the rains replenish the earth our tears renewed our relationship.

That weekend healed us and gave us the faith to be open to new life. It would have been easy to say we were not going to have any more children, but we felt we needed to give God a chance to work in our lives. We would be open to life and trust that everything would be in His hands.

Others did not see it that way. As my pregnant belly grew, so did the small-town gossip. Losing two children had brought sympathy because it had been beyond my control, but this pregnancy brought harsh opinions: "She should know better…How foolish to have another child when they know the risks…Don't they know what causes that?"

I gave birth to another girl. Cindy was born looking amazingly identical to Sarah. Of course there was a fear that we would one day lose her, but for the moment, we loved her with all we had. There was no test to determine if she carried the disease. Living to the age of two was the only assurance to know whether she was affected or not. When I became pregnant again just five months later, the cold shoulders of my neighbors grew frigid. Yet, our faith carried us through. God's opinion was the only one that mattered. Susan was born looking exactly like Theresa did at birth.

Raising my beautiful daughters under a cloud of uncertainty was hard. But every time I was tempted to fear, I recited part of the Lord's Prayer over and over: "Thy kingdom come, Thy will be done." I also prayed: "I can do all things through Christ who strengthens me."

Our girls are twenty-one and twenty now. Through our faith, joy fully blossomed in our family again. Our faith touched someone else, too. For twenty-four years, on May Day—the anniversary of Sarah's death—a lady in town sends us a card and flowers. She knew our precious Sarah and she never forgets. In her cards she expresses how much our example has helped her to grow in her own faith. "I truly know that there is a God and through your faith, you have helped me find my way to Him," she wrote one year.

Our pain strengthened us because we allowed God to work in our lives. Without Him, we would have quit church, and stayed away from people with young children. Our losses could have driven Pat and me apart. Instead, we gradually learned to trust and embrace life again. God rewarded our trust and gave us two more little angels.

—Madonna Silvernagel

Madonna Silvernagel and her husband, Pat, are both the tenth child in their families. They farm and ranch west of Braddock, North Dakota. They provided foster care for six years and daycare for nine. Madonna has been parish secretary for St. Katherine's Church for eleven years, and also serves as head of the vocations program for four surrounding parishes.

A mother is recognized by the capacity to give of self.

—Pope John Paul II

Help Is on the Way!

It was a moody fall day in early September with the wind gusting in every direction, pushing dark low clouds in billows above my head. Summer was gone in the Southwestern mountain community, yet it had the newness of spring for me. I was new to the area and new to motherhood. My daughter, June, was just four months old— a happy, chubby baby. Life took on the feeling of a grand adventure as I cared for her, watching and participating in her change and growth. Together we explored our new home. It was as new and wonderful to my eyes as it was to hers. Each day we shared our excitement together.

On this particular day we were headed to the general store to pick up a few things. I bundled up my little June in her small jacket and hood, wrapped her in a few blankets and placed her in the high riding stroller. I threw on my coat and we were out the door. The sun made a valiant attempt to pierce through the rolling clouds above us as I pushed the stroller up the hill and onto the sidewalk. The stroller's fat tires made short work of the crumbling asphalt. I moved with leisure as I pushed June past the small, silent, neat houses set well back from the road. The houses were spread far apart from each other as the vast openness of the meadows and the endless skies threatened to swallow them up.

Once at the store our shopping went quickly. Again we were outside, retracing steps down the worn sidewalk toward home. I noticed that we were alone on the street; no one else was about. It was midweek and midday and it seemed that most of the people in this small town were either working on their ranches or employed in the mines. A meadowlark called and I stopped to check on June. She was fast asleep in a nest of warmth.

This lovely peace was soon shattered by a chorus of frantic barking. I looked up in its direction and could see across the road, beyond a backyard shed, about a dozen dogs in various sizes coming directly toward us.

They descended upon us with determination, bounding across the grass and the road, moving as one body with many voices—from insane high-pitched yapping to low, deep-chested bellows. Within seconds they had us surrounded. I felt as though I had been jolted from a peaceful dream and plunged into a nightmare. The smaller dogs were jumping and biting at my Western boots and pant legs. The larger dogs were baring their teeth in a stationary crouch with the hairs on the back of their necks standing upright.

When I kicked at the lap dogs biting my legs, the larger ones would bounce in place in an attack position. In full voice and snarling teeth, they were coming so close to me I could feel the heat of their breath and the spittle on my hand that escaped from their mouths. It was as though an invisible wall held the big dogs back. A German Shepherd mix was particularly lively. Stunned as I was, my mind was trying to conceive what was happening. My prevailing thought was, "I've got to get us home!" As seconds passed, most of the dogs quieted down but continued to pace around the stroller and me. I decided to move forward, my white knuckles griping the push bar. I took my first tentative steps when the entire group erupted once again into a murderous frenzy, yapping, snarling, jumping, and lunging. To my horror, some of the smaller dogs were leaping and hanging off the edge of the stroller. They were trying to get inside! They seemed to be after the baby!

My motherly instincts must have kicked into high gear because I completely lost all sense of control. I frantically kicked and screamed at the animals, "Get out of here! Leave us alone!" One little Chihuahua nearly made it inside the stroller, yapping and snarling at June's feet. With three of its legs inside the stroller, I struck him, sending him flying several feet across the sidewalk, only to have him recover quickly and make another attempt. There were at least four other smaller dogs trying to get inside, but the height of the stroller made it difficult. Others continued to bite at my pant legs, but my boots prevented them from penetrating my skin. The larger dogs were bouncing and lunging in place. The noise was deafening. Finally I screamed, "Somebody help me!" The next few seconds blurred as the battle went on. Behind me I heard another dog barking some distance away, but my only thought was that more were coming to join the attack. I kept my attention focused on the group around me. Suddenly, I turned as an Australian sheep dog dashed across the yard toward us at breakneck speed. *This is the leader that will tear us to pieces*, I thought.

In an instant he leapt upon the large German Shepherd mix, and the two went rolling on the ground, biting at each other's throats. Soon the German Shepherd yelped and raced off down the street. The other two bigger dogs jumped on the sheep dog. The fur flew as the three of them dropped and rolled to the ground, clamping on to skin and fur, making furious guttural sounds as they drew blood.

June and I were no longer the attention of the smaller dogs. They were now in a frenzy barking and yapping at the fighters. Soon the two larger dogs were racing down the street howling in pain. The sheep dog snarled at the lap dogs; again, as in one body, the small dogs leapt on him, hanging from his neck and back, desperately working together to bring him down. Soon they, too, were running down the street, bloodied and beaten. Then, once again, all was silent.

I stared in stunned disbelief at the slate blue colored dog standing before me, tongue out, panting heavily. I looked into his dual colored eyes and simply said, "Thank you!" The dog seemed satisfied and began to walk in circles around the stroller and myself as I pushed forward toward home. He behaved like a protective centurion, walking circles around us all the way to our doorstep.

It is not easy to forget an event like this, which has served to remind me that I am not alone in this vast universe; I am loved and will receive help when I need it and ask for it. This holds true for my daughter, too. I can't be everywhere to protect her as she grows up, but I don't need to be. God will be with her when I cannot. June and I did not receive as much as a single scratch that day, and June never even woke up once during the attack. She slept through our entire ordeal! I will always be grateful for that and for all the help we receive along our way.

—Eileen Braden

Eileen Braden currently lives in the Twin Cities area and is pursuing a degree in psychology.

Total Sacrifice

"May I see your medical booklet?" asked Dr. Gianna Molla at her clinic in Mesero, about twenty miles from Milan, Italy.

Her patient adjusted her worn shawl across her shoulders and handed the doctor her booklet. Dr. Molla stepped into her office for a moment while the poor woman waited. Dr. Molla's professional partner and brother, Ferdinand, stepped into the office behind her. "What are you doing, Gianna?" he asked, watching her tuck a five thousand lira note into the booklet.

Gianna looked up suddenly. "She needs this money so! She'll find it when she gets home," Gianna whispered walking around Ferdinand back to her patient.

Ferdinand only grinned at his sister. Gianna was a reflection of their faith-filled parents who had raised their children for service to God and the Church. Their mother had led her children to daily Mass, consecrated their home to the Sacred Heart of Jesus and the Immaculate Heart of Mary, and saw that they prayed the rosary daily.

Ferdinand watched Gianna gently escort the poor woman to the door and part with encouraging words. He recalled how at fifteen Gianna had attended an Ignatian retreat, which had profoundly impacted her life. She had written certain resolutions at that time, which she still followed. He admired her because her motivation for everything was to do it for Jesus. Every work, every trouble was offered to Jesus. She had resolved not to go to the movies unless they were modest and not scandalous; she preferred to die rather than commit a mortal sin. She prayed to the Lord that He would make her understand how great is his mercy.

Often he heard her pray, "O Jesus, I promise you to submit myself to all that you permit to happen to me; make me only know your will." Her manner at this clinic was healing for all who came. "When we touch a patient's body, we touch the body of Jesus," she often said.

"Gianna, you are better medicine than anything you can prescribe!" Ferdinand exclaimed when they were again alone.

"Medicine is what I will continue with all my life. It is thrilling to be able to help lead a soul to God in this way. It's an opportunity that even priests do not have!" Gianna's bright brown eyes shown with awe. Then her brows knit together. "I am struggling, though, to know what God wants for me. Does he want me to marry or should I go to Grajaù, Brazil, with our brother, Fr. Alberto?"

"What of me here?" Ferdinand teased.

"I love working here with you, but I can't help thinking about how much help he needs in that impoverished area. Imagine how hard he works being the only doctor there."

"As you pray about it, you will have your answer," Ferdinand told her.

Soon after, in answer to her fervent prayer, Gianna met Peter Molla at Mass on the Feast of the Immaculate Conception. Both were impressed by the other's devotion to God, and several months later they were engaged.

"I want many, many children," Gianna announced as she prepared for their wedding in September of 1951. She carefully chose a white gown of the finest quality so it could be transformed into a priestly garment should any of her sons should choose that vocation.

To the delight of Peter and Gianna, in the following years she gave birth to three children: Pierluigi, Mariolina, and Laura. Then, after two miscarriages, in the summer of 1961, Gianna became pregnant with another child.

"Something is wrong this time," she told her husband, examining her symptoms. After undergoing medical testing, her apprehension was confirmed. She had developed a tumor in her uterus, which threatened her life and that of her developing baby.

The Mollas were faced with three choices: remove the tumor and perform a hysterectomy, ending the life of the baby and all hope of future pregnancies; remove the tumor and terminate the pregnancy; or remove the tumor in such a way that would not interrupt the pregnancy, but would place Gianna's life in grave danger.

"I choose the third solution," Gianna told the surgeon resolutely.

Peter admired her for her decision. "You are doing this through your love and maternal responsibility and through the great respect you have for this pregnancy, because that child in your womb has the same untouchable rights as our other children to whom you have given birth…All of whom are gifts of God."

"Yes, Peter, for me there is no other option. I will not end my child's life." Gianna tried hard not to show the great pain she experienced in her abdomen. As the months progressed toward a full-term pregnancy, Gianna had a foreboding that there would be complications. She spent time putting her house in order as if she were taking a long trip somewhere.

As she sorted through some papers one afternoon in April of 1962 she related to a visiting friend, "I am going into the hospital, but I am not sure that I'll return home. My pregnancy is difficult. They will have to save one or the other. I want my baby to live!"

A few days prior to entering the hospital, Gianna fervently reminded Peter, "If you must choose between me and the baby, let there be no hesitation: choose—I demand it—the baby; save him."

Lent was a continuing of suffering and pain for Gianna. Then on Good Friday, April 20, 1962, Gianna entered the hospital in labor. On Holy Saturday, she gave birth to a healthy baby girl, weighing nearly ten pounds, through a Cesarean section.

"We should name her Gianna Emmanuela, after her loving mother," Peter said to his wife as they admired their new daughter. Gianna smiled weakly.

"Yes, I would like that," Gianna agreed. The joy of this new birth was soon overshadowed by Gianna's elevated fever, a rapid, weakened pulse, and exhaustion. She was dying of septic peritonitis, an infection of the lining of the abdomen. Despite antibiotics, Gianna knew full well the extent of her condition.

On Easter Sunday, Gianna took the baby in her arms and kissed her, gazing at her with sadness and suffering, knowing that she would be leaving the baby without a mother. Over the next six days, Gianna underwent excruciating suffering, refusing all pain medication. She remained conscious nearly up to the end, repeating frequently, "Jesus, I love you." In the early morning hours of Saturday, April 28, 1962, Gianna was brought home, where she died of septic peritonitis.

Thirty-two years later, Gianna Emmanuela, her siblings, and Peter Molla gathered in St. Peter's Square for the beatification of Gianna Beretta Molla. On April 24, 1994, Pope John Paul II described her in his homily. "She is a woman of exceptional love, an outstanding wife and mother, she gave witness in her daily life to the demanding values of the Gospel. By holding up this woman as an exemplar of Christian perfection, we would like to praise all those mothers of families who give themselves completely to their families, who suffer in giving birth, who are prepared for every labor and every kind of sacrifice, so that the best they have can be given to others."

In October 1997, Dr. Gianna Emmanuela Molla, the daughter of Blessed Gianna, testified during the Second International Celebration of the Family in Brazil, "Dear Mom, thank you for having given me life two times: when you conceived me and when you permitted me to be born, protecting my life. Dear Mom, intercede always for all mothers and all families who turn to you and entrust themselves to you."

On May 16, 2004, Pope John Paul II canonized her as Saint Gianna while Peter Molla and their children, Pierluigi, Laura, and Dr. Gianna Emanuela Molla looked on. Countless persons watched Peter Molla receive Holy Communion from the Pope at his wife's canonization Mass. One Elizabeth Comparini from Brazil and her daughter, Gianna Maria, were especially moved to be in attendance. It was through the intercession of Saint Gianna that Elizabeth carried her unborn baby for more than two months without any amniotic fluid, giving birth to a healthy baby daughter in May 2000—the second miracle of St. Gianna!

Saint Gianna Beretta Molla, pray for us!

—Joe Cunningham

Joe Cunningham is the founder and president of the Society of Saint Gianna, based in Philadelphia. The Society gives presentations on the life of Saint Gianna and distributes holy cards and literature. For more information, go to www.saintgianna.org.

Mom's Faithfulness Until the End

"Dad," I fumed one day, perturbed at his stubbornness. "I've spent most of my life without you, and I refuse to spend all of eternity without you, too!"

At the time, my father lay dying from cancer. Though raised in a culturally Catholic home, he had been away from the Church for many years. He had a number of axes to grind with the Church and, it seemed, with God. Despite his stubborn resistance to the Faith, my mother never gave up on him. She truly believed that her prayers and dedication would bear fruit in his life and that he would return to God's grace. She truly was a warrior for his soul, and fought for him until the end.

My mother was born into a Catholic family, but it wasn't until later in life that she experienced a deep conversion of heart. Shortly after I was born, Mom received a visit from Fr. Lawrence who had come with an invitation to live "the devout life." Sensing the "Hound of Heaven" calling her, she responded by living a life of intense Catholic devotion. That invitation and her "fiat" undoubtedly changed the course of our family's history—not only for my siblings and me, but for our children's children as well. Mom taught me catechism and handed on a great love of the Faith.

Unfortunately, my father hated the change he saw in her. After a series of very serious family issues, my mother's pastor counseled her to separate from my father in the best interest of the children—my brother, sister, and me. Although it was extremely difficult for her, she obeyed. For the next thirty-two years, my parents lived 250 miles apart, but remained on friendly speaking terms. They eventually divorced and got an annulment, leaving them both free to marry, though neither ever did. Mom felt a profound obligation to Dad. She may have known, as God did, that they would eventually become close friends. I now believe that God kept them both single because this would orchestrate the future circumstances of my father's return to the Church.

Every day Mom went to Mass and we prayed the Rosary together. Mom and I would pray for Dad constantly, that his heart would be opened to God. As a child I remember one time waiting for him to leave so we could hide brown and green scapulars in his mattress, hoping their proximity to his heart would melt the hardness there.

Mom reminded me of an army general pondering the next strategic move, always looking for chinks in Dad's armor. She employed hidden 'weapons'—hit-and-run tactics (share the Gospel in small doses, but change the subject before arousing anger), going up the chain of command (invoking saints and Our Lady), and Chinese water torture (unceasing prayer). She was in it for the long haul and Dad knew he had a formidable "opponent". He respected her.

This went on for decades—Mom trying to bring Dad back to the Church while Dad resisted. I sometimes got discouraged, but Mom would say, "I know Our Lord will see to it that he saves his soul." Then Dad got liver cancer. He lived alone and had to have a temporary colostomy after his first surgery. He was in bad shape. She drove five hours and stayed with him for two weeks to care for his personal needs, including all of his hygiene needs. She took care of him round the clock. She was careful to go to the earliest Mass while he slept so she would be back to care for him.

He often said that he would have died had it not been for my mother. I saw his eyes light up when he spoke to her. Whereas before he seemed equally glad to see me, afterwards I could see his love for her. It was beautiful. He couldn't really understand why she was so good to him. I explained that it was the love of Christ within her that he experienced. "She touches you with the hands of Jesus," I told him. "No one can love like that on her own."

As Christmas of 1999 approached, we figured it would be his last. We wanted him with us, but Dad said he was too tired to come for Christmas. We were prepared to drive down and get him, but he called and asked if he could come a few days early. He drove five hours and was so spent that he didn't have enough energy to get out of the car. The angels must have been guiding him as he drove.

Mom set up a hospital bed in her room for him, and after thirty years, they were together again. In his weakened state, he knew he was there to stay. My brother, Phil, drove him back to his apartment one last time to collect important papers and put his affairs in order. Dad brought the picture of Our Lady of Czestochowa (as she is known in Poland) which hung over his bed. We hung it over his hospital bed, just as it had been at home. We didn't understand why Dad would resist God so strongly, yet have a picture of Our Lady over his bed, but we entrusted him into her hands.

Dad would shake his head in amazement that Mom took care of him after he had refused to return to the family. He was overwhelmed at the kindness and care he received. He knew that Mom technically had no legal or moral obligation to him, yet she showered spiritual and corporal works of mercy on him. There was nothing she could have done for him that she didn't do.

To put this all in perspective, my dad had let us grow up without a father. This had placed a tremendous burden on Mom to raise us virtually alone, and he had never apologized. By the world's standards, he owed us big-time, and Mom owed him nothing. He had mistreated my brother and sister, but through the sacrificial example of Mom, they were there, loving him. Phil was there, washing him, changing his diapers. My sister, Julie, came and helped when she could.

I knew Dad had softened somewhat over the years concerning God. He even sprinkled a "God bless you" in his conversations sometimes. But still, Dad didn't have long to live, and it looked like this one was going to come down to the wire.

At Mom's prompting, I asked my pastor in early January to speak to Dad about confession. Fr. Jim said he would only come when my Dad agreed to confess. I was overcome with grief at the thought of Dad in hell, and poured out my concerns to my good friend, Sue. She said that her family and her brother's family would begin St. Faustina's Divine Mercy Novena for my Dad right away. (During an apparition to St. Faustina Kowalska, Jesus dictated a set of prayers now known as the Divine Mercy Chaplet. He promised to shower His abundant mercy upon those who recite it reverently.) I was relieved, and our family started the novena as well. On the third day of the novena—after forty years without going to confession—Dad agreed to confess!

Fr. Jim came to visit Dad. In my mind's eye, I imagined a huge reservoir of graces being held back by a huge dam. These were the graces amassed by my mother's faithful prayers, day after day, year after year, without wavering. I added my inconsistent and small contributions, made smaller by my lack of faith at ever seeing him change. Suddenly, the dam burst open as Jesus poured out torrents of His tender and infinite Mercy.

Emotionally spent, I heard the bedroom door open, and Fr. Jim came out smiling and waving us in. Mom had been in the living room, faithfully praying. We went in to see Dad, and he was transformed! He had a glow about his face, and he spoke with the innocence of a child. A fruit of the Holy Spirit is peace, and it was this peace we saw radiating from my father. After receiving last rites, Dad slept for four solid hours, the longest he'd slept since he'd come to stay with us.

For the first time in my life, my father had truly become my brother in Christ! His soul was at peace. Dad received His Lord in Holy Communion several times before he died. Mom would prepare him by reading prayers beforehand, and Dad would respond with an "Amen" or a simple grunt, all he could muster towards the end of his life.

The day before he died, Mom saw Dad (who had become increasingly less responsive) sit straight up in bed and look upward with wide-open eyes. He smiled and tried to raise his arm up toward the ceiling. Afterwards, he fell back into his comatose state. Mom thinks it might have been his Mother, Mary, his Lady of Czestochowa, who came to prepare him.

Three weeks after my father's confession, I was urgently summoned to his bedside. It was January 24th, the feast of St. Francis de Sales. I joined my mother at Dad's side, and together we prayed, sang, cried, and rejoiced. As we shared in his last moments on earth, I did something I hadn't done since I was a little girl—I pulled out my father's hairbrush and began brushing his hair. I reflected on all the time I had missed with my father. Yet I rejoiced in the opportunity at spending eternity with him. I realized that both my mothers—the Blessed Mother and my own flesh-and-blood Mother—had remained faithful to him until the end.

—Lynn Klika

Lynn Klika lives across the street from her mother in central Wisconsin with her husband of twenty years, Scott, their five children, and several dogs and cats. Exactly one year to the day after her father's death (January 24th, the feast of St. Francis de Sales), they brought home their two youngest children, adopted from Russia, provided for by the inheritance he left.

Bedtime

Mom and Dad were watching TV when Mom said, "I'm tired, and it's getting late. I think I'll go to bed."

She went to the kitchen to make sandwiches for the next day's lunches; rinsed out the popcorn bowls; took meat out of the freezer for supper the following evening; checked the cereal box levels; filled the sugar container; put spoons and bowls on the table; and started the coffee pot for brewing the next morning. She picked up the game pieces left on the table and put the telephone book back into the drawer.

Then she put some wet clothes in the dryer, put a load of dirty clothes into the washer, ironed a shirt, and secured a loose button. She watered the plants, emptied a wastebasket and hung up a towel to dry. She yawned and stretched and headed for the bedroom.

She stopped by the desk and wrote a note to the teacher, counted out some cash for the field trip, and pulled a textbook out from hiding under the chair. She signed a birthday card for a friend, addressed and stamped the envelope, and wrote a quick list for the grocery store. She put both near her purse.

Dad called out from the couch, "I thought you were going to bed."

"I'm on my way," she said.

She put some water into the dog's dish and put the cat outside, and then made sure the doors were locked. She looked in on each of the kids and turned out their bedside lamps, hung up a shirt, threw some dirty socks into the hamper, and had a brief conversation with the child who was still up doing homework.

Mom then washed her face with three-in-one cleanser, put on her night solution and age-fighting moisturizer, brushed and flossed her teeth, and filed her nails.

In her own room, she set the alarm, laid out clothing for the next day, straightened up the shoe rack. She added three things to her ten-most-important-things-to-do list. She said her prayers and reviewed tomorrow's schedule in her mind.

About that time, Dad turned off the TV and announced to no one in particular. "I'm going to bed." And without another thought, he did.

—Anonymous

No Rest For The Weary

"Your mother only wishes there was someone to
make *her* sit quietly for five minutes!"

My Angel, Brianne

Deep in thought, I walked along the sidewalk on the way to my car when a loud inner voice suddenly broke through: *This car is going to hit Brianne.*

Brianne, my fourteen-year old daughter, had just finished her soccer game. She had gone ahead of me to the car so we could drive to the other side of the field to watch her ten-year-old sister Kiersten's soccer game.

Startled by the loud and mysterious voice, I jerked my head up and saw a black car coming my way. In an instant, I spotted Brianne standing on the yellow line in the middle of the street. "Brianne, stay where you are!" I screamed. Brianne hesitated just a moment seeming to gauge if she could make it across in time or not. Then, she darted into the street right into the path of the oncoming car. I froze, helpless to stop what I realized in horror was inevitable. The car whizzed past me and struck Brianne, propelling her high into the air.

It was as if time stopped. I had the distinct impression of two angels on either side of Brianne. She seemed to understand something but then turned her head and looked back in love towards me. Her slight frame fell back to the ground half on the grass and half on the sidewalk. In reality, this had all taken place within seconds, but to me, it was if everything had been in slow motion.

A doctor who happened to be at a soccer game, made the decision to have Brianne airlifted to the trauma center. Two friends offered to get my other daughter and son Brandon, fourteen. My husband Bob was away in Costa Rica on a scuba diving trip with a friend. He was already heading home, but it was a thirty-six hour trip. The doctor then drove me to the trauma center. "We don't know what we are going to be facing when we get to the hospital," he told me calmly and quietly. "Her injuries are very severe." "Dear God," I prayed "Please save Brianne." It was a prayer that could not have had more feeling or more desperation to it. The God who had previously been little more than an obligation, suddenly made me see that Brianne's life and all life was held in His hands. I realized that it might be His will that Brianne would be with Him that day, but I so desperately prayed that we could keep her.

It was Sunday, October 18, 1998. Brianne had just had the most marvelous weekend, but then she was a marvelous girl. She was going through the teen years with such grace. I often shook my head in wonder that I should be so blessed to have Brianne as my daughter. Even though she was popular herself, she always looked out for the kids who were left out or made fun of. She saw the good in everyone and it seemed everyone saw the good in her. There was never a time that anyone told anything bad about her.

God was so present in Brianne's life. She was the one who had been prodding me to be more regular about our family's Mass attendance. I was a fence sitter—if it was convenient or I had something to pray for, I was there; otherwise, there were more important things to do. But now, all I could do was pray for Brianne.

At the trauma center, I stayed with family and friends in the waiting room. I knew everyone was working frantically to keep Brianne alive. An hour-and-a-half after the accident, a doctor came through the door with news. With great sadness, he said, "Brianne did not make it."

It was as if all life had been drained from me. I went numb. "No!" I cried. "This can't be!" Even though I could clearly understand the doctor's devastating words, they would not sink in. My emotions went into autopilot. We were told we could go in to see Brianne and say good-bye. My heart overflowed with love as I looked at my daughter. I told my kids they might want to kiss her because it could be the last time we saw her. We kissed and held her and said good-bye. Then, after just a short time, we went home. There was no reason to stay, Brianne was not there anymore.

We went home to begin our changed life, the one without Brianne. On Tuesday, I had to pick up Bob at the airport, who was returning from Costa Rica. I had made the decision not to let him know about Brianne until he arrived home. There would have been nothing he could have done and it seemed that experiencing such intense grief trapped on an airplane would be too horribly painful.

There was no easy way to tell him. "Bob, Brianne died on Sunday," was all I could say.

"What?" Bob asked in disbelief. And then there were all the questions: how, where, who. It was so hard to be with him as his shock turned into searing grief at the loss of his beloved daughter who had looked so much like him.

Somehow we got through the next days, weeks, and months. My love for my other children gave me a reason to get out of bed in the morning. In spite of my deep pain, my capacity to love began to grow: for my family, for life and for God. Yes, God who took my child from me became ever-present in my life. I came to accept that Brianne was in a better place and that God loved her even more than we did. I felt Brianne praying for us, her family, who missed her so much. Through my experience of losing Brianne,

I began seeing life through different eyes. So many of the things that I once valued I realized would one day be mere dust. I began to see that only things of everlasting value truly mattered—like my children. It was that realization that led me to have a reversal on my tubal ligation. After having three children, I had thought that was plenty. Now I realized that each child was a gift beyond measure and there was nothing greater I could receive in this world. Since it had been many years, the odds for a successful reversal were against me. Yet, when I was forty-three years old, a month after my surgery, I ecstatically told Bob, "I'm pregnant. We're going to have a baby!"

Bob smiled, echoing my joy.

I would give anything to hold Brianne once again, and yet, I can now accept that our earthly life is passing. Everyone knows that on one level, but through Brianne's death, I came to accept it. I look forward to the day when we will all be reunited in heaven. I imagine Brianne welcoming us with outstretched arms.

In spite of all the pain, I would never trade the person I am today for the one I was before Brianne's death. I can see the beauty in every day and in everything. I also feel blessed beyond measure that God has given us another little soul. Camryn Brianne is now three years old. She will come to know her wonderful big sister through pictures and through our stories.

I am so thankful for the fourteen carefree years that we had with Brianne. Suffering offers us difficult but powerful lessons. It can get our attention and help us to turn toward God. Every day is a day without Brianne. But even in her death, she has brought me so much.

Brianne's memory is also continuing to help others. Several years ago, Laurie Hissey, a friend with four boys who Brianne used to baby-sit, heard my desire that Brianne not be forgotten by others. Laurie became the leading force in organizing an annual fund-raiser, "Run for Brianne," to honor her memory. College scholarships are awarded to students from Unionville High School in Unionville, Pennsylvania. This, the sixth year, was the last run. We have reached our planned goal of a $100,000 perpetual endowment. The interest earned will provide two $2,000 scholarships every year to students who are selected based on the good qualities Brianne possessed. Athletic and academic performance count but so do compassion and service to others. It brings me great comfort that through these scholarships, the good in Brianne really will live on.

—Stacey Carter

Stacey and Bob Carter live in West Chester, Pennsylvania. Their son, Robert Brandon, 20, attends the Naval Academy in Annapolis, Maryland. Kiersten, 16, goes to Unionville High School, and Camryn, 3, recently started pre-school at St. Maximillian Kolbe.

We All Have Special Needs

Our firstborn child, John, was diagnosed with autism shortly before his second birthday. Being first-time parents, my husband, Joe, and I had not detected the signs along the way since neither of us had been around small children before. His love for spinning in circles and following the edges of rooms over and over did seem odd, but we thought that it was John's way of entertaining himself.

I first began to wonder if something could be wrong when John did not develop speech like other children his age. The doctor tested his hearing and found nothing wrong; then our physician suggested that John be tested for autism. Neither Joe nor I knew anything about this disorder, which effects communication and socialization, so we began reading about it. John showed all the classic signs: speech delays, abnormal responses to sensations, ritualistic routines. From there we learned how to raise and love our son with a developmental disability that will last his lifetime. We discovered that John was a visual learner and possesses an incredible memory.

With the daily struggle of maintaining a consistent lifestyle for John, we neglected attending church on a regular basis. John reacted negatively to noise and large spaces, and I couldn't imagine him making it through a service without creating a scene. We had previously attended a large Lutheran church, but John would not step into the huge sanctuary without screaming. Not going to church seemed the easiest way to handle the situation. However, we realized that our daughter, Rachel, who was nineteen months younger than John, needed to be involved in church life.

About that time, Joe's father died of cancer, which sparked Joe to search for his faith and return to his Catholic roots. He began reading the Bible and books on Catholicism, and finally went to visit a priest.

"Let me recommend St. Raphael's. It is a wonderful parish. Don't be afraid to bring your son there to church. People realize that we all have special needs. You need to be at Mass as well as anyone else, including your son," the priest told my husband. At first, only my husband attended, but as time went on, I began reading the books that Joe had collected.

"Honey, why don't we attend church as a family?" My husband suggested. "I know it may be hard for John, but the atmosphere there is very pleasant. If we make it a routine, I think he will get used to it."

"I'm willing to try it," I agreed, but the thought of it terrified me. "How would I handle John if he screamed during a quiet moment?" I wondered. When Sunday arrived, I was sweating before we even left for church. As we entered through the main door into the cross-shaped sanctuary, I steered the family into the very back row. So far, there was no adverse reaction from John. I felt perspiration trickling down the back of my neck, but as each portion of the Mass passed I relaxed just a little. John had not made a single loud noise. At the end of Mass when the priest announced, "Go in peace!" I did just that. We were elated that John had not been upset by the new situation.

"Maybe it was just a fluke," I said to Joe on the way home. "Do you think?"

"I don't know," he responded, "but we can try it again next week and find out for sure!"

The next Sunday I entered the sanctuary with a bit less apprehension, and again John came through with flying colors. We continued to attend Mass there and soon decided to join the parish. When Joe went to the parish office to officially sign up, he found out that the church had classes for people with special needs.

"We have an autistic son. Do you have classes for him?" he asked.

"We do. I'll have the woman in charge contact you right away," said the church secretary with a smile.

That very week our son began classes at church. Our spiritual life blossomed in the next few years. Watching the religious education coordinator work so tirelessly with John to prepare him for First Holy Communion was a blessing beyond words.

Since John has many aversions to foods due to its taste or texture, we wondered how he would react to receiving the Lord in the Eucharist. His teacher spent many hours teaching him that the host is something special, something of God, something that *is* God. John practiced receiving the Lord with unconsecrated bread so he could understand what he would physically taste on that special day.

In December of 2001, we headed for church for the occasion of John's First Holy Communion. I recalled how nervous I had been the first time I had ever entered that sanctuary, and now, amazingly, John was going to receive our Lord in Holy Communion. Our joy far out-distanced our anxiety as our priest acknowledged John during the prayers of the faithful. Then surrounded by family, John walked to the front of the sanctuary and received Jesus for the first time. As Joe and I looked on with indescribable gratitude to God, tears welled up in our eyes.

Now our family sits happily in the front of the church each week. We all have a special need to be with God, and we are grateful to be together for Mass. We find John frequently staring peacefully at the altar during the consecration. It makes us wonder whether he sees something that we don't.

—Wendy Haefliger

Wendy Haefliger has been married to her husband Joe for fifteen years. They and their two children reside in Minnesota with Oscar, their Yorkshire Terrier.

A mother is not a person to lean on,
but a person to make leaning unnecessary.

—Dorothy Canfield Fisher

This Too Shall Pass

Recently, I watched images on TV of military men being sent overseas to a war-torn area of the world. Wives tearfully hugged and kissed them goodbye while their little children wrapped themselves around Daddy's neck in fond farewell. The cameras would follow these men across the globe, but it was the families returning home without husband and father on whom my thoughts rested. They, too, are among this country's brave souls—I know firsthand.

It was April 1, 1963, when my Army sergeant husband, Albert, called home. "Hi," Al said. "Just wanted to tell you I received orders this morning that I'm being sent to Vietnam for a year."

I thought for a moment and then laughed. "April Fool—right?"

"No joke," he answered. "We have only a month to prepare."

I did not even know where Vietnam was. It was only the preliminary days of chaos over there, so it had not yet become a household word. Within a month we moved with our seven children, ages ten and under, off the Army post into a three-bedroom subsidized housing project. Families could not remain on post while the men were deployed elsewhere. We sold the car (I did not drive), gave away our pets, and registered the children in a new school.

The day of my husband's departure arrived like any other. It was a warm May morning. In between sweeping up Cheerios, I readied the four oldest children for school, and dressed and fed the two preschoolers and baby. Amid the normal routine, my husband dressed and packed last-minute items. A friend would arrive shortly to pick him up.

A sick, hollow feeling filled my stomach. My husband would soon be leaving, and all I could do was threaten my boys that I had better not see any more Cheerios fly across the room. A horn beeped in the driveway, signaling his departure. Al slung his gear over his shoulder, said goodbye to the kids, gave me a quick kiss and stepped out the kitchen door. "Bye-bye. Take care," was all I could get out of myself. In a daze, I walked to the window to watch the car slowly disappear down the street.

Everything remained the same—the Cheerios, the bantering of children—and yet, suddenly everything had changed. I was so alone. I was David abandoned and distressed in the wilderness; at the same time I was Custer at the Little Big Horn, overwhelmed by the odds. Anger churned up within me at the Army and spilled out to include God. "Dear Lord, how did I ever get myself in such a mess?"

I picked up the baby for comfort but he squirmed away. He also needed his diaper changed. There was no time for a pity party. I grabbed a diaper and announced: "Karen, John, Trisha, Mark—get your coats. It's time for school. Remember to stay together and come right home afterwards. Mary and Susan, finish your breakfast. And will someone catch Jeffrey so I can change him?" I was now on 24-hour active duty as Colonel Mom, with no reserves in sight.

Schools, stores, and neighbors with daughters who babysat were the plus side of our new apartment. Housing projects, however, are also inhabited by an interesting assortment of people. Soap operas had nothing on them. We came from very different worlds.

A municipal park program kept my kids well occupied with games, crafts and swimming most of that first summer, while we all adjusted to life without Albert.

My greatest fear was having to face any kind of accident or serious illness without the support of my husband. Hence, I guarded the family's health like a watchdog. Regardless, we had colds, one black eye, a toothache, a small head cut, strep throat, a kick in the groin, stitches, and a three-day virus that forced me to direct my troops from the couch. Not a day passed without thoughts of my husband and concern for his safety, especially as the Vietnam conflict intensified. Listening to the news one night, I learned a bomb had exploded in Saigon and an MP was killed. No name was given pending notification of next of kin. My husband was both an MP and in Saigon. I had no option but to spend a sleepless night worrying, hoping and praying. How many others did the same that night, I wondered? Plans on how to proceed as a widow assembled in my head. "I need to get out of this housing project, but where should I move?" I wondered. "I need to get my driver's license. How can I support the family as a secretary?" There was so much to figure out.

As the morning played out and I neither received a phone call nor a visit from a chaplain, relief ensued. The man that I married must still be alive! I prayed for the one who did lose his life. The sun seemed to shine brighter while my children played happily outside on that beautiful spring day. I was on the short end of my ordeal now.

Then, the phone call I had long awaited finally arrived. "I'll be home in a few hours," Al announced from American soil. I sank weakly into my easy chair, hardly believing the year had actually passed and I had made it through. I had felt so inadequate so many times, but God had given me the grace to persevere. I may not have always been successful, but I had always been faithful to God, to our country, and to my family. Tears slid down my smiling face as I began to contemplate my next happy dilemma: How was I going to operate with a man around the house now?

—Jeannette E. Akin

Jeannette E. Akin has been married to Al Akin for fifty-one years. He was in the Army for twenty-two years, seven of which were spent in Germany. After his tour in Vietnam, they had two more children and retired to a farm for a time before returning to city life. Their nine children and fifteen grandchildren are scattered around the country.

Motherhood Gave Me the Will to Live

While deep sea fishing in Panama waters there was a tug on the line. Judging from the immense pull and fight, it had to be a blue marlin.

My husband and I had joined twelve other friends for a week-long fishing excursion in Central America. Each day we rotated into different pairs and departed from the ship onto seven smaller boats. On this particular day, I was with my best friend's husband, Mike.

It had been a slow day for fishing. The sun was getting low so we decided to try one last spot before calling it a day. That's when the marlin hooked the line. "Here, Mike," I said. "I have already caught a marlin on this trip. You can reel this one in."

A fierce fighter like the marlin usually takes a couple of hours to exhaust enough to reel in. It was late afternoon and the boat's captain wanted to get back before dark. He put the boat in reverse, which allowed slack in the line to reel in faster. We had the still-green fish to the boat within about half an hour. The first mate estimated her to be twelve feet long and approximately six hundred pounds.

I had grabbed the video camera and focused on the water. The first mate was getting ready to tag and release the marlin. As he leaned over to grab the lure, the fish and I made eye contact. Her angry eyes glared at me. Then, in a flash, the marlin catapulted up out of the water and lunged right at me. Her razor sharp bill gored through my right arm, through my right breast and out of my side. I was literally skewered. The enraged creature violently jerked me back and forth, lifting my body off the ground, as if trying to flip me back into the water with her. Instinctively, I put my only free hand out behind me to grab onto something. Incredibly, my hand went straight for a pole and I braced myself. The bill slid out and the fish slipped back into the ocean.

I felt my life ebbing away. The mate cut the line and the captain put the boat into high gear. Mike made a tourniquet and applied strong pressure to my chest and arm while I lay flat on the deck. The captain radioed the ship to notify the nearest clinic that we were on route. The clinic was more than two hours away; on Coiba Island, a penal colony for men.

The pain seared through me as I lay on my back, gasping for air. "This is it," I thought, "I am going to die, and there is no one to take care of Michelle." My oldest daughter Jennifer, fifteen, was fairly independent, but my nine-year old, Michelle, still needed me.

I became angry. "Damn you, God," I furiously cried out. "You know Michelle needs me! How dare you? How could you do this to her!" With death only a breath away, most people would have prayed to God rather than damn Him, but then, most people had not lived my life. I had lived a life of pain and bad choices, but it was my motherhood that gave my life meaning. Otherwise, it seemed most of my life was one long chain of pain.

One of my first memories occurred when I was three. My mother was dressed in a long pink robe, washing dishes in a comatose state. No one could get her to stop. Men in white coats came to my house and strapped my mother down onto the stretcher. She was diagnosed as a paranoid schizophrenic and went in and out of mental institutions.

My father kept his own apartment in another town where he worked, and only visited my mother and us eight kids on weekends. Later, during my teen years, when he became part of an FBI investigation, I learned that he was involved in the Mafia.

I never had much of a sense of family. We were cared for by governesses and maids. The only sibling I was close to was my oldest sister Darlene, whom I adored.

My father divorced my mother when I was nine years old. He moved us into the town where he worked and attempted to be our parent. After just a few months, his drunken, violent fits at my four older siblings, impelled them to plead for the release of my mother from the mental institution. He happily relented and the nine of us tried to survive in a three-bedroom house. My father left with his money and his womanizing really took off. Although he lavished gifts on other women, his own family usually went without even basic necessities.

Mom was not there mentally, but she did care a great deal for us. I heard her call my father many times on the phone to beg for money for groceries. When that did not work, she got on the phone to priests, nuns, and members of her prayer group.

When I was fourteen, my father was diagnosed with brain cancer and needed surgery. Although the doctors gave him slim odds, he not only survived but a spiritual experience changed him dramatically. I finally had a father. He often took me to visit my sister Darlene who now lived in Las Vegas. These were my happiest childhood memories.

Within a few short years, however, my father died of lung cancer; I was furious at God. "It took my whole life to get this man to love me and now you've taken him away from me!" I cried out.

Over the next decade, my life became a series of failed attempts at finding love. Two marriages, an abortion, miscarriage, and two children later brought me to my next devastating loss—Darlene. She died quickly of breast cancer when she was thirty-seven and I was thirty. My rock, my idol, the sister who understood what it was like to be me, was suddenly gone. I could not even yell at God this time. I thought, *This was typical of Him. Why wouldn't He take her? He never cared about me before, why would He start now?*

I sunk deep into depression and turned to gambling. Over the next two years, I blew over $130,000 although I only made $60,000 a year. I loathed myself but could not stop. I drove to a lake and sat on a rock contemplating suicide. *"What kind of mother gambles away her children's electricity?"* I asked myself. Then I thought of my daughters, Jennifer and Michelle. I loved them more than anything I had ever loved. They were a gift. It was then, through my motherhood, that I found a reason to survive. My girls needed a real mother to take care of them, not an out-of-control compulsive gambler.

The next morning, I sought help. I began seeing a therapist. I was going to do whatever it took to give my daughters the mother they deserved. I also went to Gamblers' Anonymous for a few months, but could not complete the step that required me to give everything over to a Higher Power. There was no way I was going to give everything over to God. I finally pulled my life back together and I did it for one reason—my daughters.

So on the boat, believing that at any moment death could rob my daughters of their mother, I cursed God. But as I cursed, a most indescribable feeling overcame me. I was completely enveloped in a love that was more intense and at the same time gentler than anything I ever imagined. My anger and fear evaporated, replaced with a radiating sense of peace and trust in God. I was in His hands. Whether I lived or died, I trusted God fully. Whatever happened, my daughters would be all right. I knew God loved us and He was with me.

My nightmare was far from over, but the powerful touch of God—although it lasted but a moment—sustained me. I came in and out of consciousness through the jolting two-hour boat ride. I could barely breathe, but an inner peace kept me calm.

It was getting dark when we arrived on Coiba Island, a minimum security penal colony where prisoners were allowed to roam freely. I had heard earlier that the village part of the island was full of murderers and rapists—the worst of the worst. Soldiers with guns kept them at bay.

By the time we got to the village, it was dark. Prisoners were everywhere. The front of the makeshift clinic looked like a chicken coop. The bottom was wood and the top was chain link fence. I made Mike promise not to let them butcher me, or leave me there. There was no electricity, only candles. I was met by the so-called "doctor," also a prisoner. There was a rusted gurney on a dirt floor and very few supplies. He roughly sutured my arm with fishing line without benefit of anesthesia. A sea of dark faces and penetrating stares watched me through the fence as I lay screaming. I refused treatment to my breast.

It was recommended that I stay on the island until morning when a plane could come. I grabbed Mike by his shirt collar and said: "Don't you dare leave me on this island. I don't care if I bleed to death. I'm going back to the mother ship until morning!"

A fierce storm doubled the usual thirty minute trip and made the rough ride more painful than the first one. At day break we returned to the island where we were picked up by an old single-engine plane. It arrived two hours late because of engine trouble.

I was transported to a Panamanian hospital. My right silicone breast implant had burst and x-rays showed fluid in my chest cavity. The doctors said the bill of the fish grazed my lung and tore the membrane. I was treated with antibiotics and stabilized. After five days, I was flown back to New Orleans, Louisiana. The fluid in my chest wall remained so the doctors treated me for possible pneumonia.

During the next couple of months, my recovery remained at a standstill. My doctor decided that the fish had not penetrated through my chest but only punctured my breast. He surmised the fluid was possibly caused from infection and my body being in shock. Plagued with pain and fatigue, I spent most of my days lying on the couch. After two and one half months, I went in for reconstructive surgery.

As the surgeon looked around, he was shocked. He discovered a five-inch a hole in my chest wall, big enough for him to see my lung moving. He closed me up immediately and transported me to another hospital. There, a CT scan revealed that what was previously assumed to be fluid was actually silicone. The implant had been pushed into my chest wall.

Once the silicone was removed, the hole in my diaphragm repaired, and my chest wall sewn up, I immediately began to feel better. The recovery was slow but today, the only lasting physical effects are scars and mild nerve damage to my arm. The surgeons surmised that the implant saved my life. When the marlin's bill hit it, the implant deflected the bill off to the side rather than going in the same trajectory. This, coupled with the coating from the silicone on the bill, allowed it to graze my lung tearing only the membrane, rather than puncturing it. After the bill tore up my diaphragm and came out, it left the implant in the chest wall hole plugging it up like a cork. Had it not plugged up the hole, my lungs would have collapsed and I would not be here.

"It was a close call," according to both surgeons, but I knew it was really God's call. Every amazing coincidence that saved my life, from the pole on the boat, to the plugging of my chest wall, did not occur by chance, but by God. From the moment God made His love known to me on that boat three years ago, everything has changed. A lifetime of living without Him had heaped layers upon me that needed to be peeled away. But little by little I started walking on the path that led me to Him. The rosary, prayer, meditation, spiritual readings, religious music and Eucharistic adoration has become my source of strength as I give everything over to the Almighty. Once, it was only my motherhood that gave my life purpose and power. Now, God is at the helm.

—Denise LeBlanc

Denise LeBlanc is now a grandmother helping to raise her grandson. She says the joy that her children and grandson bring to her life is enormous. Denise knows that when she leaves this earth, her children will have never doubted her love for them. She thanks God every day for the privilege of allowing her to watch over them.

Chapter Four

A Mother's Tears

For Just a Short Time

How would you answer if God asked you this: "Would you be willing to accept a precious soul who will only be on the earth a short while?" I do not know what my answer would have been before I knew my daughter, Rachel. But if I could have seen into the future and known the graces that flow from having been trusted with such a responsibility, I would have said: "Yes, Lord."

My pregnancy had proceeded normally, just like my previous one. It touched me that the first time I felt the baby stir in my womb was at Christmas of 1981 during Mass. "Just like John the Baptist," I thought. "She leaped in the presence of Jesus."

Rachel entered the world to the joyful shout: "It's a girl!" Then it was quiet. Everyone immediately knew something was wrong. Rachel would not cry. She could not breathe. "What's wrong with my baby?" I cried. No one answered; they were too busy working on her.

It was quickly determined that Rachel's nasal passages were too small. She was whisked to the Neonatal Intensive Care Unit. Once I recovered enough from labor (it turned out I was also suffering a gallstone attack), I was wheeled in to see my baby. "She's probably not going to make it through the night," the doctor had solemnly warned me.

Looking at my little girl's fragile life, I was numb. All I knew was that she was a child of God, not just my child. "She's not going to live," I thought in shock. My husband, Robin, agreed to baptize her immediately. "How long does she have?" I wondered. As yet, no one knew.

Not until the next morning could Rachel be removed from her oxygen-fed incubator so I could hold her. With my baby girl nestled in my arms, a flood of motherly love washed over me. I was filled with joy. "She's alive," I thought. "At least I can hold her." No matter what the future, she was my baby and I could not help but to love her with my whole heart.

Genetic testing revealed Rachel had partial-trisomy 13—a very rare disorder that meant she had no eyes. Her eyelids were closed and sunken. She would be severely developmentally delayed and have weak muscle tone, among a host of other problems. No baby with this condition had ever lived past six months of age. Most of these babies were only five pounds at birth. Due to Rachel being a month overdue, she had been almost eight pounds. I did not know what the future held, but deep within my heart, I felt she was born to beat the odds.

When Rachel was two weeks old she came home. We did not bring her home to die; we brought her home to live. Our two-and-a-half year old, Jessica, was thrilled to have a little sister to help care for. Robin and I sent out birth announcements. We had already started grieving the inevitable loss of our beloved baby, but for the time being, she was alive. We were determined to celebrate that life.

Through Rachel, we experienced what it truly means to live each day to its fullest. I would think: "Today is a day we will take and live joyfully, because I have a healthy child, because I have a happy marriage, because my baby lives, because, because, because…" Rachel gave me an ability I never possessed before—to truly experience and appreciate life.

We took Rachel with us everywhere we went. I was determined not to stop living or stay trapped at home because I had a disabled child. Some times people would look at her and say, "Oh, the poor thing." I always responded patiently that she did not know any different. And Rachel did seem happy, especially in the arms of her daddy. With Robin, Rachel smiled often and became completely relaxed. There were so many things Rachel could never learn to do, but one gift she did have was laughter. Her angelic giggles and laughs were infectious.

One morning, when Rachel was two years old, I checked on her before going to the kitchen to make breakfast. I smiled to see her contentedly rock herself back and forth in her crib. When I returned a short while later to check on her again, she had stopped breathing. Robin began CPR and I called 911, but Rachel had already left us. It was time.

I cried, not for Rachel but for myself. Now God had my little girl in His loving arms. Now she knew things she could never have known in this world. She was experiencing God and loving me from heaven. I missed holding her in my arms, but now I knew she was holding me in hers.

Jessica was four when Rachael died. She missed the part of life that had once included her little sister, yet there was an acceptance. Jessica talked about Rachel a lot and when she was in second grade, and her teacher let her do a show and tell about her little sister.

Two years after Rachel died, our new daughter Becky was born perfectly healthy. As she grew, she came to understand that she has a sister in heaven watching over her.

Rachel brought our whole family a little closer to heaven. Through her beauty and through the pain we had to suffer, we learned to see life for what it really is: a gift from God to be fully lived moment to moment.

—Brenda Vogsland

Brenda and Robin have been married for 25 years. Jessica is now 23 and Becky is 17. Although Brenda works a little on the side, she describes herself as a stay-at-home mom who is quickly working herself out of a job as her baby is soon to graduate from high school.

No Longer a Child

At baby showers and women's socials the conversation always seems to come around to childbirth stories. We easily laugh at the tales of misery and discomfort as though it's a badge of honor, now that the physical pain has passed and is nearly forgotten. However, you will rarely find mothers swapping hysterical stories about the day their first child left home permanently. That bit of memory is a pain that lingers.

When mothers-to-be prepare for delivery, no one ever mentions in the childbirth classes that this little necessary event of motherhood is nothing compared to the other end of the spectrum: the day your child steps *out* of childhood. There are few classes to prepare you for that. There are no mental breathing techniques to help you through that pain.

When the August weekend finally arrived for my husband, Jeff, and me to drive our oldest daughter, Carly, to college, I felt like I was in a fog, though the days were hot and sunny. I had no choice but to go through the experience, ready or not. The nearly 1,000-mile drive was filled with little reminders for Carly about college details and constant questions of "Are we there yet?" from her two younger sisters. I was thankful for their distraction because if I thought too much about our destination, my eyes would mist over. I could feel a tangible tug of emotion toward Carly, who was sitting in the backseat of the fully packed van.

I reminded myself that college was a great opportunity for her and she would excel in whatever she did, but that thought moved over every time I imagined a petite little girl, twirling around in our living room, laughing and leaping. Carly was

going to step out of childhood forever! Now, I understood
how my mother felt when I left home at eighteen, and how
my grandmother felt when my mother married my father and
moved to Switzerland for four long years. The unavoidable
cycle surely has continued through the generations.

After the flurry of unloading at the dorm, purchasing
books, and trudging in the heat from building to building to
revise her schedule, it was time to think about our departure.
On this Catholic campus, an enormous steel cross stood
upon a hill. It was visible from Carly's dorm room. Jeff and I
decided that would be the best place to say our goodbyes.

"Before we go we wanted to pray with you," Jeff said
bravely, leading the way up the hill toward the cross. Carly
and I could not even exchange a glance without tears welling
up as we followed behind. *So this is how it feels to have a
child grow up,* I thought, disliking the heart-squeezing pain
immensely.

When Carly was a child, every morning Jeff had blessed
her before school with the blessing of Aaron, "May the Lord
bless you and keep you and cause His face to shine upon
you and grant you peace." Here on the hill, Jeff began this
familiar prayer, but after the first phrase, only tears came
out. We all three blubbered for a while as the younger girls
watched, not able to grasp the poignancy of the moment.
Jeff managed to choke out the rest of the prayer. I squeezed
Carly so tight, words of love gushing out, "I love you and I'm
so proud of you and I know you'll do just great here!"

After we regained a bit of composure, Jeff said, stroking
Carly's long, chestnut hair, "We want to leave you here at the
foot of the cross, because we can trust Jesus to take care of
you when we are not here."

Carly nodded in assent, looking up at the towering cross.
To escape the 100-degree afternoon temperature, we drove

her over to her dorm before we left the campus. She posed at the front door of her dorm to wave a farewell.

A glimpse of her from afar imprinted her beauty upon my memory forever: her creamy white complexion, her large green eyes trimmed with thick, long lashes, her thick straight hair blowing like the mane of a thoroughbred—free and windswept. *Could there be anything as lovely as she?* I thought. It was impossible to verbalize anything for several miles. After an hour of our lonely journey, the cell phone rang. It was Carly, and she was as lonely as we were. *Maybe we should go back and get her,* my heart cried, but in the course of the conversation, a dorm RA heard her sniffles and invited her over for popcorn and to meet other just-as-lonely freshmen. "Bye, Mom, I'll talk to you later! I'm going over to somebody's dorm room!" her now cheery voice exclaimed while I was in mid-sentence with some word of comfort.

"OK! Have fun!" I squeezed in before she hung up. "Well, we did it," I said looking over at Jeff. "She's on her own now and she's going to make it."

Jeff and I jumped a parenting hurdle as Carly stepped out of childhood, never to return. That one moment of separation is a hurtful spot that will stay buried in my heart along with all the delightful memories of Carly. Now we can cherish each facet of her sweet life in our memories, photos, and movies and watch her continue to spread her wings and fly away. How bittersweet.

—Emily Cavins

Emily Cavins is co-editor of Amazing Grace for Mothers. *Her biography appears at the end of the book.*

Cold News

I was giddy with delight after my husband, Gary, announced that we were moving back to our home state of New York now that he had left the military. It had been eight years since we had lived near my parents. I began to imagine all the fun things I could do with my mother again.

Soon, we were unpacking in our new home on a large parcel of land adjoining my parents'. They lived in a historic wooden house that at one time had been a stagecoach stop. The two-story white house was a frequent stop for our girls, who could easily walk over to visit. Just as I had imagined, Mother spent time with my daughters and me, creating memories together.

About a year after we had moved back, I drove over to Mom's to pick her up for an afternoon of shopping. She didn't come out, so I ran in to see what was keeping her. "Mom? Are you ready to go?" I called, poking my head in the front door.

There she stood in her floral nightshift with a look of confusion in her usually bright eyes. "Mom?" I said stepping inside to get a closer look. "What's wrong?"

"I can't remember!" she cried, her eyes widening with fear. "I'm confused. I…I…I can't think to say what…" Her voice trailed off and she looked around the room as though she might find an answer somewhere.

A feeling of dread washed over me as I tried to link her symptoms to something. Stroke? I didn't take another moment to ponder. "Mom, come in the car right now. We're going to the hospital!"

The emergency room doctor said confidently, "Her blood pressure is normal, heart rate normal. She is not having a stroke." He looked into her eyes and asked me more health questions. A nurse brushed open the curtain to our little chamber. "The tests all came back normal," she told the doctor. "Just keep an eye out for this type of thing happening again," the doctor told me. Mom seemed to be regaining herself as the afternoon wore on. Instead of shopping, we went to her house and sat at the kitchen table until my Dad came home.

"Have you ever noticed her do that before?" I asked my dad.

"Everyone gets forgetful. Especially at our age," he said, dismissing the notion that this was a problem. I followed his lead and tried to put the incident out of my mind, but every time I was around her I looked for signs of abnormal behavior. Within a few months my list grew. She couldn't remember a friend's name; she began to tell me something and forgot completely what she had said; she did not read anymore; she often stopped in mid-sentence. I was afraid to keep track any further.

"Dad, are you sure Mom is okay?" I tried to coax him into telling me what he had observed. "You are doing all of her chores."

"She's the same as always," he said shortly. He would not match my gaze; I knew this conversation was over.

A sense of foreboding hung over me. "It must be old age," I would conclude, only to counter the thought with, "Other women mom's age still hold jobs, do volunteer work, talk on the phone." As I was brooding over these thoughts, an old friend of mine caught my attention at the grocery store.

"Mary Lou? How are things going now that you are back home?" she asked.

"Pretty well," I said, trying to look optimistic as I bagged up my groceries. "We're glad to be back in town, but I'm worried about my mother," I confided to her. "She seems to be forgetting things lately."

My friend's eyebrows rose. "Really? You know, I have a friend going through something similar. They diagnosed her with Alzheimer's disease," she finished.

Those words stabbed me in the heart. "Alzheimer's! Oh, I pray it isn't that!" I gasped. My friend gave me a sympathetic squeeze.

"I hope it isn't either."

My father agreed to bring Mom in for an examination. "Mr. Elderkin, your wife has the early stages of Alzheimer's," the doctor reported, confirming my fear. I could barely listen to the rest of his diagnosis as I envisioned her with her energetic step and her sweetness beyond compare.

"Sixty-eight is still so young," I lamented to Gary at home. "What is going to happen?"

"Didn't the doctors say to keep life as normal as possible? That's all we can do," Gary said, trying to be reasonable. I was too numb and overwhelmed to think of it reasonably.

"I wanted to spend the rest of her life with her the way she was!" I cried, trying not to feel bitter that we had lived so far away for many years. I knew Gary was right. All of us endeavored to make life normal for Mom; keeping her on even keel was her only medicine.

One cold night in March, I awoke with a start. "Gary, someone is knocking!" We both flew out of bed. Gary flung open the door to find my parents shivering in their pajamas!

"What happened?" I asked, ushering them into the living room and finding some blankets to wrap around them.

"Our house burned. It's gone! By the time the fire department came there wasn't much left to save," my dad explained as Mother nodded. "I tried to call, but the phone was knocked out. We came over because everything is gone." My father dropped wearily down on the sofa.

Our daughters appeared from their rooms to hear the awful news. "It's all gone," my father repeated.

"You'll stay here as long as needed," Gary said, taking charge.

We pulled together and got through the loss of their house and possessions, but the fire had robbed my mother of so much more. It destroyed her daily routine and her predictable paths and connections. With that stripped from her, she declined rapidly.

In the course of a couple of months, Dad replaced the ruins of the old house with a modular one. However, he might as well have put it on the moon, because my mother couldn't grasp the fact that this was now home. This was a foreign place for her and she couldn't remember anything about the fire.

"I'm afraid to sleep," Dad nearly cried not long after. He looked so fatigued. "Mom doesn't sleep. She wanders around and I'm afraid she'll hurt herself! I can't leave her for a minute!"

I would stay with her so Dad could rest, but she continually wanted to know where Dad was and would become very upset. She slipped further and further from who she had been. Each day seemed harder than the last, until one evening she suffered a seizure.

We finally had to make the difficult decision to put her into a nursing home for her sake and for my dad's.

I had never seen my father cry, but now he began to sob inconsolably. Making this decision was a time of mourning for all of us. Since the facility was close by, we could visit her every day. They took great care of her, and it was evident that she was not going further downhill. We spent every holiday there with her, including my parents' 50ᵗʰ wedding anniversary.

"Hi Mom, it's me! I love you," I told her every time I came to visit. I had read many books about how Alzheimer's progresses, but it was still hard to face her blank look the day she didn't recognize me.

Even though I missed her so badly, when I sat with her in her bright, cheery room, just hugging her and being with her was a comfort. That frail woman was still my mother. After twelve years in the nursing home, I thought I would be ready when the time came for Mom to die, but when we received news she was not doing well, I realized I wasn't ready for it at all.

As we gathered around in Mom's room, our priest came to give her last rites. I knew she was ready, but I wasn't. While I sat by her bed praying with her and holding her hand, I must have dozed off. In a dream I saw my mother holding someone else's hand. They were both dressed in long white robes, walking away from me into a cloud. My mother turned to give me a big smile as she waved good-bye. What a wondrous dream to be given that day, the day she died. I entered into a new phase of missing her physical presence. The finality was tremendously difficult, but I knew that Mother was happy and no longer suffering, and that someday I would once again be reunited with her—and she would remember me.

—Mary Lou Smith

Mary Lou Smith and her husband, Gary, live in Richfield Springs, New York, with her father Lincoln Elderkin. Mary Lou and Gary have two daughters. Mary Lou owns and operates a dog grooming shop called Kreative Klippers.

Thirty Minutes

The year might have been 1990, or it might have been 1995. I don't remember anymore. Nor do I recall the name of the woman who packed a lifetime of mothering into thirty minutes' time. Was it Karen? Cathy? Jennifer? Truly, I don't remember. During my sixteen-plus years as an obstetrical nurse, I was privileged to know many courageous mothers, to be with them in the most intimate moments of life and death.

I have often said that labor and delivery nursing was the best of the best...and the worst of the worst. Its joys were exhilarating and tremendous; its sorrows agonizing and intense. Yet even in situations that one might look at and categorize "the worst," a closer examination would reveal a glimpse of the divine.

This story isn't about me, it's about a woman—let's call her Susan—who gave birth prematurely. Susan had been transferred in from another hospital because she was very sick, and so was the baby inside her. I was Susan's nurse when the specialists were valiantly trying to maintain her pregnancy with bed rest and strong medications. But in the way that these things often go, it became apparent that delivery was the most prudent course for both mother and child.

I wasn't on duty when Susan's baby was delivered, but I worked a few days later. I was saddened to learn that there were unexpected complications with the baby and mother— he was gravely ill, and Susan wasn't recovering as quickly as expected, either.

I often visited my former patients and wanted very much to see Susan, but my shift that day didn't permit a break to do so. It wasn't until the evening shift had started and I was on my way home that I was able to stop by her postpartum room.

Susan lay on her bed, weak, pale, and heartbroken. I recall that her hair was long and blonde, and it hung limply around her face. She was alone in her room, for her husband was over with the baby at the Neonatal Intensive Care Unit (NICU), located in the children's hospital two blocks away. Fresh tears flowed as she told me of her baby's condition, confessing that she hadn't yet been over to the NICU to see him. "They said that until today I was too sick to make the trip; now that I can go, I'm too scared."

We talked for a few minutes, and I held her hand while she expressed her fear and sadness. When the bedside phone rang, interrupting her words, she closed her eyes and drew in a ragged breath.

"Do you want to answer it?" I asked.

She shook her head "No," but still reached slowly for the receiver. Her "Hello" was filled with apprehension, and only seconds later her face and body crumpled with the weight of the words she received.

Her breathing was distressed when she hung up the phone. In her eyes was stark fear. "He's dying," she managed to say. "They want me to come right now so I can see him... before..."

She broke down completely, sobbing in my arms. Just then the charge nurse appeared in the doorway with a wheelchair, having received a phone call from the NICU, as well. "Someone will be here shortly to take you over to the unit."

"This can't be happening." Susan gripped my forearm. "I can't go...I can't do this!"

"Yes, you can," I reassured her. "You're his mother, and he needs you."

"Can you take me?" she pleaded. "I know you're off duty, but can you please take me over?"

"Let's go," I said. I brought the wheelchair to her bedside.

As physically fragile and emotionally wrought as she was, I worried that the trip might bring on a worsening of the condition that had initially brought her to the hospital. In a little kit I brought with me were the emergency medications I would need should that occur. From the sixth floor we took the service elevator to "G" and began the long underground trek to the children's hospital.

Anyone who frequently traverses the tunnel between the two hospitals has seen the NICU team rushing to attend an emergency delivery, or whisking a tiny, critically ill newborn back to the unit. The parents, grandparents, and loved ones of these newborns are likewise easy to spot. Their hurried steps and anxious, sometimes tear-stained faces cause the conversations of passers-by to still into respectful silence. Some people look away, either uncomfortable with the sight of suffering or politely offering whatever privacy can be afforded in such a public place. Others, perhaps those who work frequently around sickness and death, seek eye contact, making a brief, compassionate, human connection.

Susan was so distraught that she noticed no one in the busy tunnel. The nearer we drew to the elevators of the children's hospital, the more panicky she became. "I can't do this," she said over and over, trembling, gulping for air. "I can't, I can't."

We reached the second floor and entered the first set of double doors that would admit us to the NICU. Her husband was waiting there, and he collapsed into her arms. Together they cried.

"He's going to die, Susan," he wept. "He's too sick to make it. There's nothing more they can do for him. The doctors want to take him off life support so he can die peacefully."

Once we were at the baby's bedside, the doctors came to meet with Susan and her husband. Though Susan's husband had been able to find a degree of composure, his wife had not. She was wholly hysterical in her grief. A bewildered young chaplain intern, hastily summoned, stood a few steps behind the doctors, nervously shifting his weight from one leg to the other. In his hands he gripped a prayer book, and I watched him steal several deep breaths.

As the respirator was switched off, the chaplain tentatively put his hand on Susan's shoulder. She wailed all the more. Silent tears slipped down her husband's cheeks while he watched a pair of neonatal nurses gently remove his son's IVs and EKG leads.

The tiny boy was still breathing, but barely. One nurse swaddled him in warm, soft blankets and held him toward his father. He shook his head.

"Susan," he said. "It's your turn to hold our son."

Susan was silent. When she looked up, her face was blotchy and swollen. With the sleeve of her blue-and-white striped hospital bathrobe she wiped her eyes. "I can't," she whispered, but she held out her arms.

In that moment, a grace befell Susan unlike any I had ever seen before. Until the baby quietly died, she held her son and poured out her mother's heart of love for him. She was calm and serene, filled with the same kind of dignity I imagine another Lady must have possessed when she watched her Son die.

The chaplain intern wept openly as he prayed. So did the nurses and the doctors. In the midst of such tragedy, we realized we were witnessing something holy and extraordinary, a transformation that could have been wrought only by God.

When the baby's heart stopped beating, Susan fell apart once again. Yet she triumphed in her motherhood, and I will always remember her as one of the finest and bravest mothers I have ever known.

—Peggy Stoks

Peggy Stoks is a wife, mother, registered nurse, and the author of several novels. Her story "It Stops Here!" appeared in the first book in the Amazing Grace *series,* Amazing Grace for Those Who Suffer. *She and her family make their home in Minnesota's Twin Cities area.*

The Long Road

As my teenage son, Peter, handed me a small gift, he looked into my eyes with a smile and said, "I love you, Mom. Thanks for everything." I dissolved into tears as we embraced. Thinking back over all that we had gone through in the past year, I experienced true joy at his words. One year ago I never thought this scenario would have been possible.

During Peter's sophomore year, he began to change from a loving and obedient son to being belligerent to my husband, Bill, and me. He refused to obey our house rules and wanted to argue continually. He also was not able to concentrate on his schoolwork and was failing in many subjects. We knew something must be wrong, so we had him tested for learning disabilities. In the process our pediatrician suggested we test him for drugs. To our surprise, the test turned up positive.

Immediately Bill and I tried to talk to Peter, but he said he would rather leave than talk about it. That afternoon he left the house. I was in shock. I had never seen a child act so bizarre. He was entirely unreasonable, and I felt so unprepared for this situation. We knew that Peter needed to be placed into treatment, but how could we force him to go?

I waited anxiously for Peter to return, but by late evening, we called the police and filed a runaway report. That night Peter slept in the park, however, and the next day he returned to school. The counselors there asked him if he wanted to go home, but he said, "No."

The police brought him to a runaway shelter where he stayed for two days. This threw me into such a state of confusion and fear. Peter had never been around youth from tough backgrounds. I couldn't sleep wondering what was happening to him. Life had to go on as normally as possible for the sake of our other three boys and infant daughter, but Peter was a constant concern on my heart.

Finally after two days, Peter called and asked to come home. "You can come," we told him, "if you will go in for an assessment." He agreed, but once home he showed little desire to cooperate. His assessment diagnosed him as an alcoholic, and we learned he frequently used marijuana.

Bill and I wondered for how long and where he had been using drugs and alcohol. Obviously his group of friends from school were involved. We spoke to some of the other parents, but they denied there was any problem with their children.

Due to the runaway charges we had filed against Peter, the police met with him, reminding Peter if he went to treatment and stayed out of trouble, he wouldn't have to go to court. I hoped that this would bring about some change, but Peter continued with his belligerent behavior. I was on guard every moment so he would not sneak out to get in trouble. One evening he begged to go rent a movie, so I broke down and gave him permission. Instead of going to the video store, a friend picked him up at the end of the street and they ended up burning down someone's garage!

I was home alone when I found out what had happened. "Peter, you lied to me! What were you doing?" I demanded. He began swearing so violently at me that I took a step back. Then he spit at me and stormed to his room. I was so stunned and hurt that I could do nothing but cry.

That summer, Peter was ordered by the court to go to treatment. He attended an outpatient program, but no change in behavior occurred. He was so far from the loving and respectful son we had known. We then tried an inpatient treatment center covered by our insurance, but eventually Peter was asked to leave because he was not cooperating. Peter promised us he wouldn't use any more if we let him go back to Catholic school for his junior year. His former school graciously made every effort to help Peter, so I had a hopeful attitude that the worst was over.

Two weeks after school started we received a call from the principal. "I have Peter here with me," she said. "He is very drunk." Bill brought him home. It was awful to see Peter totally out of control. We couldn't keep him at home in such a condition, so we called the police to arrest him for disorderly conduct. I have etched in my mind the horrible scene of Peter standing on our front porch that dark night yelling at the police.

"Do you want to talk to your mom?" one officer asked.

"No," Peter shouted. "Why would I want to talk to her, that…" he finished his sentence with degrading names. Words had never hurt me so badly as those. Where was my adorable baby who used to write me love notes? I hit an all-time low.

After a night in jail and sobering up the next day, he realized what he had done and he was truly sorry. My heart wanted to rescue him, but I knew we had to be tough and press charges. He spent four days in juvenile detention. I did not go to visit him, although Bill did. I just couldn't bring myself to face him. Peter admitted to Bill that he needed help and they had a breakthrough moment together.

After that we decided to find the best treatment center we could, even if it meant re-mortgaging our house. For twenty-eight days Peter was at a terrific treatment center, where Bill and I were also helped by attending sessions to learn how to separate Peter from the addiction and see him as the person God had made. This helped me to be able to love him, even though I was deeply hurt. I had to remember that he was God's child more than mine. It was still hard to fight the sense of shame I felt for failing as a parent, but I also learned that we were powerless to change Peter. All we could do was to place Peter into God's hands and trust Him. During this time I put up a picture of the Divine Mercy with the simple prayer at the bottom of the figure of Jesus that says, "Jesus, I trust in You." This was my daily prayer.

After Peter finished the initial treatment, there were still three months of after-care living away from home. The holiday season was approaching, and I grieved to think Peter would not be part of our celebrations. We visited him on weekends. Then one Sunday evening in November, we received news that Peter had run away with a boy who had a criminal record.

My heart felt as though it would break. My emotions were on a roller coaster as Bill set off to find Peter's trail. First he called the mother of the other runaway, but she didn't care at all that her son had run off. She did, however, show Bill a drug house where her son used to hang out. Bill questioned the boys there until finally one mentioned that Peter had been there and had been crying. He had let him use his cell phone. "Please, give me the numbers off your phone," Bill asked. The boy cooperated and Bill found the number Peter had called. It was a friend he had made at the treatment center.

The friend was very concerned about Peter and said to Bill, "Peter said he would call me again. He wants to go to California. They plan to catch a ride from a trucker. When Peter calls, I'll get him to meet me and I'll tell him I'll give him money. Instead, you can be there to pick him up." Paul thanked the young man for his help.

The whole ordeal lasted two days. I'm sure I aged a few years in that time. Our extended family was ready to put up posters and begin searching for Peter. To everyone's relief, Bill's plan worked. When Peter saw his father's car instead of his friend's, he gladly went with his dad.

The experience was eye opening for Peter. The police issued a warrant for his arrest for violating the court order to finish treatment. That landed him in jail for ten days in a locked cell with only drawing utensils and a window. It was humiliating to visit the jail because we had to be patted down several times. It was so sad to see Peter sitting there in a uniform and slippers. I was frightened for his life and for his soul, so I tried to be encouraging and as always I would tell him, "God has not given up on you. God has a plan for you. Trust God for your future."

"I drew this, Mom," Peter said, sliding a picture toward me. He had sketched a praying hand entwined with a rosary. I knew somewhere inside him was a desire for God. This picture is now one of my treasures.

After his jail stay he went back to the after-care program and finished it. Bill and I attended his graduation from treatment and brought Peter home again. Still I was worried and anxious. How can you monitor a seventeen-year-old and still raise the rest of the family? Peter was highly unmotivated and seemed lost at home. It was so difficult to watch him struggle and struggle. He didn't want to go anywhere for fear he would start using again. I prayed and cried so often to Mary because I knew she understood my pain. I asked her to be my Mother and comfort me. This would calm my anxiety so that I could love my son and be patient with him.

In the spring, on Mother's Day, the whole family went to dinner. Each child gave me a small gift, but as Peter handed me his I was overcome with gratitude that my loving son was back. "Mom, the biggest thing you and Dad have taught me is to believe in God."

By the end of summer, Peter celebrated his eighteenth birthday. For a while I wasn't sure he would live to see it. Instead of partying with friends, he willingly spent his birthday with our family and grandparents. He acted so nice and hugged everyone.

I don't know what the future will hold for my son, but I will continue to put him in God's hands everyday.

—Sharon Lee Wagner*

Sharon Lee Wagner lives in the Midwest with her husband, Bill, and five of their children. Peter has moved out on his own and works with animals.

Name has been changed.

Behold your Mother.
—John 19:27

A New Saint in Heaven

For most people it was another ordinary day in the span of time, but for my husband Marc and me it was the day that marked the birth of our second child. After a long and difficult pregnancy, Dominic Fulton was born on March 30, 2000. When I first held his tiny body in my arms, I was taken aback at the simple yet profound beauty of life! My very excited, two-year-old son Joseph soon joined us, immediately covering his new brother with kisses. Our family was growing and I was so thankful to God for this new gift of life that He had sent us.

Shortly after the birth of Dominic, I began to journal about our family life.

Saturday, May 13

"Dominic was baptized today, the feast of the miracle of the sun at Fatima. My precious child became a child of God."

Wednesday, July 19

"…Dominic is now three–and-a-half months old and Joseph is two-and-a–half years old. My children daily bring me so much happiness. I love them dearly and I marvel at the beauty of my vocation as a mother and a wife every day …Praise the Lord for His goodness, especially for Joseph and Dominic; what true blessings they are!"

Sunday, August 6

"Dominic rolled over today; he was so excited and so was I! Both of my boys bring me such delight. Certainly there are times when mothering my two boys can be challenging, but it never outweighs the blessing that they are, the incredible joy that they daily bring to my heart. It is so beautiful to look at Dominic—to hold his tiny head up as it wobbles around and his big blue eyes stare at everything. To see his bright smile as he looks at me, like he is so happy to see me, just warms my heart. Yet, to hold him—yes to hold him, and cuddle him close to me as I nurse him, as my body provides nourishment for his—makes me wonder at the beauty of life that God has given me to raise and love…Oh, how truly blessed Marc and I are!"

Wednesday, August 9

"Dominic becomes a SAINT! Our baby goes back to the Lord!"

Wednesday, August 16

"One week ago today, the angels came and took my little Dominic to see Jesus. He is a saint now. He died suddenly of Sudden Infant Death Syndrome. My heart aches so much. I have never felt so much pain in all my life. I love being a mother and I loved my little Dominic more than words can express. I am still in shock, like maybe he is coming back; maybe he did not really die. It has not all quite registered. The pain is so deep, I cry often. I miss him terribly! It is hard to believe that it all happened—it was so sudden. I would give anything to have him back. So many things remind me of him: his favorite toys, the smell of baby shampoo, his clothes that are still in the laundry basket, certain lullabies that I sang to him, plans that we had, etc. Please God help me! I hurt so much inside. I give my pain to you. Saint Dominic, intercede for us all! In one night, my whole life was turned upside down. My heart feels so empty; my breasts want to nurse. I have milk coming in, but no baby to feed. This is a harsh reminder to me and especially difficult. I want to forget this all happened and have Dominic back.

He was such a good baby. He brought me so much joy. That joy is gone now and it is hard to imagine ever being that happy again."

I was now in uncharted waters. The journey of loss is so painful that it has the power to either destroy you or completely transform you. I knew in my heart, by the very gift of faith that had been given to me, that somehow I had to let Dominic's death transform me. I believe the transformation began the night Dominic died.

It was a warm summer evening, and I had just finished cleaning up after dinner. Marc went outside to cut the grass and I decided to go out and join him with the boys. I knew I had a lot to do with a move to a new house scheduled for that upcoming Saturday, but I thought it was best to make sure we had some family time that day.

Before we went out, I changed Dominic's diaper while Joseph lay on the bed next to him. I clearly remember at that moment looking at my children and thinking how blessed and happy I was just to be a mom. We soon joined Marc outside where he was trying to fix the riding lawn mower. Realizing it was too big of a job for that night, Marc decided to spray the front bushes for spiders instead. Joseph played on his swing set while I pushed Dominic around the yard in his stroller. After a short while, we all went inside. Marc took a shower while Joseph played, and I got Dominic ready for bed. It was a hot night so I put Dominic in a short-sleeve outfit. Around 7:30 p.m. I nursed him. He wanted to keep sucking even though he was done nursing, but I was feeling so overwhelmed with all that had to be done that I gently unlatched him and laid him down for the evening. I thought he would be up again in a few hours wanting to nurse, and then we would be able to cuddle a bit more. Little did I know that would be the last time that I would be able to nurse him or to hold his precious body, so alive in my arms. Marc bathed Joseph while I made a few telephone calls. About 25 minutes after lying Dominic down, Marc checked on him. He was lying face down, so Marc rolled him over and realized that Dominic was not breathing. He could see froth like blood coming from Dominic's nose and his body was limp when he picked him up. "Kathleen!" he screamed. I will never forget the way that Marc yelled for me at that moment and the look of terror that I saw in his eyes when I met him in the hallway and he handed me my lifeless child. As we scurried to find the telephone to call 911, my heart was in complete agony begging God to help Dominic wake up. While we waited for the ambulance to arrive, we laid Dominic on the living room floor and Marc performed CPR on him. There was no sign of life. All the while our son Joseph sat on the couch and watched, not really saying anything. We thank God that he did not realize the horror of what was going on at that moment.

The ambulance soon arrived and the medics laid Dominic on our cocktail table with attempts to revive him. They never verbalized at this point that he was already gone, and so in my heart I had a small glimmer of hope. They loaded Dominic up in the ambulance and Marc encouraged me to ride along. He said he would follow us in our minivan, as there was not enough room for both of us in the ambulance. It all happened so fast that I did not even have time to put on my shoes. It seemed so weird not using Dominic's car seat as we pulled out of our driveway. The ride to the hospital seemed like an eternity. Half way to the hospital another ambulance met us along the country road and the paramedics joined us in our ambulance. I sat in front, as there was no room for me in back. There were so many people working on Dominic that I could only catch a glimpse of his little head from behind. The cold air from the air conditioner chilled me to the bone as I attempted to pray. I called on Our Lady's intercession as I prayed the "Hail Mary" repeatedly interspersed with cries of "Please God, do not take my baby!"

When we arrived at Pekin Hospital, I jumped out of the ambulance hoping to catch a glimpse of Dominic as they rushed him into the emergency room. Back at home Marc called some friends to come and get Joseph, and then he drove alone to the hospital to meet us. Upon arriving at the hospital, I was immediately taken to a little room and Marc, many dear friends, and our parish priest soon joined me. Both my family and Marc's family were called, but they all lived too far away to join us at that moment. A woman doctor soon came in, sat down next to us, and very lovingly said as she touched my arm, "I'm so sorry; we did all we could." Those words pierced right through my heart. My son was officially pronounced dead at 9:31 p.m. How could this be? Just two hours before he was smiling, laughing, and apparently healthy? What happened? There were so many questions. Did he eat something? Did he inhale some of the bug spray? Did he suffocate? How could God allow this to happen? We had tried to be so faithful to Him.

The nurse said we could hold Dominic one last time. As I sat in that tiny hospital room and waited for them to bring me my son, my mind was flooded with many memories from Dominic's four short months with us. It was all over now. It seemed so cruel.

When the nurse placed Dominic's lifeless body in my arms that night, I felt a unique closeness with our Blessed Mother. She knew the pain, the anguish, the feeling of loss. I thought of that holy image, the Pieta, with our Lady holding her lifeless Son, our Savior, in her arms. From that moment on, I knew that my life would be forever changed, and that Dominic was now in heaven. According to Church teaching, he was now a saint.

The first week after Dominic's death, I spent a considerable amount of time in our bedroom just staring at the place where my child died. This was the place where he met Our Lord face to face and entered from this life into the next. When I lifted my gaze from this earthly place where my son had once been sound asleep up to his heavenly home where he is now forever alive, peace came to my soul and I began to find hope. I found hope in the resurrection of Christ that assures me of the possibility of reuniting with my son someday and together enjoying the eternal splendor of God. Although hope did not remove the deep pain that I experienced over such a great loss, I came to discover that hope has a unique way of ultimately transcending my pain.

The sting of Dominic's death has given me a new vision of life. I have come to understand that my pain over his loss goes as deep as my love for his life. The mixed feelings of sorrow over his death and joy over his new birth have by far been the most profound experiences of my life. The night Dominic died I was acutely aware of the words of Job in scripture, "The Lord gives and the Lord takes away, blessed be the name of the Lord." God gave Marc and me a precious soul to care for, if only for four brief months. We now forever have a child in heaven watching over us. What bittersweet pain it is to meaningfully echo Job's cry, "Blessed be the name of the Lord!"

This awful tragedy has awakened me to what is truly important in life. I have seen God's glory in the midst of my grief. Life has moved on, and yet Dominic will be forever deeply embedded in my heart. I am his mother, and I cherish my child. We now have a beautiful little girl, Gemma Marie, who was born thirteen months after Dominic's death. Her birth brought us great happiness and yet at the same time there was a lot of fear to work through. Joseph often speaks of Dominic, and last year he wondered if they were going to have a birthday party in heaven for him. Marc has walked his own journey of grief, though closely united to mine. I have found joy again and truly, "The joy of the Lord is my strength."

I have learned a lot over the past few years from my son's life and death, and I trust that God will continue to show me what more I am to learn throughout my lifetime. Daily as a family we ask our little Dominic Fulton to pray for us, and daily our love for God grows deeper; for prayer begets love, and love brings forth new life in our souls.

—Kathleen Miller

Kathleen Miller has a theology degree from Franciscan University of Steubenville and lives in Peoria, Illinois with her family. Since the death of Dominic, she has become a certified SIDS Risk Reduction Educator for the state of Illinois.

In Search of My Mother

My mother's screams of pain had ceased only to be replaced with my own screams. The woman who gave me life died in 1959 when I was twelve years old. I have no memory of her last birthday, her last Thanksgiving and Christmas, or my own last birthday with her. I felt abandoned and alone. I hated God and was very angry with my mother for dying and leaving me. I felt horrid that I had all these feelings and no one to talk to about them.

Back then, children were treated as though they did not need to grieve. I was expected to go on with life as though nothing happened. One day at school, I began crying uncontrollably. The teacher came over and asked me what was wrong. A boy sitting in the next desk told her that he heard some kids making fun of me at recess because I did not have a mother. There were times I just could not keep it all bottled up inside.

My mother, a woman I hardly knew, affected every aspect of my life, and I had to face that life without her. I wanted her with me, especially at the birth of my children. I wanted so much to pick up the phone and ask her advice or simply watch her hold my children like she used to hold me.

I never realized how profoundly my mother's death affected me until I became a mother. It was then that the memories of her dying that I had repressed for so many years came to the surface. They had been buried deep, but once they began to surface, there was no holding them back. Finally, so many years later, I could begin to grieve what I had lost. When the memories of my mother's death came back, I allowed the little girl in me to cry and cry. I wrote a letter to my mother telling her good-bye. I asked God to forgive me for hating Him and to help me heal. I know that He did both.

When my children were all in school, I believe I was guided spiritually to apply for a job at a hospice. A friend encouraged me to apply for the job because he thought I would be good at it. I applied, having no clue as to why. I certainly did not want to talk about or deal with death, but I felt compelled to do so. Surprisingly for me, I was hired; my life forever changed. Through this experience, I began to truly accept my mother's death and understand the dying process. I learned about her death through the death of so many other mothers. I felt my mother saying good-bye to me when the patients reached out to hold my hand and smile. I saw my mother's spirit and faith inside of these wonderful people. Death no longer was an evil that took my mother away from me. I came to understand and accept that death is a passage to another life, not an end.

I also became involved with grief sessions for children. We connected immediately. I understood their anger, their aloneness, and their depth of sorrow, and they understood mine. We were able to help each other work through our grief and know that we were not alone on this kind of journey. I could help them understand that sorrow comes and goes, and that it is OK to feel sad sometimes even when grown-ups think they should feel happy.

My memories of my mother are few, but I sense her presence with me often. A day does not go by that I do not talk to her and ask her for advice. My answers do not come over the phone but through incidents that happen or words I read or hear. I especially see her in my children and my grandchildren. Sometimes it is her energy, her determination, her creativeness or just her basic physical features. She speaks to me through them in many ways.

Through no choice of her own, my mother left behind a loving husband, two grown daughters and a little girl. But just as the tree roots are deep within the soil, my mother is rooted deep within my spirit.

—Susan Handle Terbay

Susan Handle Terbay lives in Dayton, Ohio. She is the mother of six wonderful children and grandmother of four spectacular grandchildren. She is a columnist for catholicmom.com and co-author of Gifts *(New Horizon Press, 1997), which contains stories of the final journey of many extraordinary people and the families and friends left behind. Susan collected them during her thirteen years working at a local hospice.*

The Freedom to Love All My Babies

I tensely mumbled good-bye to my boyfriend who sat in the clinic waiting room while I stepped through the next door. I was not prepared for what greeted me. Before me stood a long line of women in various stages of pregnancy all waiting their turns to have an abortion. I had not expected the line. It was like a scene out of the Holocaust where people waited to board trains that led to death.

When I told my boyfriend that I was pregnant, he responded that he was not ready for a family. He asked if I would have an abortion. Neither was I ready. I was only twenty, and we both had big hopes and dreams for our futures. I wanted to be a dancer, an actor, and a writer. Having an abortion seemed like my only choice.

Even though we had spent four years together, my boyfriend's reaction sealed my conviction that he was not the man for me. I wanted someone who was strong and would stand by me no matter what. As for me, I was too afraid to face pregnancy alone.

I numbed my mind and emotions in order to stay and wait my turn to have my baby's life taken. A clinic assistant had showed me an ultrasound of a fetus around the age of my own. She had pointed to an area and said, "See that? It's just a cluster of cells."

I was put to sleep and awoke in a recovery room full of women with the same stricken looks. It's the only time I can remember being in a room full of women where no one was talking. I looked around and vowed that no one would ever know what I had done. I would go to my grave with this horrible, humiliating secret.

The relationship with my boyfriend quickly deteriorated. In order to start over, I moved from New York to Florida where my dad lived. In Florida, I began the Dare to Dream dance company that served children from the Naval base. I have always called my students my kids because I do more than just teach dance. I believe if you can teach a person one dance step, they can dance their whole life. And if they can dance, they can dream. I often wrote poetry that I recited at my kids' recitals. For instance the poem, "My Child" in which I say:

A child, oh a child, don't hide them from the light.
Love them, care for them, teach them how to pray...
A child, oh a child, give them all your love.
Welcome them, cherish them, and teach them to dream.

Even though I had buried the pain from my abortion, my poem was a hidden plea to my kids not to make the same mistake I had of failing to love and cherish a child. Ironically, in spite of the pain of my abortion, I still considered myself pro-choice. By burying the pain, I did not have to think it all through.

During this time I became an American Red Cross volunteer at the naval hospital. One day a good-looking doctor attracted my attention. Tom seemed a little put off by my bold invitation to dinner, but within five days of our first date, we knew we wanted to marry. Actually, it only took me the first date. When he showed me his car, outrageously painted in multicolored patches, I spotted a square that was not filled in. Instead, it had a picture of a shark and a dinosaur. When Tom explained that a little boy from his apartment building had painted the picture, I knew he was the man for me. The last guy I dated did not even want anyone eating in his car. I knew Tom had the qualities I wanted in a husband.

Tom transferred to Connecticut and we married in a civil ceremony within the year. By the following year I had joined the Catholic Church and we married again in the Church. Although Tom and I both wanted children, the first year of our marriage he was sent to serve in Japan for seven months. Before his departure, I visited a doctor and explained I had severe abdominal pain and sickness during my monthly periods. He suggested giving me a shot of Depo-Provera—a contraception that works for several months. The doctor determined that it would prevent an untimely pregnancy since Tom would be away for so long and also take care of the monthly pain. I did not tell the doctor that it was only since the abortion that my periods had become so painful.

When Tom returned home, he was a very different man. He had grown spiritually and had become fully convicted in all aspects of his Faith. Tom also became actively pro-life and eventually refused to prescribe any form of contraception or do sterilization surgeries. His stance caused great persecution from his colleagues but Tom steadfastly refused to go against the teachings of the Catholic Church. During this time, I was still quietly pro-choice. I kept my feelings to myself as I watched my husband's faith and convictions solidify. Once, when Tom asked me if I had ever had an abortion, I lied to him. He was the man of my dreams and I desperately wanted to be the woman of his dreams. One day, Tom brought home a picture of an aborted fetus dumped on a garbage pile. The baby was fully formed at thirty weeks and had weighed two pounds and two ounces. The sight sickened me and I became completely pro-life from that day on.

Tom and I tried for three years to conceive a baby. I kept busy, but my failure to give my husband a child devastated me. My intense abdominal pain continued and I had also developed a dull aching pain in my left breast that never went away. The only thing I was told to do regarding the breast pain was to avoid chocolate and caffeine which never helped. Finally, a doctor diagnosed me with having endometriosis as the cause for my abdominal pain. I have since learned that this medical condition is common in women who have had abortions.

Surgery to remove the endometriosis required the removal of my left ovary and fallopian tube. Now my chance of pregnancy was even slimmer. I was put on a drug that duplicated menopause in order to rid my body of the endometriosis that surgery could not reach. Amazingly, I became pregnant at this time. Tom and I were ecstatic. He was at my side for the ultrasound when the baby was six weeks. When the nurse pointed to an area and explained it was my baby's heart beating, I broke down and sobbed. Tom put his arms around me, convinced my tears were from joy. In reality, I realized at that moment that the "cluster of cells" pointed out to me before my abortion had actually been my baby's heart.

My pregnancy was healthy and I again pushed away thoughts of my other baby until the moment of Gabrielle Anna's birth. As I experienced the miracle of her entry into this world and beheld her beautiful face, my first thought was, *I killed someone.*

Through Gabrielle, I experienced love like I never had before—as a mother. It was getting harder to pretend I never had an abortion. Tom was now heavily involved in the pro-life movement, however, so I could not imagine breaking the truth to him.

Three years later I was again having difficulty conceiving and my medical problems grew. After a surgery to remove a polyp on my uterus and remaining fallopian tube, I developed a rash on my left breast—the one that always ached. I was diagnosed with breast cancer. Then, the next day, I learned I was also pregnant. I knew I needed

Tom's support now and the only way he could fully support me was to know everything. "God please give me the strength to tell the truth," I prayed. "I need your help to love all three of my children."

I went to confession and talked to three different priests to get the courage up. Tom knew I had something to tell him, but the words kept getting caught in my throat. Finally one morning, he asked, "Did you have an abortion?"

"Yes," I cried, afraid of his reaction. Tom put his arms around me and gently said, "Honey, so many women are hurting from this. We both lost a child." My tears released a floodgate of pain and brought relief. We melted into each other's arms and I fell in love with him all over again. Tom's strength and love was deeper than I imagined possible.

Tom asked if he could adopt my aborted child. We named her Sarah Eve Messe and had a plaque for her placed on the Memorial for the Unborn in Tennessee. Now, I was free to love all three of my children. I also felt God's grace and love holding me up through the ordeal of my pregnancy.

During the pregnancy, I had a mastectomy and modified chemotherapy. I had to delay radiation and full chemotherapy until after the baby was born. I joined a support group for pregnant women with cancer. I also went through Post Abortive Counseling Education (PACE.) I learned that women who have had abortions or been on Depo-Provera have a huge increased risk in getting cancer. I was angry that women are never told this. But through all the support and counseling, I was no longer a slave to the pain of my abortion. Even though I became bald and now had only one breast my heart sang the praises of God and with the joy of carrying a new life in my womb. Getting cancer actually gave me freedom; the freedom to grieve, heal and love the child I lost to abortion.

I had a sureness that God would keep my baby safe. As for me, I prayed for survival, but I knew if the choice came down to my baby or me, I would lay down my life for my baby. There was no fear in this realization, only a deep sense of peace and love.

At thirty weeks, I developed preclampsia so the baby was born early. This had no connection to my cancer and took everyone by surprise. Christian was born weighing three pounds, two ounces, fully formed and so beautiful. I wondered why God had chosen to have him born early. *"Is there a message in this?"* I wondered. As I looked at my tiny son, something about him looked so familiar yet I did not know what it was. When I returned home without my son, I opened a drawer and pulled out a picture. *"That's it,"* I realized. Christian was the same age and almost identical in weight to the aborted baby in the picture that had made me pro-life. I knew what God's message through Christian was now: Life is precious at every stage.

Christian is twenty months old now and healthy. My cancer is in remission so my health has returned. I will never stop thanking God for the gift of my family. Together, Tom and I will work try to prevent other woman from making the mistake I did. And through my testimony, I hope I can help other women who have had abortions to heal and experience the freedom to love the babies they lost.

—Charnette Messe

Charnette Messe is currently writing a book about her battle with breast cancer entitled, A Brilliant Performance: A Mother's Battle with Breast Cancer and Pregnancy Defines Her Diginity in the World. *Her husband Thomas is a family practice physician in the Navy, and they have three beautiful children—Gabrielle, Christian, and Sarah (who is in heaven).*

Please Hold Him for Me

At 2:00 a.m. Monday morning the phone ringing jolted me awake. My daughter, Robin, said through sobs that she had received a call from the hospital that Randy, our oldest son, had been in a horrible accident late Sunday night. Robin's phone number was found on a slip of paper in Randy's wallet. They would not give further details over the phone and they wanted us to call them at a special number. My husband, Gene, reached over and took my hand. He hugged me tightly and quietly told me to pray while he called the hospital. I watched the blood drain from his face as he listened to the doctor.

A drunk driver had run a red light and slammed broadside into my son's truck. Randy owned a carpet cleaning business and was headed to clean a restaurant when it closed at midnight. The impact had totaled the truck. The doctor explained that a series of X-rays, an MRI, and CT scans revealed a broken neck, broken ribs, and perhaps a punctured lung. Randy was having great difficulty breathing on his own.

The doctor asked us to go downtown to the spinal injury hospital because as soon as he was stabilized, Randy would be flown there by air ambulance. As we rushed out the door, I picked up my prayer book. With our hearts in our throats, we made the drive in silence. I began to pray: "Jesus, be with my child! Jesus, I trust in You." All of a sudden, I felt a great calming peace come over me. The panic evaporated.

When we pulled up at the emergency entrance, the staff was waiting for us. A special phone line had been set up with the other hospital to keep us posted minute to minute. But the minutes turned into hours. Randy would not

stabilize enough to be moved. We continued to be assured
that it was better to stay where we were. As the sun came up
we continued to wait and quietly pray. Randy still was in no
condition to be moved. The calming presence of God stayed
with us and we felt no fear, just an ever-present need to pray
and to trust. My greatest distress was that my son was alone
on the other side of town. We could not hold him, nor assure
him of our love.

At almost 7:00 a.m., I made a quick call to Father Joe
Mancuso, my parish priest. I left him a message to please
offer the morning Mass for Randy. At 7:30, I found a quiet
bench outside. I sat there saying all the prayers of the Mass
and imagined myself at my parish, St. Andrew's, taking part
in this wonderful sacrament of love. I knew God was the
only one who could save my son. And yet I knew He might
well decide to call him home. I had to accept whatever God
thought best.

I surrendered my will and my son to God and prayed:
"Jesus, I trust You. Only one thing do I ask. Please take my
son's broken body and lay him in Your mother's arms. Let
her hold him as she held You when they removed Your body
from the cross, for I cannot. I give him back to You, Lord.
He is Your child more than mine. But please Lord, let him
feel Your mother's arms around him so that he will not be
afraid."

Then I went back inside to take up the vigil and see if we
had any news on Randy. Within minutes the line between
the two emergency rooms was buzzing. The doctors at the
other hospital said Randy wanted to talk to us. He was
kicking his legs and said he wanted out of the contraptions
they had him in. The medical staff was flabbergasted. The
doctor said, "This cannot be! There is no way! The X-rays
clearly show his injuries have rendered him paralyzed. We'll
get back to you. We have to take him back to X-ray."

The second set of X-rays showed no broken neck. His ribs were just bruised a bit and his lungs were fine. "I have no explanation for this," the doctor said. "The first tests we ran clearly showed that your son's neck was broken in the very worst place for a spinal injury. I have compared the X-rays from Sunday night and the ones we just took. They are completely opposite from what we first saw. I am baffled beyond words," he said.

"This young man must have a very powerful guardian angel looking out for him. The only injuries he shows now are the facial cuts, which we had not tried to treat as they were minor compared to the other injuries when he came in." He concluded, "We just have to stitch up his face and he can go home this afternoon."

Needless to say, the depth of my thankful heart was bottomless. Jesus had laid my son into His mother's arms and she gave him back to me.

—Christine Trollinger

Christine Trollinger writes for pleasure from her home in Gladstone, Missouri. After working as an insurance agent for twenty years, she now enjoys maintaining the Adoration Society she founded at her parish, as well as building up the parish library she helped establish. Christine is the mother of three grown children, a wife of forty years, and the former host of the website Catholic Chronicles. *She contributed several stories to* Amazing Grace for the Catholic Heart, *the second book in the* Amazing Grace *series.*

Tiny Handprint

At sixteen weeks gestation with our sixth child, I awoke one morning to the overwhelming feeling that something was wrong. "I think I need to head to the doctor's this morning," I alerted my husband over the phone. "Are you going in with all of the kids? Are you okay? Should I come home?" Dan asked, his voice strained. "I just feel strange," I replied, "but I can get the neighbor to stay with the little ones while I run to the doctor's. I'll call you from there if it's anything serious." I didn't want to upset him if there really wasn't anything wrong.

As I sat in the waiting area, I kept trying to feel any sort of movement in my womb, even the tiniest flutter. "Gretchen, why don't you come on back now," the nurse summoned me. I was trained as an obstetric nurse, so my fears compounded as the nurse listened with the Doppler for the baby's heartbeat. Her expression relayed she found none.

"Let me try it," I insisted. I ran the wand over my slightly bulging stomach, but the only beat I detected was the rhythm of my own heart.

"We'll have you head over for an ultrasound," the nurse said. "They'll see what's going on for sure."

I phoned Dan and he reached the doctor's office before the scheduled ultrasound. There we viewed with sadness the motionless image of our baby, her hands hanging straight at her sides.

"She probably died about two weeks ago, judging by her size," remarked the radiologist as she studied the form of our tiny baby in the darkened room.

Dan squeezed my hand as the obstetrician stepped in. "In a situation like this, the safest thing for you to do is to have a D and C as soon as we can schedule you." I knew the soul of my sweet baby was nestled close to Jesus in heaven, but the idea of having her sucked from my womb was not what I had envisioned for her tiny body. After some thought and discussion with Dan we went ahead and scheduled the surgery.

"What will happen to my baby's body?" I asked the obstetrician. "I want to have a burial for her."

"Well, someone tried it a few years ago and was able to get the remains, but you have to jump through a lot of hoops. It's possible," he said, but he didn't sound confident.

I felt peculiar asking for my baby's remains, but I was determined. In calling the lab to find out what was protocol, I came in touch with a lab technician named Marcia.

"I had a miscarriage several years ago," she confided to me. "I really wish I would have had a burial for my baby. I think what you're doing is great and I will help from this end to see that you get your baby's remains."

With that bit of comfort, I went in for the scheduled surgery. As I lay in the pre-op room, I clutched my husband with one hand and my small wooden bead rosary in the other—both of great comfort. "Can you make sure they don't take away my rosary?" I begged my husband. "I'm really afraid."

My husband gave me a soothing kiss on the forehead as they wheeled me to the operating room. I held fast to my rosary as the orderlies strapped my legs straight out and stretched my arms open to the sides, securing them to a board. I remember vividly the anesthesiologist telling me, "In thirty seconds you will fall off to sleep." At that moment my eyes flooded with tears. I realized that *this* was it. This was the final moment with my baby—then she would be gone from me. I could not protect her as my instinct screamed, *Don't let go of her!* I then fell asleep.

In what seemed only seconds, I awoke to someone saying, "Wake up, it's over." Immediately I felt angry to awaken again to the situation. They had done it—she was gone. Again, I wept—I sobbed—like never before. My mouth was parched and my emotions were raw. *I thirst!*

When I was again up and around, we held a memorial service for our baby in a portion of the cemetery just for infants. On a sunny but windy early March afternoon, we gathered around the tiny coffin with our pastor and immediate family. A woman who oversees the cemetery approached me and delivered an envelope and small, delicate box. "The funeral director said this came with the baby's remains," she whispered and left. I opened the envelope to find a card with no writing in it, just little black hand and foot prints—awesomely perfect. The box contained soft white clay with a hand and foot impression—each toe distinguishable from the other. Marcia, the lab technician from St. John's Hospital, had worked with the perinatal outreach nurse to create these cherished treasures for us. I felt grounded for a time having these in my hands. I held something that my child had actually touched. That was as close as I could physically get to her. It felt so good.

A few days following the burial, I stood in the kitchen reflecting on the recent events, when suddenly I was stuck with the image of the last few moments of Christ's life. Then I saw myself with my arms and legs stretched out on the operating room table, in the same position as Jesus on the cross. In a flash, I saw Him and then again me. I remembered the mental pain I felt just before I slipped under the anesthesia, and then, from Christ's eyes, as if they were mine, I saw Him hanging, stretching out and saying, "My God, My God, why have you forsaken me?" This was what I had felt laying on the table—wearing my own crown of thorns of mental anguish and torment. While I knew that my suffering came nowhere near to Christ's suffering, it was the closest feeling to what I as a human being and as a mother had felt thus far in my life. Again, I felt my child being taken from me, and again that initial anger and an incredible thirst. Then I heard Jesus' words: "Into Thy hands I commend my spirit."

What followed in the next minutes, days, and weeks was my desire to fulfill those words. I would commit my baby and myself to Him. As Christ then hung His head and died, I, too, needed to die; not a physical death, but a death to self. While it was not *my* will for our child to die, God allowed it, and that is where I began to find great peace. I needed to accept His commands for my family, our baby, and for me.

Now, I use the precious handprint of our baby as a tool to show the humanity of the unborn. This baby was a real person. Anyone looking at this print cannot deny that. While counseling outside abortion clinics I can show many women and men her handprint and give them the chance to reconsider their decision to abort their child. I also have been able to help other families grieving from a miscarriage and can suggest the many possibilities available for commemorating their baby. I have spoken to small groups of obstetrical and family practice residents regarding how they can best help their patients.

I leave you with this beautiful handprint of our daughter, Christina Katherine, at twelve weeks from conception. God has blessed us. He allowed us to cooperate with Him in the creation of a new soul, to glorify Him in heaven. God is good. Not only did He bless us with this child, He blessed us with many people who showered us with much comfort and love.

—Gretchen Thibault

Baby Christina Katherine's handprint

Gretchen Thibault is married to Dan and is the mother of six children. They reside in Minnesota. Her primary activity outside the home is her involvement in the pro-life movement.

Chapter Five
A Mother's Lighter Side

Planet Magazine

About six months ago we received a letter from an airline. They were tired of hanging on to 1,000 frequent flyer miles we accumulated four years ago. Would we please accept a few magazine subscriptions and call it even? Delighted to get some freebies, I signed up for several women's magazines. No, not the sort that feature blurbs like, "Six Ways to Make Your Man Dissolve into a Puddle of Passion," but the more sedate, wife-and-mother variety, whose front covers promise so much assistance with one's health, beauty, housekeeping, cooking, and parenting skills. I'd always been foiled in my attempts to garner this wisdom while in line at the grocery checkout. I'd flip the pages frantically, finding nothing but ads and reply cards. Then it would be my turn at the register, and, cheapskate that I am, back the magazine would go onto the rack. But now the secrets of feminine perfection would come directly to my home.

I've come to realize that not only will I never measure up, but that I shouldn't even try. The magazine people apparently inhabit a parallel universe.

Citizens of "Planet Magazine" are able to set aside an inordinate amount of time to an activity called exfoliation. They rub themselves with mixtures of goo and grit for the purpose of removing dry skin. Different formulas are needed depending on whether one wishes to exfoliate the hands, feet, face, or lips. Of course, thriftier ladies are encouraged to make their own exfoliating scrubs by mixing sugar and mineral oil "to the consistency of cake frosting" or by using mayonnaise and cornmeal. The greater part of one's exfoliating hours is devoted to the feet, along with subsequent soaks, massages, and pedicures. Now in my world of real women with families, only minutes a day are available for self-beautifying activities. It seems sensible to spend these on areas my husband will notice, such as face and hair, rather than my feet. Maybe the men of Planet Mag are of a different sort as well. Perhaps electric blue toenails and the lingering scent of mayonnaise drives them wild.

Planet Mag women put white carpets on the floors of children's bedrooms. They "perk up" the living room by loading the couch with so many decorative pillows that no one can sit on it. They actually remember to go and stir the sorbet in the freezer every twenty minutes. They save yogurt containers and use them to organize their hosiery drawers. I don't pretend to understand, but I do admire.

Maybe these interesting ladies would be just as stupefied by my own favorite tips. But for the benefit of earthlings who need a few laughs, here are Daria's Hints for Harried Homemakers:

Beauty

Nothing has enhanced my looks more than having seven children. Really. All I have to do is mention the size of my brood to strangers at parties. They invariably go slack-jawed, pop-eyed, and then, after gathering their wits, gasp, "Seven children! But you look *fabulous!*" In fact, they are only noting the contrast between a mental image of a haggard, gap-toothed hillbilly in a faded cotton dress, and my own healthy, cheerful but decidedly un-fabulous self. Still, it's a tremendous ego boost, and I don't need an expensive makeover, or even an exfoliating scrub, to obtain it.

Diet/Weight loss

Try the remarkable children's leftovers diet! Stop fixing yourself breakfast and lunch. Instead, graze on soggy cereal, sandwich crusts, cold chicken noodle soup, and half-eaten apples. This will either prevent waste, thus saving valuable landfill space, *or* kill your appetite so effectively that you very well may drop one dress size in a month.

Easy Kid-Pleasing Dessert Idea

After dinner, hand each child one piece of hard candy (sour balls, root beer barrels, etc.). If you teach them to suck, not bite, the candy, it will last much longer than cake or mousse or sorbet. Fewer calories, too, and so economical!

Housekeeping

An ice scraper such as you use for car windows is great for removing the old Cheerios that have bonded to the kitchen table. It's also good for old ketchup, pancake batter, etc. (Note: These items are not included as part of the children's leftovers diet above.)

Home Decor

The world's best carpet color is mud brown with little flecks of beige scattered throughout. We put this in our boys' bedroom six years ago. It has yet to look as if it needed shampooing, and rarely appears to need vacuuming, either. The beige flecks disguise lint, and the mud brown, everything else. If we could only afford it, we would probably carpet the entire house this way, and possibly paint the walls to match.

Entertaining

Whenever possible, entertain with low lighting or candle light. It creates an elegant mood, and what your guests can't see won't bother them.

Stress Reduction/Parenting Skills

The pot is boiling over. The TV is blaring. A pre-schooler is crying because the grade-schooler called her favorite show *dumb*. The grade schooler insists on explaining to you why it really *is* dumb, while a teenager simultaneously holds forth on how unfair it is that you let those little kids watch so much TV compared to how *he* was treated at that age. Fear not. Turn down the stove. Lean against the counter, resting your forehead gently against a cabinet. Close your eyes and say one Hail Mary, out loud and very slowly. The children will be startled into immediate silence and tiptoe away. They may even play nicely together until dinnertime. Your serenity will be restored. Prayer is powerful.

I could go on with gems like these, but you've got the idea. Undoubtedly you have a few of your own. But I have to go now. I've got some exfoliating to do.

—Daria Sockey

Daria Sockey's biography appears after Mother's Day *at the beginning of Chapter 3.*

Dear Santa

Dear Santa,

I've been a good mom all year. I've fed, cleaned, and cuddled my two children on demand, visited the doctor's office more than my doctor, sold sixty-two cases of candy bars to raise money to plant a shade tree in the school playground, and figured out how to attach nine patches onto my daughter's Girl Scout sash with staples and a glue gun.

I was hoping you could spread my list out over several Christmases, since I had to write this one with my son's red crayon on the back of a receipt in the laundry room between cycles, and who knows when I'll find any more free time in the next eighteen years.

Here are my Christmas wishes:

I'd like a pair of legs (in any color, except purple, which I already have) that don't ache after a day of chasing kids. I'd like arms that don't flap in the breeze, and that are strong enough to carry a screaming toddler out of the candy aisle in the grocery store. I'd also like a waist, since I lost mine somewhere in the seventh month of my last pregnancy.

If you're hauling big ticket items this year, I'd like a car with fingerprint-resistant windows and a radio that only plays adult music; a television that doesn't broadcast any programs with talking animals; and an invisible closet where I can hide and talk on the phone.

On the practical side, I could use a talking daughter doll that says, "Yes, Mommy" to boost my parental confidence, along with one potty-trained toddler, two kids who don't fight, and three pairs of jeans that zip all the way up without the use of power tools. I could also use a recording of monks chanting, "Don't eat in the living room" and "Take your hands off your brother," because my voice seems to be out of my children's hearing range and can only be heard by the dog. And please, don't forget the Play-Doh Travel Pack, the hottest stocking stuffer this year for mothers of preschoolers. It comes in three fluorescent colors guaranteed to crumble on any carpet and make the in-laws' house seem just like home.

If it's too late to find any of these products, I'd settle for enough time to brush my teeth and comb my hair in the same morning, or the luxury of eating food warmer than room temperature and not served in a Styrofoam container.

If you don't mind I could also use a few Christmas miracles to brighten the holiday season. Would it be too much trouble to declare ketchup a vegetable? It will clear my conscience immensely. It would be helpful if you could coerce my children to help around the house without them demanding payment as if they were the bosses of an organized crime family. Could you please make my toddler not look so cute sneaking downstairs to eat contraband ice cream in his pajamas at midnight?

Well, Santa, the buzzer on the dryer is ringing and my son saw my feet under the laundry room door and wants his crayon back. Have a safe trip and remember to leave your wet boots by the chimney and dry off by the fire so you don't catch cold. Help yourself to cookies on the table, but don't eat too many or leave crumbs on the carpet.

Oh, and one more thing Santa: you can cancel all my requests if you can keep my children young enough to believe in you.

Always,
Mom

—Debbie Farmer

Debbie Farmer's biography appears after A Halloween Angel *in Chapter 1.*

Just Like Mother Used to Say

"Get down from there before you break your neck!" Sound familiar? I'm sure you heard this growing up and have probably repeated it to your own children. There are certain sayings in a mom's lexicon that seem to have infiltrated homes throughout the land. Some you promised you would never repeat once you became a mom—and yet, the sayings were stowed away on your tongue and pop out of your mouth quicker than you can say, "Because I said so, that's why!"

I suppose even top anthropologists would be hard-pressed to track down the origins of these "mommy" sayings. My own theory is that they were a product of spontaneous generation. There are some things that just need to be said.

Your face will freeze like that if you don't stop it! Did you ever wonder where all the kids with frozen faces were kept?

Don't make me come in there! This is an interesting statement. It assumes the child has an invisible yet powerful control source in which the parent could be forced, beyond any personal desire, to "come in there."

It looks like a hurricane (or tornado) swept through here. Wouldn't all the debris have been blown out of there?

I've worked my fingers to the bone. Now this was an icky saying for children who did not appreciate all their mother's hard work. Children likely missed the point and perhaps had nightmares with bony fingers in them.

You are going to (eat this, clean up this mess, etc.), and you are going to like it. Why wasn't compliance enough?

This is going to hurt me more than it hurts you. Then why was the child the only one crying?

The starving children in India (or Africa or China or Russia) would be happy to eat this. Food that activated the gag reflex never became tastier when starving children were brought into the equation.

Shut your mouth and eat. This would usually bring a confused look to the child's face.

Were you born in a barn? Why would a mother ask such a question? Wasn't she there at the birth—notwithstanding adoption.

Do you think I'm made of money?—or, Do you think we have a money tree out back? I always wondered who the lucky people were with money trees and how we could grow one.

Shut the door; we're not paying to heat the whole neighborhood. Once we understood we were not made of money, we began to understand why our mother did not want to pay the heating bill for the whole neighborhood.

Stop crying or I'll give you something to cry about. We actually were under the impression we did have something to cry about.

If you fall, don't come running and crying to me. We already knew that if we came crying to her she would give us something to cry about.

If so-and-so jumps off a bridge, are you going to jump, too? Look at the result this question produced. A generation later, these kids grew up and started the bungee jumping fad. Instead, Mom could have said something like, "If so-and-so gets a hole pierced in his face, are you going to do it, too?"...Oh, wait a minute, what am I saying? Never mind. No wonder we mothers have to resort to the sayings we heard as kids.

—Patti Maguire Armstrong

Holy Humor

Birth Announcement

Due to a power outage at the time, only one paramedic responded to the 911 call. The house was very, very dark, so the paramedic asked Katelyn, a three-year-old girl, to hold a flashlight high over her mommy so he could see while he helped deliver the baby.

Very diligently, Katelyn did as she was asked. Her mother, Heidi, pushed and pushed, and after a while her brother, Connor, was born.

The paramedic lifted him by his little feet and spanked him on his bottom. Connor began to cry. The paramedic then thanked Katelyn for her help and asked the wide-eyed little girl what she thought about what she had just witnessed.

Katelyn quickly responded, "He shouldn't have crawled in there in the first place. Spank him again!"

The Thunderstorm

One summer evening during a violent thunderstorm, a mother was tucking her son into bed. She was about to turn off the light when her son asked with a tremor in his voice, "Mommy, will you sleep with me tonight?"

The mother smiled and gave him a reassuring hug. "I can't dear," she said. "I have to sleep with Daddy in mommy and daddy's room."

A long silence was broken by the boy's shaky little voice: "The big sissy."

A Prayer for Dinner Parties

One night, a woman invited some people to dinner. At the table, she turned to her six-year-old daughter and said,

"Would you like to say the blessing?" "I wouldn't know what to say," the little girl replied. "Just say what you hear Mommy say," the mother said. The child bowed her head and said, "Dear Lord, why on earth did I invite all these people to dinner?"

Thank You For This Food

A four-year-old boy was asked to give thanks before a big dinner. The family members bowed their heads in expectation. He began his prayer, thanking God for all his friends, naming them one by one. Then he thanked God for Mommy, Daddy, brother, sister, Grandma, Grandpa, and all his aunts and uncles. Then he began to thank God for the food. He gave thanks for the turkey, the dressing, the fruit salad, the cranberry sauce, the pies, the cakes, and even the Cool Whip. Then he paused, and everyone waited ... and waited. After a long silence, the young fellow looked up at his mother and asked, "If I thank God for the broccoli, won't he know that I'm lying?"

New and Natural Barbie

I thought it was a joke when I first heard that Mattel planned to give Barbie a makeover by widening her hips, reducing her bust, and flattening her facial features. I was pleased that my daughter would finally have a plastic role model that resembled me, but I couldn't believe a child would want a Barbie that couldn't fit into jeans, was constantly on a diet, and hung out in the Barbie camper wearing a moo-moo in front of the television because she never got asked out by Ken.

Mattel planned on creating six new dolls with the new "natural and today look." This was a real turning point in the fashion world, although I wasn't sure if she was invented to show little girls a diverse standard of beauty or if the other Barbies needed someone to make fun of. I couldn't imagine a doll with my "natural and today" look: purple calves, crows feet, and a stomach with its own fanny pack.

I bought the updated Barbie for my daughter because I thought it would be good for her to have a realistic role model, and I harbored a desperate, maternal hope she would transfer her idolization to me.

"It's a new Barbie!" my daughter said as she pulled the doll out the box.

"Mommy," said my three-year-old son, pointing to the doll.

"I call her the 'Working-Mother-of-Two Barbie,'" I said. "Look in the box, I think she comes with a plate of leftovers and a Thigh Master."

"Where's her bathing suit?" My daughter shook the empty box.

"She doesn't have one," I said, "but she has a nice, sturdy pair of sensible shoes."

My daughter frowned.

I quickly tried to find something positive to say about a Barbie that needed support hose and an elastic waistband. "Look! She has a wardrobe just like Mommy!" She didn't look impressed, so I added, "And she's really, really smart, just like you."

She considered her new Barbie for a moment, then said, "I'll call her Francine."

While my daughter introduced her to the other Barbies, I congratulated myself on making a brilliant doll selection for my daughter.

Everything was going great until Ken asked Francine out on a date.

"Mommy!" my daughter said, "We need to get Francine nicer clothes."

"But I have a dress just like that," I said.

"She only has one outfit that fits," she said. "Jeans won't go on, and her feet are too wide for high heels."

I seized the teachable moment.

"Francine doesn't need to go anywhere with Ken," I said. "She's going to go to college and get a high-paying job, so she can support herself without being dependent on a good looking, muscular man with plastic hair."

My daughter stared.

"She doesn't need new clothes or stiletto heels to be beautiful," I continued. "Her inner qualities such as kindness, confidence, and integrity are what matters." I felt important and proud as I bestowed my motherly wisdom on my daughter.

She considered Francine for a moment, and then tossed her over her shoulder into her closet.

"Ken will take Gymnastic Barbie instead."

Francine was dumped for a doll with small thighs. I chided myself for making such a stupid purchase.

That night, when I went into my daughter's room to kiss her good night, I found Francine tucked in beside her and Gymnastic Barbie lying haphazardly on the floor.

"See, good legs aren't everything," I whispered.

—Debbie Farmer

Debbie Farmer's biography appears after A Halloween Angel *in Chapter 1.*

If evolution really works, how come mothers only have two hands?

—Ed Dussault

My Favorite

"You know you are my favorite, don't you?" I often whispered to a son or daughter whenever we had a quiet moment together.

"Uh-huh," they always nodded and smiled impishly. "I know."

Then, I added my usual caution: "But we can't tell the other kids or they would cry."

Feeling benevolent at the special status bequeathed upon them, each child always readily agreed to the pact. It was a secret just between us—my favorite and me.

When my children were young, I read an article about Pope John XXIII, who came from a family of eleven children. The Pope was quoted as saying that as a child he would ask his mother "Whom do you love best?" She always answered, "All of you."

John XXIII said he used to wish that, just once, she would name him. He yearned to be the apple of his mother's eye. This story struck at the core of my biggest desire as a mother—to make each child feel special, as if they were all only children. I wanted to give them everything. So, the Pope's tale gave birth to the white lie that I would tell to each of my kids.

Whenever one was in need of my attention, I made sure to conclude with a surreptitious whisper of, "You know you're my favorite, don't you?"

Somehow the whole truth eventually slipped out—that they were all my favorites—and my little secret turned into a family joke. A teen would often give me a wink and announce: "I'm your favorite, right Mom?"

"Of course you are," I would agree with a sly wink to the other kids.

One Christmas after my seven favorite children were all grown up, I presented each one with a framed copy of a poem I had written:

You're my favorite, I would whisper, and your eyes lit up with glee.

Gee, ain't it great, to participate in your mom's conspiracy?

It's a secret you must keep; I said that I love you above all the others.

Now hurry to bed with that in your head. I've something to tell your brothers.

That evening, as they were packing up their gifts I gave them each a kiss goodnight and whispered in their ears, "Yours is authentic, the rest are counterfeit."

—Barbara Winters Pinto

Barbara Winters Pinto is wife to Al, mother of three daughters and four sons, and grandmother to twenty. Now that they are old enough to handle it, she tells them it took seven "imperfects" to get twenty "perfects." Barbara is also an award-winning professional actress. (And, by the way, Matthew Pinto, co-editor of this book, is really *her favorite.)*

A Grimy Greeting

"Don't worry about me getting my clothes dirty,
I'm not wearing any."

Baby Gauge

Your Clothes

1ˢᵗ Child: You begin wearing maternity clothes as soon as your ob/gyn confirms your pregnancy.

2ⁿᵈ Child: You wear your regular clothes for as long as possible.

3ʳᵈ Child & Beyond: Your maternity clothes *ARE* your regular clothes.

Baby's Name

1ˢᵗ Child: You pour over baby-name books and practice pronouncing and writing combinations of all your favorites.

2ⁿᵈ Child: Someone has to name his or her kid after your great-aunt Mavis, right? It might as well be you.

3ʳᵈ Child & Beyond: You open a name book, close your eyes, and see where your finger lands.

Preparing for Birth

1ˢᵗ Child: You practice your breathing religiously.

2ⁿᵈ Child: You don't bother practicing because you remember last time—breathing didn't do a thing.

3ʳᵈ Child & Beyond: You ask for an epidural in your 8th month.

Layette

1ˢᵗ Child: You pre-wash your newborn's clothes, color coordinate them, and fold them neatly in the baby's bureau.

2ⁿᵈ Child: You check to make sure that the clothes are clean and discard only the ones with the darkest stains.

3ʳᵈ Child & Beyond: Boys can wear pink, can't they?

Going Out

1ˢᵗ Child: The first time you leave your baby with a sitter, you call home in five minutes after you depart.

2ⁿᵈ Child: Just before you walk out the door, you remember to leave a number where you can be reached.

3ʳᵈ Child & Beyond: You leave instructions for the sitter to call only if she sees blood.

At Home

1st Child: You spend a good bit of every day just gazing at the baby.

2ⁿᵈ Child: You spend a bit of every day watching to be sure your older child isn't squeezing, poking, or hitting the baby.

3ʳᵈ Child & Beyond: You spend a little of every day hiding from the children.

—Anonymous

It will be gone before you know it.
The fingerprints on the wall appear
higher and higher. Then suddenly they
disappear.

—*Dorothy Evslin*

Relish the Moment

Children have an endearing way of making you feel special. When my middle daughter Jaki was five, her older sister Carly, whom we call "Sissy," was leaving on a trip with her friends from church. Jaki didn't think Carly should be allowed to go, so she solidly planted herself at the front door and told Carly that she would be severely punished if she left. After we dragged Jaki away from the door, she followed Carly out with a warning, "You're going to be in big trouble for leaving!" Carly smiled and waved goodbye out the car window. As she drove off, Jaki shook her long, curly hair and hollered, "Sissy, as part of your punishment I am going to make you look like your mother!"

I was stunned at the severity of this punishment. "Is that so terrible, to look like me?" I gasped.

Jaki replied matter-of-fact, "Sissy will think so!"

Well, I spent some time in front of the mirror after that remark, considering plastic surgery.

Not to be outdone, my four-year-old Toni informed me at the breakfast table one morning that I was boring. She gave me a look of pity and said, "Mom, Dad is fun, but yo'w bowwing," she said in a drawn-out manner.

"I am?" I gasped again. "What about all the games I play with you and the books I read you and the Play-Doh sculptures I make for you?"

She continued looking at me with that pitying look as if to say, "You can't help it that you're boring." Apparently having her belly eaten by a bearded man was a good time, and being chased and wrestled all around the house was a blast, but my feeble attempts at fun were simply boring.

After this experience I considered taking a circus-training course. But then one hot day I offered the two smaller girls a Popsicle, to which they declared, "You're the best mother in the world!" Their eyes lit up as though I just created the universe. I stood for a moment relishing their compliment. In their eyes at that moment, I was terrific! I knew this status would not last long, but that moment for me is reward enough to last for years. I can imagine those happy faces during the times when they don't like what I cooked for supper or when bedtime comes too early in their estimation.

Even though I'm "ugly" and "boring," I can still be the world's best mom!

—Emily Cavins

Mother's Day Breakfast

It was an eventful Mother's Day when my young boys broke out of the mold of giving me presents orchestrated by their teachers. For many years I had received numerous little handprints dried into clay or pressed with paint onto paper, accompanied with the same old poem about this being a handprint that did not need to be wiped off. For the first time, they had planned something on their own.

As the day began, I could see through the slits in my bedroom blinds that a sparkling blue morning was underway. Accompanied by the early birds' breezy chirps, the house hummed of silence. With a husband, four boys eight and under, a dog, and a parakeet, it was a tune rarely played. I lightly tiptoed my way across the room, avoiding any floor-creaks that could wake a slumbering household. Once in the hall, I exhaled deeply, only moments away from a cup of warm tea and a spot of leisure with the newspaper.

When suddenly, what to my wondering ears did I hear, but a whispering child, blinking back a tear. "Mom," my oldest son Aaron called from the top of the stairs. "We were going to surprise you with breakfast in bed." His forlorn face looked down at me and asked, "What are you doing awake?"

"Me? Awake? No, no, I just thought I heard a noise. I'm going right back to bed."

So back to bed I went, this time taking no care to avoid the creaky floor boards. I laid on my back and stared at the ceiling's cobwebs that danced in a breeze emanating from my husband's rumbling snores. Perhaps if I stuffed Kleenex in Mark's mouth I could both silence and wake him, I thought.

The Kleenex temptation became moot when the baby sounded his alarm. "Mamamamamamama," he called out. "Mark," I nudged, not quite gently. "Jacob is calling for you—and remember, it's Mother's Day." Mark obligingly rolled out of bed. "Happy Mother's Day," he mumbled, bobbing and swaying his way into the baby's room.

"And now that you are up, would you mind bringing me the newspaper?" I did not get an answer but moments later Luke, son number two, bounded in with several pages from the paper. "I think you dropped some of it," I commented holding up a crumpled TV guide and the sports section.

He left to retrieve the rest, but his mind apparently wandered with his feet into the kitchen, which now was abuzz with small voices and clatter. By the time I had memorized the week's TV programming and the Minnesota Twins' batting averages, breakfast arrived with each boy carrying a plateful.

"We need to buy a serving tray next year," explained Tyler, son number three. "But don't worry," he assured me. "The food is great. We made it ourselves."

I flashed a concerned look at my husband. "I was reading the paper," he explained. I manufactured a motherly smile for my three wide-eyed little fellows.

"Well, let's see, what do we have here? French toast, my favorite, "I gushed, sampling a forkful. "Oh, it's crunchy."

"See, I told you that you couldn't get all the eggshells out using a towel," Aaron complained.

"Never mind," I said moving on to the next dish. "This cereal looks perfect, and the peanut butter toast is certainly thick and creamy. Wow, you must have scrambled a whole carton of eggs. Oh, boy, two bananas, and oh my, you boys certainly went to a lot of trouble to pick all the seeds out of this slice of watermelon. But what's this in my cup? There's not much in there."

"Tyler drank most of the chocolate milk he made you," Luke tattled.

"I did not," protested Tyler. "It spilled!"

"That's OK. Lets not worry about a little spilled milk," I comforted. "Well, I can see I'm going to need plenty of help eating this big, delicious breakfast," I said to my crowd of well-wishers.

"No thanks, I'm not hungry"..."Neither am I"..."Me neither," they responded. Mark waved the food away, "You know I never eat breakfast," he said in a panicked voice.

"We made it all just for you, Mommy," yelled Tyler. "Mother's Day is sure fun," said Aaron. "I'm having a great time," agreed Luke. "Happy Mother's Day," said Mark.

"Thank you everyone," I smiled, "God has certainly blessed me." But then gazing upon my big Mother's Day feast, I was suddenly overcome with a new appreciation for all those little hand prints I had received over the years. There were never leftovers to worry about.

—Patti Maguire Armstrong

The Many Faces of Mom

When I was pregnant, I vowed the most important thing I could do for my family was to be consistent. Now two children later, my moods swing faster than a tennis racket at Wimbledon, my children are saving their allowance for an exorcism, and my husband calls me Sybil under his breath. Although he says he will never really understand me, I have finally convinced him that six moms are better than one, especially if one actually cooks.

In the morning I am Bright, Perky, Energetic Mom.

"Good morning children!" I cry, flinging open the blinds. "Are you ready for your breakfast? I made fresh-squeezed orange juice to go with the loaf of bread I just took out of the oven."

"What's today?" my pre-schooler asks, wiping the sleep from her eyes.

"It's Thursday," I chirp. "The fifth day of the week. And if you get up now you'll have time to do all the exciting adventures I have planned."

My children just stare.

Perky Mom lasts until Efficient Mom arrives at 10:30 a.m.

"OK, kids," I shout. "Enough arts and crafts! I will start three loads of laundry at 10:35, scrub the bathroom and dust your room until 11:10. Then, at 11:36, we'll leave for the park, feed a few ducks, and be eating our lunches on a bench by noon."

My children just stare.

Efficient Mom is replaced by Tired Mom at 1:00 p.m.

"What day is it again, Mom?" my pre-schooler asks.

"I dunno."

"Why is the sky blue?"

"I dunno."

"Where's Baby Ben?"

"Who?"

Reality Mom arrives during naptime. "So what if the wash isn't dry, the only clean item in the bathroom is soap, and the only thing dusted is the screen on the television so we can see the picture," I think. "We're all dressed, fed, wearing clean underwear, and we don't smell."

Frantic Mom arrives a half an hour before dinner. My children look as if they've been run over by a steamroller.

"Back off, kids!" I screech, throwing a bag of frozen peas into the microwave as the buzzer on the dryer rings and Baby Ben howls for milk.

"These hands are registered weapons!" I exclaim while karate chopping the lettuce for salad and dropkicking the oven door closed. "What do you want from me? Go back to the television. The macaroni and cheese will be done in a minute!"

My children just stare.

My favorite mom is Loving Mom who arrives at bedtime.

"Aren't they sweet?" I say, stroking their hair as they sleep. "I just can't see how you men can work all day and miss out on all of this." I slowly shake my head at my husband. "I just don't understand you at all."

My husband just smiles.

—Debbie Farmer

Debbie Farmer's biography appears after A Halloween Angel *in Chapter 1.*

A Test for Mothers

Have you ever wondered what kind of a mother you are? Here's a chance to rate yourself by taking this multiple-choice test. If you receive a low score, do not fret. Being a mother has built-in job training. So, if you keep trying, eventually you should get it all figured out.

Circle the best answer to each question below. At the end of the test, add up the number of correct answers to determine your score.

1. Your young child reports that several kids in his class went home sick with the flu. By bedtime, he is not feeling well. You:

    a) Tell your child to get to the bathroom if he wakes up sick during the night. Remind him that he almost made it the last time.

    b) Replace your child's sheets with a plastic coated table cloth and dress him in a raincoat before he gets into bed.

    Answer: "b." If you are truly a professional, the raincoat and tablecloth are neatly folded and waiting in the linen closet.

2. How many times must you say, "Stop that!" before your child actually does?

    a) Once or twice.

    b) An infinite amount of times.

    Answer: "b." Your children will never "stop that" until you place your hands on their shoulders and ask them the question, "How many times do I have to tell you to stop that?"

3. A violent temper tantrum is taking place. You:

    a) Remove your child to his or her room.

b) Control yourself by realizing that you are providing a bad example.
Answer: "b." And try not to let it happen again.

4. You are in a doctor's waiting room with your child for his or her annual physical. There are several sick looking children with runny noses walking around. Your social child will likely want to play with the other children. You:
a) Keep your child occupied with books and games.
b) Pull out a marker and draw spots all over your child's face. Tell anyone who approaches that he or she is contagious.
Answer: "b." Doing "a" would turn you into a kid magnet.

5. What is pink and sweet and used by young children to blow bubbles?
a) Bubble gum
b) Amoxicillin
Answer: "b." Even when a long medicine dropper places it down the throat, you are going to see those pink bubbles.

6. You hear screaming from a room in which two of your children are. You run in to find the older one pulling the hair of the younger one. Who is at fault?
a) The older one
b) The younger one
Answer: "b." The other kid always starts it.

7. How many ways are there to peel a banana?
a) One
b) At least twenty-seven.
Answer: "b." A child can have his or her little sister sit on it so the insides squish out, have the dog bite off an end,

use a hammer, run over it with his or her bike, eat the peel off, use a scissors, jump on it...

8. Your children refused to eat their supper because they do not like those green specks they see in it. You:
   a) Send it to starving children in India.
   b) Feed it to the dog.
   Answer: "b." The children in India will not like those green specks either. Send them a donation and give the food to the dog.

9. You discover a cookie with a bite taken out of it. You accuse your son of doing it since he is the only other person in the house besides you. He insists it was not him. Is he telling the truth?
   a) No
   b) Yes
   Answer: "b." If your son had taken a bite out of the cookie, the rest of it would not have been found. Face it, you have mice.

10. You are at a playground and it is time to go. What is your child's understanding of the phrase: "One more time?"
    a) One more time.
    b) Until my legs fall off.
    Answer: "b." The only time children understand the phrase "one more time" is when it is something they do not want to do twice.

11. Your child is annoying you by crossing his eyes and making faces. You:
    a) Explain he is getting on your nerves and should stop it.
    b) Tell him you have a brother who used to do that and his face froze that way. When he asks why he has

never seen this uncle, explain that he is too horrible to look at.
Answer: "b." Getting on your nerves was the whole idea in the first place but the story might actually work.

12. Your child has been an absolute monster the entire day. It is bedtime now and you are completely worn out. When you go to his room to say good night, you:
a) Bring in a contract for your child to sign in which he promises to support you in your old age which his behavior has hastened.
b) Give him a big hug and kiss and tell him that, no matter what, you always love him.
Answer: "b." Children cannot be held accountable to contracts. And if you want to be an expert, "b" is your only choice.

Scoring:
12 points = Expert.
You are either an expert or you figured out that the answer "b" was always correct.
10 to 11 points = Superior.
No one expects perfection, but this is close.
8 to 9 points = Poor.
Sorry, there is no such thing as average in this test.
Either you give it all you've got or you get a poor rating.
0 to 7 points = This test does not score accurately for men.
You will need to find some kind of father's test.

—Patti Maguire Armstrong

Mom's Vacation

"Your wife's completely recovered,
but she'd like a few more days off."

A Mother's Prayer

Now I lay me down to sleep,
I pray my sanity to keep.
For if some peace I do not find,
I'm pretty sure I'll lose my mind.
I pray I find a little quiet
Far away from my family's riot.
May I lie back—and not have to think
About what they're stuffing down the sink,
Or who they're with, or where they're at,
And what they're doing to the cat.
I pray for time all to myself
(Did something just fall off a shelf?)
To cuddle in my nice, soft bed
(Oh no, another goldfish—dead!)
Some silent moments for goodness sake
(Did I just hear a window break?)
And with no need to cook or clean—
(Well humph, I've got the right to dream!)
Yes now I lay me down to sleep,
I pray my wits about me keep,
But as I look around I know—
I must have lost them long ago!

—Anonymous

The Mom Olympics

I had a brief career in soccer when I was seven years old. My most vivid memory is of the absolute panic that overcame me when the ball was accidentally kicked in my direction during a game.

Just because I was not destined for stardom on the soccer field, though, does not mean that I have no athletic aspirations. We are all teammates of a sort, using our individual talents and working to further God's Kingdom on earth. I have always thought that mothers in particular have specialized athletic skills. Perhaps if there were a "Mom Olympics" these would be better recognized.

Event #1: Laundry. In this event, the mom runs up a flight of stairs holding a screaming fifteen-pound baby in one arm and a full basket of laundry in the other. She leaps over a safety gate at the top and answers the telephone before the caller hangs up.

Event #2: Road Trip. The mom drives a minivan containing an assortment of small children. She quickly and completely meets the needs of her back-seat passengers while maintaining safety on the road. This may require serving juice, finding the baby's pacifier, breaking up a spitting fight, or killing a spider. A one-point penalty will be assessed for turning up the radio to drown out the noise.

Event #3: Supermarket. Now the mom pushes a grocery cart, with assorted children attached, through the crowded aisles of a bustling supermarket. Without giving in to their pleas for various forms of sugar, she prevents the children from breaking or stealing any merchandise. She reads labels, watches for specials and remembers her husband's favorite brand of frozen french fries while completing a shopping list of a week's worth of groceries.

Event #4: Dinner. In this event the mom prepares a delicious, nutritious, well-balanced meal for her family. Obstacles include a whiny two-year-old climbing the cabinets, a ringing telephone, and a four-year-old who is "helping" by unfolding the laundry and spreading it on the dining room table. Points are deducted for overcooking the broccoli, but extra points are awarded for convincing a preschooler to eat it.

Event #5: Bedtime. Now the mom bathes an assortment of indefatigable little people, removing chewing gum from hair, sand from ears, and spaghetti sauce from faces. She brushes their teeth, wrestles them into pajamas and finds a bedtime story acceptable to children of three different age levels. She tucks them in their beds while satisfactorily answering the questions that naturally arise at this time of day—such as "Who made God?" and "How *exactly* does a baby get in its mommy's belly?"

I know the competition would be stiff, but with my daily training I feel fairly confident that I could earn a medal in the "Mom Olympics." A picture of me might appear on Wheaties boxes with a baby on my hip and a plastic sippy cup raised triumphantly above my head. On early-morning television, Matt Lauer might interview me about my training regimen and my diet of peanut butter and jelly.

But when I arrived home from swimming lessons *this* morning, Matt Lauer was nowhere in sight. Adoring fans did not mob me. No reporters accosted me on my way to the front door.

I realize that there may never be a "Mom Olympics"— and that's OK with me. When my days of mothering come to an end, I only hope that, like Saint Paul, I, too, will be able

to say: "I have fought the good fight; I have finished the race;
I have kept the faith" (2 Timothy 4:7).

—Danielle Bean

*Danielle Bean writes from Center Harbor, New Hampshire, where she is a
freelance writer and homeschooling mother of six. This story can be found
in Danielle's book* My Cup of Tea: Musings of a Catholic Mom, *©2005
Danielle Bean. Used by permission of Pauline Books & Media, 50 St. Paul's
Avenue, Boston, MA 02130. All rights reserved.*

Chapter Six
A Mother's Ephiphany

What Adorable Children You Have

"One!" yelled our two-year-old, with an emphatic jump. "Two!" I called from the kitchen. "Fwee!" (jump). "Four!" And so we went, back and forth, up to twenty. Sighing, I threw breakfast onto the breakfast bar and put the kids on their stools. The prospect of keeping up with Mr. Energy after only a few hours of sleep did not excite me.

Plaintive wails emanated from the baby monitor—the baby was awake again. As I trudged up the stairs, I was feeling pretty sorry for myself. An hour later, with everyone dressed and settled into our stroller, we headed for the park. Yup, it's Strategy A—wear them all out, and Mommy gets a nap as a reward.

All along the way, passersby smiled at my little ones and me. As each one approached, my spine stiffened in anticipation of the dreaded comment: "My, you've got your hands full!" I have a close friend who also receives this comment, and we laugh about it often. On better days, I smile and say to my audience, "Full of joy!" But, on this day, I barely smiled, and muttered under my breath, "Yeah, right."

Even though I was feeling worn out, I dared not appear to be anything but capable. It disturbed me to think that almost every stranger I met might be judging me as irresponsible because my children are so close in age. Too often in this country, children are treated as burdens rather than joy-filled prophets of the beauty of life. We truly wanted each of our little prophets. But must I witness every day?

Apparently so…"One!" shouted Mr. Energy. I was too tired to respond. "Two!" he urged me authoritatively. "Fwee!" Suddenly, I giggled. Three people had greeted us with the dreaded comment on the way to the park.

"Three!" I responded to my son. My pre-schooler chimed in, and we counted to three the rest of the way to the park. After setting my little captives free, I sat down to nurse the baby. A woman with one eighteen-month-old girl sat next to me.

I forced a smile as the inevitable comment rolled off her tongue, "My, you've got your hands full!" "Four!" screamed my brain. Just then, Mr. Energy jumped over next to the bench. My real smile returned, and I said, "They do keep me busy." Encouraged by my smile, she continued, "I don't know how you do it—just one keeps me hopping. I can't imagine having more children. I just don't have what it takes."

Sighing inside, I decided not to answer. I cringed at the mental reminder that I didn't have what it takes, either. Just that morning, I yelled at them several times and even threw a toy across the room when I tripped over it. I couldn't summon the self-righteousness to begin my usual dissertation on the joys of multiple siblings.

Suddenly, I saw my son run full steam ahead toward another child, with my daughter right behind him. Excusing myself quickly, I ran (baby in tow) to redirect their energies. The mother of the bulldozee tried to be nice, but it was clear that she thought my children were out of control. My head began to hurt as I helped the children apologize.

Actually, it felt more like I was the one out of control. By the time we were ready to leave, two other mothers had offered me the startling insight, "My, you've got your hands full!" In a foul mood, I rounded up my kids and filled the stroller. My son was counting again, and banging his feet on the footrest of the stroller. I echoed him in my mind, "Five! Six!" Would this day never end? Mentally shouldering my cross, I headed for home. Across the street, an elderly couple lurked on our homeward path. Sighing again, I headed straight for them. They smiled broadly at me as we approached one another. "My," the older woman began—and I promised myself I would not scream—"what adorable children you have. How lucky you all are to have one another!"

Dumbfounded, I responded, "Thank you." I pondered her words for several blocks. God had sent me a Veronica to wipe my brow and to encourage me to continue following Jesus to Calvary. I realized that God's glory is shown through my weakness. The burdens we take on for His glory are simultaneously carried by our Lord. I had been trying to carry the whole load—for my own glory. I wanted to look capable. God only wanted me to lean on Him.

"Count it all joy...when you meet various trials," declares James 1:2, "for you know that the testing of your faith produces [perseverance]."

"One!" began my toddler again. This time, I joined in right away. My children beamed up at me. Joyfully, we counted all the way to twenty.

—Kristen McGuire

Kristen McGuire lives in Milwaukee, Wisconsin, with her husband, Daniel (a retired U.S. Marine), and their seven children. She holds a B.S. in Psychology from Georgetown University and an M.Div. from Wesley Theological Seminary. She converted to the Catholic faith in 1992, and is the author of The Glory to be Revealed in You: A Spiritual Companion to Pregnancy *(Alba House, 1995).*

Sunny Above The Clouds

It was a dreary, January day at the Columbus, Ohio, airport. The oppressive clouds matched the condition of my soul—blah and burdened by unworthiness, fatigue, and hopelessness. I was ready to crumble under the weight of single parenting, wage earning, and loneliness. The long nights and cold days of winter had drained my emotional reservoir. Even if I could have found my boot straps, I didn't have the emotional energy to pull myself up.

I climbed aboard my plane and out of habit selected a window seat. The nose of the plane began its ascent into the gray cotton, and I settled into reading the in-flight magazine.

I don't know what I expected to see out the window that day. Clouds and more clouds, I suppose. But fifteen minutes after take-off, I looked out the window and stared in awe: We had broken through the clouds and were cruising through a panorama of bright blue sky. I could feel the sunlight beaming on my face and trickling down my body to fill my empty soul.

It's sunny above the clouds, I marveled. It's sunny *above* the clouds.

In all my gloom and doom, I had projected my grayness everywhere. I'd forgotten the clouds were only a finite covering. They didn't reach all the way to the heavens, and they certainly didn't reflect the sum total of my life.

In many women's lives, the clouds of family responsibility, financial worries, and work demands threaten to block out the sun. It's easy to lose perspective and to dream of life without diapers, dirty dishes, and self-absorbed husbands. We wonder if our efforts really matter. Would anyone notice if we checked out of life?

At times like this, we have to remind ourselves that it's sunny above the clouds. My friends do this in a number of ways. One of them breaks out the bubble bath. Another fixes her thoughts on those who are less fortunate, like the couple who makes $20 a month in Cuba or the child who works fourteen hours a day in Pakistan, and she offers her sufferings for them. A third spends time before the Blessed Sacrament to regain her sanity.

While I'm convinced God created me to live in the Caribbean or Hawaii, the reality of my life in Ohio is abrasively different. I have to embrace the season of winter and acknowledge that even it has a purpose. Instead of complaining, "I hate winter," I oblige myself to push beyond the gray clouds to winter's divine purpose—to draw me closer to the Body of Christ.

In winter, I no longer have the personal and emotional resources to be self-sufficient. I need my spiritual brothers and sisters to encourage me, pray with me, and carry me through this time. Just when I want to hibernate in the misery of my self-pitying cave, I need my friends to draw me out.

That January plane trip took me to more than my physical destination. It gave me a new spiritual destination—above the clouds. However, I learned I can't get there on my own. I need a lift from a friend or a break from parental responsibilities. I need words of encouragement and sympathetic hugs. And most of all, I need to believe in faith that the clouds are just a temporary covering.

—Katrina J. Zeno

Katrina J. Zeno is co-foundress of Women of the Third Millennium *(www.wttm.org), an organization that promotes the dignity and vocation of women through one-day retreats. She is a freelance writer whose articles have appeared in* Our Sunday Visitor, New Covenant, Catholic Parent, *and* Franciscan Way. *A native of San Diego, Katrina now lives in Ohio with her 12-year-old son, Michael.*

Coming to Sunday Dinner

When I was a little girl, I would begrudgingly set the table for the traditional Sunday dinner that my mother insisted on serving after church each week. She always spread the crisply ironed tablecloth over the dining room table and took the china from the hutch. The silver was polished, the cloth napkins arranged, the wine glasses placed, the candles lit. Why did we always have to have such a big fuss over Sunday dinner? My two sisters, two brothers and I gathered hungrily at the table as soon as mother announced all was ready. I disliked all the preparation, but I could never deny how wonderful it was to sit like a princess at the table and eat a lovingly prepared meal with dessert to follow.

That dinner table expanded as girlfriends and boyfriends would come, evolving from friend to fiancée to spouse, followed by several grandchildren. When I brought my future husband to the table, it was the place where my family learned to love and accept him. Then it was our turn to bring our babies. No matter where we went, we somehow would make it back to the Sunday table as often as we could.

After moving several hundred miles from my parents' home, Sunday dinner became a fond memory. By now I was a busy mother with five children of my own spread over several years. Each year seemed to become more hectic than the last. In the busyness I sought counsel from a spiritual director once a month. During one session, the priest suggested that I make my home a place to where my children would love to come home, even after they leave for college. He said, "Especially make Sunday a celebration." Inspired by his suggestion, I looked for ideas in several books but I didn't find a thing that seemed to fit our family. As far as planning activities, there wasn't a lot that would please all of the different age groups at the same time. My mind drifted back to Sundays when I was a child. I saw Mom bending over the oven, armed with potholders, to pull out the roast while everyone greedily inhaled the aroma. It suddenly struck me! My mother was a genius! Every family member of any age wanted to be part of that event— Sunday dinner! "I could do that, too!" I realized as the light bulb went on. "This is a gold mine! Everyone is home Sunday afternoon. We don't allow the teens to work Sunday so they'll be here. And everybody loves a good meal!" I couldn't believe I spent all those years of my married life thinking my mom was a fool to put the burden of all that work on her shoulders; now I wanted to do the same.

That next Sunday I dusted off our china, tossed on a tablecloth, and brought out the candlesticks. Each pair of delighted eyes took its place at the table. The pot roast was revealed. No one hurried away, no one claimed to be bored. Out came the apple crisp and ice cream. The little ones marveled at the decorated table, the teens happily ate their fill. My middle son soaked it all in and is now the Sunday monitor to make sure we don't scrimp on any of the trimmings. My husband and I smile at each other across the table and thank God for our beautiful family. And now I look down the road for the day when we will expand our table for new family members to come.

—Jean McGinty

Jean McGinty is a stay-at-home mom with five children. She is an active volunteer at her local parish, and she, along with her husband, Mike, coordinates their parish's Perpetual Adoration chapel.

The Most Important Job

Once, when the job of motherhood felt especially difficult, I reminded myself that anyone can do a job: proofreader, German teacher, or whatever I would be doing if I worked outside of the home. But no one can be Roger's wife, or Robert's mom, or Gabrielle's mom, or Mary's mom, or Ryan's mom. If I died while I had a job, my employer would simply post an ad, conduct interviews and hire someone else. But if I died today, my children's lives would never be the same.

A mother cannot be replaced. There is no work more important.

—Jeanne Gilbert

Jeanne Gilbert and her husband, Roger, have four children, ages fourteen to five months. They have been home schooling for six years. Jeanne is a graduate of the University of North Carolina at Chapel Hill with a masters degree in German literature.

A mother is she who can take the place of all others but whose place no one else can take.

—*Cardinal Mermillod*

The Blessings I Almost Missed

I was one of those little girls who hovered around babies waiting for a chance to hold them. Baby dolls were real babies to me. Even though I had the joy of caring for my two little brothers, I often wished we had even more than six children in our family.

So when my first son, Aaron, was born, my heart brimmed with happiness. As he grew, I was thrilled with his quick mind and curiosity of the world. Son number two, Luke, was a cute, cuddly little blond with a sweet temperament. Our third boy, Tyler, showed his lively personality and athletic prowess early. I loved my little boys with all my heart, but were three little bundles of joy enough? I decided that they were. Or rather, I was influenced by the world around me to think that three was plenty.

My husband, Mark, was not so sure. I knew the Catholic Church taught that contraception was contrary to God's plan, but being surrounded by Catholics who had no qualms with it, I comfortably ignored that teaching. I decided to have surgery for a tubal ligation. Two days prior to surgery, during the pre-op exam, the doctor explained the failure rate was *only* 1 in 500. Those odds were unsettling. "Not bad odds for the lottery," I thought. A failure could result in a tubal pregnancy, which could result in death. I canceled.

The next line of attack was birth control pills. I experienced physical problems so I stopped taking them. I became pregnant the following month. When Mark heard the news, he announced: "I've been praying for this." I wanted to know if he meant that figuratively or if he had prayed behind my back. It turned out the big sneak had literally been praying on the sly. Regardless, a diehard baby lover like me could not help but rejoice at another little soul.

Jacob was born on May 13, the anniversary date of Our Lady of Fatima's first appearance. It was also Mark's birthday and Mother's Day that year. Mark, too, had been born on Mother's Day, thirty-three years earlier. Happy birthday, Mark—from God.

During this time in our lives, we had begun reading about various Marian apparitions and were inspired for the first time to pray the rosary. We stopped missing Sunday Mass and started to learn more about our faith. Still, we were not fully converted yet—particularly when it came to family planning. I had insisted Mark have a vasectomy. He finally relented and went through with the procedure.

Initially, I was oblivious that we had done anything wrong. But gradually, as I grew to desire God's will in my life, I started making visits to Jesus in the tabernacle and continued praying the rosary, a feeling grew in me. I realized that the Church, which Christ had founded to guide us until the end of time, had authority to teach on spiritual matters, including matters relating to sexuality. I had been given no such authority.

I shared my feelings of regret over Mark's sterilization with him. He was less than thrilled since he never really wanted to go along with it. As a matter of fact, he accused me of being like Eve. "You are right," I agreed. "But remember, Adam was kicked out of the garden, too." We began praying that God's will would be done in our lives, including whether we would have more children. We determined that if it was God's will, Mark's vasectomy would fail.

One night, I had a dream in which I saw two babies— one blonde and one dark-haired. I felt an intense love for these babies as if they were my own. At the end of the dream I realized that these were babies God had planned for us, but because of our sin, they would never be born. I woke up feeling like a mother who just lost her babies. I knew the only way to get to them was to convince Mark to have a reversal of his vasectomy.

When Mark came home from work the next day, I approached him with my idea for a reversal. He would have none of it. I barely got two sentences out of my mouth before he announced the subject was officially closed. Even if we could afford it, he was completely unwilling to subject himself to another surgery. Now, it was my turn to pray behind Mark's back. "OK, God," I prayed. "I want to do Your will but I am powerless to change Mark's mind. I'm putting everything in Your hands." Then, I just kept praying.

Several months had passed when one morning we went out for breakfast after Mass, Mark casually wondered out loud how much a reversal operation would cost. "I know," I announced. Before Mark had shot my idea down, I had called the doctor's office to get all the information.

"Well, I can't get off from work this month," Mark said, "but next month I could go in and get it done." I was shocked and thrilled. We did not have the money to pay for it, but we determined that we could probably make payments.

"What changed your mind?" I finally asked, wondering what had caused such a drastic change of heart. His answer took my breath away.

"I had a dream last night," Mark said. "I saw two babies that God had planned for us." I had never told a single soul about my dream.

Three months later we were expecting a baby. I had a strong feeling that it would be our first girl and God wanted us to name her Mary after the Blessed Mother who had intervened for us. We had never considered the name with any previous pregnancy.

Our blonde-haired baby girl, Mary, was born on December 22, 1993. A few months before her birth, we inherited the exact amount of money we needed to pay for Mark's reversal surgery in full. Dark-haired Teresa was born on my birthday, April 18, 1996. I thought we must be done now that we had the babies from our dreams. Mark, as usual, said he thought ten would be a good number of children. While praying about it, I recalled that when St. Maximilian Kolbe was young, he had received a vision of Our Blessed Mother. She had shown him two wreaths of roses—one of red representing martyrdom, and one of white, representing purity. She asked him which he would like to choose. He chose both. I wondered, if like St. Maximilian, could we volunteer to take on more than God asked? We prayed for guidance.

John was born on August 31, 1999 and Isaac was born on his sister Mary's birthday, December 22, 2001. There could be no greater blessing on our family than our precious children. The kid's love for each other runs deep. The older children—and even their friends—especially delight in these two littlest boys. Our oldest is in college and the youngest is still in diapers. I know that one of the biggest draws for my oldest son to come home for visits is to spend time with his younger siblings.

Most mothers would say there is nothing more precious or valuable in their lives than their children. I am so thankful to God that He opened my eyes to what I had almost missed out on—the opportunity for Him to bless us further.

—Patti Maguire Armstrong

Words from Mother

Beatified by Pope John Paul II in October, 2003, Blessed Teresa of Calcutta (1910-1997) is a shining example of spiritual motherhood. Here are some of her most inspiring sayings:

∽ Joy is a net of love by which you can catch souls.

∽ It is not how much we do, but how much love we put in the doing. It is not how much we give, but how much love we put in the giving.

∽ Everybody today seems to be in such a terrible rush; anxious for greater developments and greater wishes and so on; so that children have very little time for their parents; parents have very little time for each other; and the home begins the disruption of the peace of the world.

∽ Smile at each other; smile at your wife, smile at your husband, smile at your children, smile at each other—it doesn't matter who it is—and that will help you to grow up in greater love for each other.

∽ I have found the paradox that if I love until it hurts, then there is no hurt, but only more love.

Lasting Legacy

When I joined the ranks of motherhood at the tender age of nineteen, I did not have a clue that I was signing on for a lifelong commitment of the most important assignment of my life. My husband, Randy, and I were immediately captivated by the four-pound, seven-ounce miracle entrusted to our care. Baby Chris had arrived several weeks prematurely.

Chris gained weight quickly and soon came home to be part of our little family. It didn't take long for romantic notions about motherhood to wear thin. Chris had colic and usually cried all night. Randy and I took turns walking back and forth across our postage stamp apartment to quiet our squalling infant. I'm not sure how we survived those early parenting days, but I'm sure it had a lot to do with the legacy my mom gave me.

I was fortunate to have a role model who taught me about the kind of selfless giving for which moms are noted. I like Jill Churchill's comment in her book, *Grime and Punishment*: "There's no way to be a perfect mother— and a million ways to be a good one."

That was true of my mother. She was not perfect, but she lived out her faithfulness and commitment day by day. Mom did not have to work outside of our home, so she was always there. Lunch waited for my brothers and me on school days: triangular-cut sandwiches, steaming soup, little glass dessert dishes filled with pudding or fruit, and homemade chocolate chip cookies. Mountains of laundry piled up with a family of seven, but Mom always had our clothes neatly folded and put away.

Her sewing machine often whirred late at night, and I would wake the next morning with delight to find a brand-new outfit hanging on my bedroom door. She sat patiently with us kids during measles, mumps, chicken pox, and other childhood ailments, bumps, and bruises.

Mom insisted I take piano lessons and practice regularly. I often complained, but learning to read and enjoy music was a gift. Mom introduced me to a belief in God and the priority of weekly worship. Seeds of faith planted in my heart led me to a relationship with the Lord Jesus Christ when I was a young adult.

Growing up, I did not realize how much of Mom's nature had permeated mine. I did recognize motherhood was not for the faint-hearted. Sometimes it seemed like an endurance test. I thought I'd be changing diapers forever—especially when our second son, Jeremy, came on the scene. I lamented to my mother and mother-in-law that older brother Chris was not getting the knack of potty training.

My mother encouraged me with her optimism. "Don't worry," she said. "By the time Chris goes to college, he'll be out of diapers." How could she be so nonchalant? After all, I was the one hauling pails of diapers to the laundromat each week. (Pampers had barely been invented.)

I, too, had the privilege of "being there" for our sons. We survived chicken pox, wisdom tooth extractions, colds, and the flu. Chris learned to play electric guitar while Jeremy attempted to master the bassoon. I gave those familiar sounding talks about being true to godly standards, caring for those less fortunate. We attended church on Sundays where we all learned what it means to be a Christian.

Years passed as quickly as the more seasoned moms had predicted. Why had I not believed them? One day I was sitting at high school graduations, then walking past empty bedrooms with that hard-to-swallow lump in my throat, facing a new dimension of motherhood. I've made lots of mistakes, but it's heartening to observe some of my mother's legacy being passed along.

On a recent visit to Chris and Jeremy's apartment that they share, my heart was touched by Chris taking time to fold his brother's laundry. I don't recall such gestures while they lived at home! Jeremy often e-mails to ask for prayer regarding work situations or other concerns. Despite busy schedules, they always find time for family and friends.

I observe our now-grown sons, more keenly aware that the opportunity to influence a child is the most demanding, most heartrending, most rewarding job a woman may have in her lifetime. Though there were days when I was tempted to turn in my "Mom Badge" and resign, I'm thankful being a mom is a forever assignment.

I will always be my mother's daughter. "Don't forget to call when you get home," she'll say when I have been visiting. Rather than resist her maternal concerns, I comply. It's always a joy to have another chance to hear her voice.

I confess I am the same way with our sons. "Call when you get home," I say, sounding like my mother's clone. I don't even have to ask them anymore. I think they enjoy hearing my voice as well.

—Deb Kalmbach

Deb Kalmbach is an author and speaker. She is co-author of Because I Said Forever: Embracing Hope in a Not-So-Perfect Marriage. *She and her husband, Randy, live in Washington's beautiful Methow valley with their "second" family: Kramer and Kosmo, lively Jack Russell Terriers, and their cat, Nip. Grown sons Chris and Jeremy live in the Seattle area and phone home regularly.*

A Mom's Workout

"My mom can't talk right now.
She's pumping iron."

Learning Patience in the Pews

As a child I had memorized the sweet words of Jesus, "Bring the little children unto me," but I had no idea then what He was really asking. Those seemingly uncomplicated words became more complex when I stepped into motherhood and our family size grew.

After the birth of our third child, my beloved husband, Albert, and I settled into a routine of sitting in "our pew" at a rural church in Texas. There was a pillar on one end that kept the older boys from slipping out the other end unnoticed. We would sit with a boy on each side of us and one between us. When our fourth son was born, my husband and I were suddenly faced with something completely unexpected (besides the fact that no one asked us over for lunch anymore): we could no longer completely separate the boys at church.

We later moved to the community where I grew up and began to attend another parish. Our family quickly settled into our new pew, where I ended up sitting on one end and Albert on the other as sort of pew-sentinels.

As the boys grew, as often as not, it seemed that the grace I received from attending Mass had leaked out by the time the final blessing was given. Instead of praying along with the liturgy, my attention was turned, time and time again, to correcting recalcitrant youngsters. Get up, sit down, sit still, shush, stop that, don't touch your brother, don't look at him, don't breathe on him. Misbehavior meant that the offending child would be unceremoniously (but often comically) hauled from wherever he was sitting and re-seated at the far end of the pew.

Then there was the weekly issue of whose turn it was to sit by Mom. It's an honor and a bane. So much went into the simple act of taking four small people to church. But take them we did, Mass after Mass, until the Sundays turned into years.

Now I actually get to sit by Albert at Mass, but occasionally I still have to settle the heathens down. Inattention at Mass these days is usually *my* fault.

As my children are almost grown, I find myself lending encouragement to a new generation of parents who are struggling with bringing small bundles of energy to Mass.

Albert's sister sometimes attends our church with her young son. There are mornings when he is less than thrilled to be at church. Sitting still and being quiet for a whole hour is a real challenge for him. He wriggles and squirms, chatters and cries, claps, sings and sometimes sleeps. Mostly he, like my children before him, is there to teach his mom patience.

Oddly though, I don't find his delightful little distraction a disturbance the way my own children perturbed *me* when committing the same offenses. Neither are the twins who sometimes attend our tiny parish bothersome. These toddlers sing at the top of their lungs and often whisper "Is it over yet?" quite audibly. They are a joy, not a bother.

I am grateful for all the hours I've spent in church, teaching my children about the love of God. I think, though, that they ended up teaching *me* what love really is about. I guess the grace I received from all those Masses didn't really leak out after all. It just took a while for it to manifest itself.

—Jackie Zimmerer

Jackie Zimmerer has been married to her beloved Albert since 1985. They have four sons, ages 22, 18, 17 and 15. The Zimmerer family has been homeschooling since 2000. Jackie's columns can be found at www.catholicmom.com and www.texashomeeducators.com

Jewels in My Crown

"We've got to get you on the Pill, girl!"

I received these words with silence, stunned by my friend's reaction to the news that I was pregnant with my third child within four years. Recovering quickly, I babbled something inane that I hoped would convey my belief in being open to life. Inside, though, my true response to my friend was pressing against my mind like an inflating balloon: *Why? Why aren't your first words ones of celebration? Why shouldn't I bear another child?*

My mother, who was usually supportive of me, was also upset that I was pregnant with my third child. She agreed with my dad that it was not in my best interest to have more children, though she loves all of her grandchildren very much. She took offense at my assertion that contraception was wrong. She passionately defended the committed Christians we knew who had used contraception, including my husband and me before we converted to Catholicism. I argued the Catholic position until she finally stormed out of the house, crying, "Birth control is not wrong!" Our quarrel left me discouraged and hurt, but I understood her viewpoint.

Since becoming Catholic the previous year, I grasped the tragedy of the contraceptive mindset. I had grown up as an evangelical Protestant believing contraception and sterilization to be responsible ways of using medical advances. Yet, in spite of realizing how immoral both actions really were, the old Protestant part of me whispered agreement with my mother and my friend. The truth was that I was deeply upset by this third pregnancy and angry with God for not understanding that two young children were all I could handle.

I had done my best to follow my newly forming conscience by surrendering my will and committing to Natural Family Planning. A year before my husband and I were confirmed in the Catholic Church, I had even asked my husband to cancel his vasectomy on the day of his appointment. And how had God rewarded me for my obedience? By allowing me to make a charting mistake and conceive again! How could He?! Didn't He care?

Still, I was honestly ashamed of my inability to be open to life, knowing that some of my resistance came from pure selfishness. I knew that countless women longed for children and could not conceive. Children were a gift and fertility was a blessing. I knew that I would love this child just as much as I loved the other two. Still, I could not pretend that I was truly open to life, and neither could my husband.

I had dreams for the future, plans that did not include an expanding family. I wanted to fulfill my lifelong goal of writing children's books, continue my step-dancing lessons, travel, be financially comfortable, and perhaps return to teaching after my girls were in school. Not only that, I had been raised as an only child and was accustomed to large amounts of solitude and silence. My personality and temperament were not suited to a large family, although I did love visiting the only one I knew. I wanted a small, intimate family, and so did my husband, who had grown up with one sibling. The constant busyness and material needs of a large family—which in my mind meant more than three children—were overwhelming to me.

When I finally gave birth to our third daughter, I found myself struggling. She was not the problem; it was the shifting dynamics of my life. Suddenly, all of my responsibilities exhausted me both mentally and physically. In spite of part-time work, our financial picture was extremely bleak. I was often overwhelmed and driven to the point of breakdown more than a few times.

Worst of all, I had no one to talk to. My husband was too close to the situation and experienced many of the same things, anyway. I was developing a base of Catholic friends, but I did not know any women who could relate to my struggle. It was pointless to talk to Protestant friends and relatives because they did not agree with either my conversion or Church teachings on sexuality. I couldn't afford counseling and was afraid to share my problems with a stranger, anyway. Though I read some helpful Catholic books on sexuality and marriage, none fully addressed my issues.

That left only one option—God. But confiding in Him while I was blaming Him for everything did not seem helpful. Feeling alone, I finally decided that all I could do was continue to obey as best I could and pray for a change of heart. Then came another shock: I became pregnant, again. It had only been a year, and we were still not doing well financially. This time I had done everything right with NFP to avoid a pregnancy. Even my doctor, who understood NFP, was surprised when he examined my chart.

One thing was obvious, though. We could not doubt God's will for us this time. This pregnancy could not be simply dismissed as a mistake or an accident. We may not have chosen it, but we knew that God had. We also believed that this new life would bring glory to Him. In His mysterious wisdom, He had called us to receive this gift. What could I say to that?

This realization comforted me somewhat, but the intense stress continued throughout my pregnancy. How would I ever be able to handle another child? What about my dreams and goals? They had to be put on a high shelf that I would not be able to reach for many more years. Why would God let me dream and then make them impossible?

I dreaded telling Mom about this pregnancy. She responded to the news with a three-month-long silence that somehow seemed just as loud as our argument earlier.

God did begin to break through my confusion during this pregnancy, however. As it progressed, I began to realize that God was working to make me more like Jesus, as I had often asked Him to do. He was asking me to give of myself until I had nothing left to give and follow Him even when I did not know where He was leading me. Slowly, I began to understand what I was meant to do with my dreams and goals. Everything I was and everything I wanted needed to be surrendered to God. As my Bible study teacher helped me see, I had "Isaacs" that needed to be given back to God, just as Abraham was asked to give back his only, precious son. My dreams were to be laid at the foot of God's throne.

As I write this, my baby is three weeks old; another jewel in my maternal crown and just as precious as the other three. I would not hand her back for any amount of riches or freedom. Still, it would not be honest for me to say that I am fully now open to life. My faith is strong, but it often battles with my willingness to trust and surrender fully to God. I know His wisdom is far greater than mine, though, so I seek to fully trust and surrender to Him. I do it imperfectly, but I pray that He will perfect me.

The time may come someday when God will return my dreams to me, as He gave Isaac back to Abraham. Yet, I realize that my temporal dreams do not reach into eternity as the perfectly created souls of my children do. He has entrusted me with the job of leading at least four precious, eternal souls to His heavenly throne. If I can be faithful and someday hear the words, "Well done, good and faithful servant," then my own dreams will mean nothing at all. Of all the stars to reach for, none are brighter than this.

—Anna Wind*

Anna Wind is a full-time mother and part-time bookseller. She lives with her husband and four "Little Women" in Minnesota.

Name has been changed.

Modern Mom

"Oh, hi, Helen, I'm just multi-tasking.
How about you?"

For Mothers Who Stay

"The roof could cave in!" bellowed my mother.

My teenage sister and I howled with laughter. "Mother! Just because some YMCA roof three hundred miles away caved in onto a swimming pool doesn't mean it will happen down at the YMCA today! Don't be ridiculous! Please let me go swimming!" begged my sister. The argument continued as Mom peppered her with more questions until finally she allowed her to go.

Mother lived in a constant state of fear in the midst of raising eight children. I never realized how frightening motherhood could be until I became a mother myself. Then my mom's outrageous concerns didn't seem so funny anymore. The YMCA roof may very well cave in while my son is there swimming!

I hadn't intended for life to make me into a single mother, but after my husband left me while our son, Eric, was barely walking, I was alone to make the world a safe place for him.

Watching the news would convince me of how unsafe the world is. When Eric was a baby, every news report seemed to include information of Sudden Infant Death Syndrome. When he was a toddler, children his age were being crushed by garage doors at an alarming rate. When he started school, there seemed to be an epidemic of pedophiles snatching school-age boys.

The day I made the appointment for Eric to get his driver's license, I learned of a teenage couple that had crashed through the ice of a frozen lake and perished in the frigid water. I toyed with canceling his license appointment, but knew that wasn't possible. Instead, I made Eric promise he'd never drive on a frozen lake. While sitting in the waiting room as Eric took his driving exam, I read a story about a carload of teenage girls on the freeway when the driver lost control of the car. All the girls were either dead or dying in the hospital. When my son returned, elated that he passed his test, I wanted to lock him up in the house for the next five years. Of course I told him about the terrible accident and made him promise he wouldn't drive on the freeway with a car full of his friends.

By far the most troubling news reports for me, however, have been about the fate of fatherless children. My son was six years old when Dan Quayle, then U.S. Vice President, made his infamous speech against Murphy Brown and the evils of single parenting. By then I had struggled through the worst of a bad divorce. I had obtained a good job, a new car, and my son and I had a home of our own in a quiet neighborhood. I was proud of how well we were doing under difficult circumstances, and resentful that anyone would berate me for the wrenching choices I had made.

A year later when the *Atlantic Monthly* cover displayed in large print "Dan Quayle was Right!" I read (and reread) every word of that excellent article with angst and dismay. I also took mental notes and planned my parenting strategy accordingly, hoping to offset this statistic in my child's case.

I doubt there is any experience as overwhelming and humbling as parenting a child. I knew before I had a child that I was not perfect, but parenting forced me to accept how drastically imperfect I am. And as difficult as parenting is, parenting alone is guaranteed to reveal the full extent of every shortcoming of your personality.

One evening, I watched a show about Catholic parenting. My ears perked up immediately as they began discussing the question of single parenting. The expert sighed before answering, "Single parenting is like standing in the middle of the Mississippi River and trying to hold back the water with your bare hands." I realized he was right. Successful single parenting is impossible, but so is parting the Red Sea, and Moses managed it with God's help. With the help of God, my son was growing into a responsible teen.

A dear friend of mine is also a single mother whose ex-husband vanished after the divorce. During one of our conversations, she lamented her mistakes and shortcomings as a mother, blaming herself for some difficulty her child was experiencing. Even though I felt the same way about my own parenting, I found myself leaping to her defense. "Don't blame yourself," I chastised her. "You are not the parent who left, you are the parent who stayed!"

It was good advice, for her and for myself. We are parents who stay, even though it's hard and humbling and terrifying and sometimes overwhelming. We face our responsibilities and we sacrifice everything to provide for our children. I think God honors that, whether you are a single parent or a married one. Despite the social stigma and the seemingly inescapable failure we faced as single mothers, we stayed. We did our best every day and trusted God for the rest.

Still, I am like my own mother. I fear that tragedy could strike at any time, and sometimes that overwhelms me. Now when I voice my concern, my son rolls his eyes and repeats the teenager's chorus, "Mom, that is not going to happen to me." It's exactly what my siblings and I said at that age. Though I may fear, I know I can still call on God for help in protecting, guiding, and caring for my son.

—Kathleen R. Fitzgerald

Kathleen Fitzgerald is a single mother, a chronic worrier, and a marketing manager in the Twin Cities area. She works to develop life safety and personal emergency response systems that help other worriers feel more secure. Eric recently celebrated his 18th birthday and graduated from a Catholic high school. He is interested in fitness and nutrition, and plans to become a personal trainer.

A Luxury I Took for Granted

We had hours to kill between the hearing test and the follow-up appointment with the ear, nose, and throat specialist. Five months after my first grader's tube surgery, she heard perfectly (albeit selectively), so this would be a routine visit with the doctor. What wasn't routine was the gap between appointments—they didn't tell me we would need sleeping bags and a toothbrush.

I was peeved they wouldn't just squeeze us into the morning schedule so we could get in and get out. I had a million things I should have been doing, and we all knew the actual appointment with the doctor would last about thirty seconds. But no matter how nicely I asked, the schedule could not be changed because the *computer* said it couldn't. It may as well have been etched in Greek on the outside of the building.

So lunch it was. The nurse directed us down the hall to the cafeteria that served the medical complex, where we crossed the main lobby of the children's hospital. We knew we were on the right track because she said we'd pass a statue of Big Bird, and here it was.

There, sitting next to Big Bird in a well-worn wheelchair, was a boy of about four. His bright eyes danced under a baseball cap resting atop his thick, curly hair. He was dressed in soft sweats, surrounded by bags of toys and helium balloons.

His face was happy and eager, but profoundly disfigured. He wore a shiny, plastic mask designed to keep his skin intact as it healed from what must had been a horrible fire.

I took a big breath and hoped my daughter didn't say something loud or insensitive. We walked within two feet of his chair, but even after we passed, she didn't say a word. I sensed she was thinking about him, so I asked, "Did you notice that boy wearing the mask? It looks like he was burned in a big fire and he's going home now. I'll bet he's really brave."

We talked about fire safety as we ambled toward the lunchroom. It was a crowded, busy place and before we knew it, we were swept into the line, deciding what to eat and where to sit.

I was munching my chicken salad, but I couldn't stop thinking about that little boy. The suffering displayed behind the mask was unspeakable, and the fact that he sat in the lobby with his mom waiting to go home was a testament to his heroic determination and her incalculable love. She must have been grateful for every breath he took.

Suddenly, I was glad for the time with my six-year-old to eat a leisurely lunch and await an uneventful visit with the doctor. I am so blessed, it's embarrassing.

Most days, I don't remember this. I'm too busy lecturing about unmade beds, towels on the bathroom floor, toys on the driveway, and dishes in the sink. My kids are expensive and exhausting, and they talk to me through the bathroom door, which is really annoying.

But being annoyed was a luxury I took for granted.

My daughter and I finished our lunches and cleaned our table, moving together in a familiar rhythm. As usual, her hand sliped easily into mine as we strolled down the long corridor toward the doctor's suite. Back in the lobby, Big Bird towered from his pedestal, but the little boy and his mom had moved closer to the door. His hat and mask were off. He looked like he was getting tired.

We were just about to take the corner when the mom leaned across the wheelchair, tickled her son's tummy and gave him a big snuggle. "I love you so much!" she said. Her voice was pure joy.

I knew just how she felt. I squeezed my daughter's hand, and we headed off to spend an hour together with nothing to do but live gratefully.

—Marybeth Hicks

Marybeth Hicks is the author of the feature Then Again. *A wife of 17 years and mother of four, she uses her columns to share her perspective on issues and experiences that shape families and the communities we share. Marybeth began her writing career more than 20 years ago in the Reagan White House. She also has worked in marketing and public relations positions in corporate and agency settings. Mostly, she spends a lot of time in her mini-van, where the real work of parenting actually happens. Learn more about Marybeth and her column at www.marybethhicks.com*

Surrendering To a Better Plan

When Ash Wednesday arrives and finds six children at home with the flu, it's clear what I'm giving up for Lent. I'm just giving up. Surrendering. Taking all that I hold tightly and giving it to God. It's time to recognize again that His plan is always better than mine. It's time to acknowledge that I am not in control, nor should I be.

So often those things that frustrate me are products of my own tendency to want to play God in my life. Frequently, I do this without even recognizing it. When I meet obstacles to my plan, it vexes me. Rarely do I stop to consider that the obstacles might be part of a bigger, better plan. They might be God's plan.

I can hold so tightly to my own plans that I am closed off to God. I am a bit of a proud perfectionist. It has taken seven children to teach me that pride will always stand between God and me. To live out my vocation faithfully in the suburban world means that I have to wrestle daily with the imperfect appearance of my life.

I have friends and neighbors whose hair and nails are perfect, whose homes are perfectly decorated, whose wardrobes are perfect for their perfect bodies. I want my life to look like that. My revolving wardrobe frustrates me: the clothes I love, the just-getting-out-of maternity clothes and the maternity clothes themselves. I have mornings when my shower gets pushed back until noon as I deal with one mini-crisis at a time. My house looks more like something from *Chaotic Home Today* than *House Beautiful*.

Over time, I have come to recognize that my life appears odd, out of control and somehow sad to people who think that perfect appearances and human control are important.

I never consciously put aside perfectionism; instead, I had to recognize that I am outnumbered and it is humanly impossible to keep up the appearance of being perfect. A friend whose life appears so perfect said to me, quite matter-of-factly, "I could never have another baby. I am too much of a perfectionist. One more, and I'd lose control." She would. She'd have overwhelming days, and bad hair days and extreme laundry days. She would not be perfect. She would not be in control. But she would be driven to her knees and she would, in her openness to life, be open to God. His power would be made perfect in her weakness.

He would meet her there, where she desperately needed Him. He would not whirl through her house like some sort of spiritual Mr. Clean. He would not magically liposuction the last ten pounds of baby weight. But He would bless her with the comfort of knowing that He is in control and He has a better plan.

She would be frustrated some days. She'd feel misunderstood by most of the world. She would look with longing at catalogs and decorating magazines, but she would know that she and God had a deal. She would do things His way and He would bless her in ways that are beyond the understanding of the woman who tries to stay in control.

I had grand plans for Lent that February. Instead, I surrendered. I rubbed a lot of backs, gave a lot of baths, wiped a lot of noses, read a lot stories. I don't like it when my children are sick, but I always find that we are brought closer by the experience of weathering the storm together—even though it appears that I got nothing accomplished.

My house is dusty and I am sorely in need of a haircut. But my children are feeling better today. And they know that I was there every step of the way, day and night. They are better for it and so am I. It felt very out of control at times. I offered more round-the-clock prayers than a monk. I had plenty of opportunity to listen to God above the noisy breathing of sick babies. And I am certain that this wasn't my plan for February, but it was a better plan.

—Elizabeth Foss

Elizabeth Foss' biography appears after Ballet Lessons *in Chapter 3.*

Chapter Seven

A Mother's Prayer

A Cana Wedding

It was a beautiful spring morning in May of 1995 as I gazed out across the fields from the deck behind our house. The birds had just begun to twitter and the sun was peeking above the horizon. But I had little appreciation for the morning that was dawning. I had wrestled half the night with a big financial problem. Finally, I gave up trying to sleep and got up to calculate finances instead. There had to be a way to come up with some extra money.

Our only daughter, Robin, was engaged to be married after a five-year courtship to Michael. The memory of the day she called us from Hawaii to tell us the news still brought me joy. Robin and her boyfriend, Michael, had gone to Hawaii for a winter vacation with a group of their friends. Michael had met her that morning in the lobby of the hotel where the girls in the group were staying. He told her he had planned a very special day for just the two of them. He also had a gift for her.

When Robin opened the present—a pair of hiking boots—she hid her disappointment. Swimming, water skiing, or snorkeling were right up her alley, but Michael's idea of hiking for hours over rough terrain to the top of a volcanic mountain did not interest her. Yet, Michael's excitement forced her to put up an enthusiastic front.

Robin had valiantly appeared cheerful while sweating it out until they finally reached the top of the mountain. It was there that Michael got down on one knee and proposed to her. He then revealed an engagement ring—a diamond ring presented on the peak of Diamond Head mountain.

But Robin's tearful phone call the previous night had not been so happy. The florist wanted a deposit of $100 paid by the following week. The week fell between paydays for the kids and we had no extra money for at least the next month. Robin had shopped carefully for a reasonably priced florist that could deliver the red and white roses for her bouquet and the other flower arrangements. Originally, she had wanted Cana lilies also, but with their money constraints, they had to leave that out. The kids had already put down money for the wine and food for the reception and nothing was left over at the moment.

My husband, Gene, and I wanted to help with the expenses as any parents would. However, years of battling cancer had left us financially strapped most the time. Other than paying for part of her wedding dress and making the wedding cake, I could see no other way we could help. I had also made a deposit on Gene's black tux and dress shoes. There were other expenses I had planned to help with over the spring and summer, but I had nothing to contribute for the flowers at the time.

Later that morning, I called my beloved retired former pastor, Father John Giacopelli, to cheer myself up. Father John always gives me good advice and has been a special prayer partner and spiritual director for me since he retired in 1992. Father was struggling financially himself so I often sent care packages to him and his sister whom he lived with back in his native New York. We chatted a bit. I mentioned my daughter's dilemma and we commiserated on the fact that money could be a wicked thing when you have too much and a real pain when you do not have enough. Before we hung up, Father John said, "I really feel bad for Robin and Mike. I will offer a special prayer to Our Lady that you will find the deposit. I think I shall appeal to her under the title of 'Our Lady of Cana.' Tell Robin not to worry. Just trust Our Lady to handle the problem and it will all be fine."

The following week dwindled to a mere twenty-four hours remaining for the deposit to come due. None of us had been able to come up with the money. I felt guilty that I could not even pay a little deposit for the flowers for my own daughter's wedding. I tossed and turned most the night, before giving up on sleep once again. I decided to take an early morning walk as long as I was up.

Soaking in the early morning sun and saying my morning prayers allowed me the peace to accept the fact that some things just are not necessary even if they seem important to us. God had given us so much; it was ungrateful of me to stay grumpy over the wedding flowers. The very fact that my husband had beat the odds with his cancer and was still alive and healthy was blessing enough for me. Turning toward home, I felt a renewed spirit.

I returned just in time to take the mail from the mailman. Seeing a letter from Father John lifted my spirits even further. With a happy heart, I went inside and poured myself a cup of coffee.

I read Father's quickly scribbled note, dated from the day of our talk. "I offered prayers for the kids' needs after we hung up this morning. Then, I went to the store to buy a quart of milk. As you know, I do *not* condone gambling, but I had an overwhelming urge I could not ignore. I bought a lottery ticket for a quarter and won $100. I knew it must be from Our Lady for Robin's wedding—so don't thank me, thank Our Lady of Cana." Enclosed was a check for the money.

Not only did Robin and Mike have a wonderful wedding, but on the day of the wedding, as if to punctuate Our Lady's intercession, the florist delivered the flowers with Cana lilies tucked into each arrangement. The florist said she had a cancellation that weekend. The order was loaded with these very rare and expensive flowers. Because she recalled how much Robin liked the exotic lilies, but could not afford them, she decided to make up Robin's flowers with them as a special surprise wedding gift. And so Our Lady showed us that not only can her Son turn water into wine, He is also very good at arranging flower bouquets when His mother asks Him.

—Christine Trollinger

Christine Trollinger's biography appears after Please Hold Him For Me *in Chapter 4.*

A Modern-Day Monica

When my twelve-year-old son, Donnie, became involved with drugs and alcohol, as far as I could tell, he was still the same obedient and kindhearted son he had always been. We had been close during his childhood but I failed to recognize the changes he was going through.

In many ways, Donnie and I grew up together. I was only eighteen when I had him, so I went from being a teenager to a mother. We always had a strong love and bond between us. When Donnie was ten years old, I married Don Calloway, an officer in the Navy. The two Dons in my life took to each other with great affection. Don soon adopted my son as his own.

A year after our marriage, our son, Matthew, was born. Donnie was ecstatic. He helped me decorate the baby's room and could not wait to hold his little brother shortly after the birth. As Matthew grew, the boys spent hours together playing, bike riding, reading, and laughing. They rarely used one another's name, instead preferring to always call one another "brother."

Because Donnie seemed to be his same old self when we lived in California, I never saw the dangerous changes taking place. But shortly after our family transferred to Japan, the problem became obvious. Donnie lost no time getting acquainted with the local criminal element. He grew distant from us and became defiant and hostile. His grades at school dropped, and his friends were all that mattered to him. Donnie refused to talk with me about anything. My heart broke and I often cried out in anguish. We were at a loss for what to do.

During this time of conflict, some friends in the Navy invited us to attend the Catholic Church on base with them. Religion had been largely absent during my childhood. I lived back and forth between divorced parents with only sporadic church attendance of various denominations. But I did have fond childhood memories of my beloved Catholic grandmother taking me to Mass. I had hoped that Don would go with me, but my mind was made up to go whether or not he came.

The moment I walked into that church, peace filled me. I knew that I had found a home. Don felt it, too. We were where we needed to be. The Catholic Church became our comfort and grace to get us through what awaited us.

After we had been in Japan for two-and-a-half years, Donnie ran away one night. We did not search alone for our wayward son, however; the Japanese government also wanted him. It did not take long for them to figure out that the white boy frequently witnessed at crime scenes was responsible for them. The military transferred our family to Pennsylvania to get us out of there. Although I felt incomplete leaving Japan with just one son, my newfound faith gave me the strength to trust that my prayers for help would be heard.

As I boarded the plane in tears, Don looked at me and promised: "I will not leave Japan without Donnie." He was true to his word, but it took a pair of handcuffs and a police escort to get Donnie on the plane.

Donnie agreed to be admitted to a drug and rehabilitation center in exchange for the Japanese government not pressing charges. He did not like us any better than before he had run away, but my heart rested in the faith that God would take care of Donnie. At least we were together as a family again. And Don and I were determined to do everything possible to help him.

In Pennsylvania, we officially became Catholic and gained assurance from an arsenal of spiritual resources: Mass, the Eucharist, prayers, the Bible, and the intercession of Our Blessed Mother. "Dear God," I often prayed. "Please help my son. And hear the prayers of Your Mother, the Mother of Our Lord and Savior, Jesus Christ. She gave us the gift of Your Son. Now I plead to You that my own son be saved."

Upon completion of Donnie's rehabilitation program, we rejoiced. Our son seemed better, and our new membership in the Catholic Church brought us much comfort. But before long, Donnie was back to his old ways. During his junior year, his school performance both academically and behaviorally was so poor that he finally just gave up altogether and dropped out. Waist-length hair, an earring, and a Grateful Dead tattoo gave the world an impression of my seventeen-year-old son that I refused to accept. I knew that underneath the rough exterior was still my kind and loving son.

Even though Donnie offered no outward sign of it, I believed it with all my heart that he was going to be something very special when he finally came out of this. God would give Donnie the grace to turn his life around. I loved him so much; I knew that this child was a child of God and that all the destruction was from the devil.

We had often tried to encourage Donnie to turn to God, but he would have none of it. "I will never set foot in your church," he once announced. Another time, he had been embarrassingly rude over the phone when our pastor called.

After he dropped out of school, his life continued on a downward spiral. On his own, he chose to enter drug treatment for a second time. It did not take, although at the

time I was hopeful. Shortly after completing the treatment
program, Donnie left for Louisiana to bum around with a
friend. He had another brush with the law and continued
down the wrong path. Donnie called only sporadically. My
heart broke that he was so far from us both physically and
spiritually.

My prayers were unceasing now. Not a half an hour
went by that I did not talk to God about my son and ask His
Blessed Mother to keep praying for Donnie. He returned
home at nineteen. If nothing else, at least he was home
with us, I thought. Shortly thereafter, my husband was
transferred to Virginia. Donnie came with us.

Matthew settled into fourth grade at a Catholic school,
Don was sent out to sea on a six-month tour, I kept up
my never-ending conversations with God and the Blessed
Mother, and Donnie returned to his destructive lifestyle.
Then, suddenly everything changed overnight. "Mom,"
Donnie said as I passed by his bedroom early one morning.
"I want to talk to a priest."

I stopped in my tracks. This was the moment I had
waited for so long, but when it finally happened I was
shocked. "What did you say?" I asked, afraid to believe my
own ears. Donnie repeated his request. There was a light
in his eyes and his face was radiant.

Dumbfounded, I just stared at him. "Mom, I read this
book last night," he said, holding up a book of mine on
apparitions of the Blessed Mother.

"You read *that* book?" I asked, amazed.

"Mom, I consumed this book," Donnie said. He did
not understand it all, but somehow, through the beauty and
love of the Blessed Mother, Donnie was overcome with the
reality that her God was his God.

I made arrangements for him to talk to a priest on base. Donnie flew out the door and ran the half-mile to the chapel. Something miraculous had happened to him that night. My spirits soared in wonderment as I thanked God. Words cannot describe my joy—it was so complete. Now I prayed that what had begun was for real and would continue without distractions.

Later, I learned that all the pain, the sadness, the desire for any alcohol, cigarettes or drugs had evaporated overnight. Donnie was left only with a craving for the Almighty. The Blessed Mother had come to him with her Son, Jesus, who washed Donnie and healed him. Tears of joy dripped onto the letter I wrote to my husband. "You will be coming home to a very different Donnie." I wrote. After that, everything happened very quickly. Donnie immersed himself in Catholic books and began practicing the faith. It would be another six months before he could be fully received into the Church, but during that time, his all-consuming zeal never let up. Donnie told us early on that he had a great desire to serve God for the rest of his life.

On May 31, 2003, ten years after he became Catholic, I cried tears of joy again as I hugged my son, the priest. "I love you, Father Donnie," I told him after the bishop had congratulated him and introduced him as Father Donald Calloway. My son had become a priest for life with the Congregation of Marians of the Immaculate Conception. He went from being a high school drop out to earning a bachelor's degree with majors in philosophy and theology, and a master's in divinity. He plans to continue his studies and pursue a doctorate in Mariology.

So many people prayed for Donnie on his journey to the priesthood, especially from our church, Immaculate

Conception Parish in Clarksburg, West Virginia. We are immensely blessed by them all.

And, of course, our Blessed Mother Mary has interceded every step of the way on this journey of faith for our entire family. She understood a mother's pain and now she celebrates with us the conversion won by her Son.

—LaChita Calloway

LaChita Callaway is a realtor in Clarksburg, West Virginia, but says mothering is her primary profession. Don, now retired from the Navy, works for the state. Matthew, twenty-one, is attending Fairmont State College in West Virigina.

I remember my mother's prayers and they have always followed me. They have clung to me all my life.

—Abraham Lincoln

Two Gifts

I was so excited at the possibility of being pregnant that I bought and used three over-the-counter pregnancy kits before finally getting verification. I was so excited that I kept taking the test before the minimum waiting time. When the results finally confirmed what I had suspected, I ran into the living room to tell my husband, Alan. We hugged and cried tears of joy.

We had only been married six months, but both being close to 30, we did not want to wait too long to start a family. My mom and Alan's parents also cried tears of happiness at the news, even though this was to be the 26th grandchild on my side of the family. I was the youngest of ten children and the last to have a baby. The baby of the family was having a baby of her own.

The realization of new life growing inside me colored my world now. At work, as a police officer for Oak Park, Michigan, I frequently thought, "I'm going to have a baby!" At eighteen weeks, I went to my doctor for a regularly scheduled visit and a routine ultrasound. Lying on the table for the ultrasound, my heart raced in anticipation of actually seeing the baby for the first time. As the technician scanned my growing tummy she suddenly laid down the scanning device and went to get assistance from another technician.

"I'm still new at this," she explained calmly, "I just need a little help." The screen was turned away from me while the two took measurements and looked at the baby from different angles. When the screen was finally turned to face me, Alan was invited in. We were shown pictures of the baby's head and a top view, but nothing full-body or from the side. Returning home, I felt unsettled. Something was not right.

Two days later, my doctor called me at work and asked me to come in the next day to go over the pictures together. I knew the routine from my sister who was an X-ray technician. The only reason I would need to come in before my next scheduled appointment was if something was wrong. I was so upset I had to go home for the day.

An hour before our appointment, my doctor was called away to deliver a baby, so she had to break the news over the phone. "Your baby has omphalocele, a condition in which organs develop outside the body," she said. In my baby's case, it was the liver, kidneys, and intestines.

I was hysterical. Researching the condition on the Internet brought only more bad news. Fifty percent of these babies also had chromosomal abnormalities and numerous other health problems. The doctor suggested abortion as an option, but it was not an option for us. Instinctively, I began to pray. It was a pleading prayer: "Please God, make my baby healthy." It was also a prayer steeped in guilt. God had not been a serious part of my life for a long time.

I was born and raised Catholic, but I had not practiced for years. Now, I realized how desperately I needed God. There was no one else who could make everything better— not my mom, not my close-knit family or loving husband, not even the doctor.

I had not consciously decided to exclude religion in my life, it just sort of happened. After my father died when I was thirteen, I was angry with God. "Why did you have to take him?" I had cried. Everything I did after the death of my father, I did to make him proud. But God had been largely left out of the picture.

Alan was equally lax in his faith, so even though we were both cradle Catholics and married in the Church, attending Mass and praying were not part of our lives. Now, everything depended on God. We prayed unceasingly. Family, churches, prayer lists—everyone was enlisted to join in the spiritual pleading for God's help and mercy on our little baby.

Nine days later, Alan stood at my side during another ultrasound. Before, we did not want to learn the sex of the baby, but now we wanted to know everything possible. We learned it was a boy and an amniocentesis revealed no chromosomal abnormalities. For the first time since the traumatic news, we felt some relief.

Regular doctor appointments and ultrasounds showed that in spite of having three vital organs growing outside his body, the baby was otherwise progressing well. A Cesarean section was scheduled for the morning of August 16, 2001. We entered an operating room full of people: several doctors, an intern, nurses, and even a small camera crew from a local Detroit television station there with my permission to film this event as a documentary. At least twenty family members crowded the waiting room, storming heaven with prayers.

As the baby was lifted out, hearing his cries flooded me with relief. He was alive! As I gently held him, swaddled in a blanket, maternal love gushed forth. He was the most beautiful baby I had ever seen! We had not named him yet but at that point I knew right away; Victor Alan, our little victor. Then, Victor was whisked away to prepare for surgery.

I wondered if I would ever see him again. But my doctor had some unexpected news. Only the liver was outside Victor's body in spite of the fact that every ultrasound had always shown the liver, kidneys, and intestines growing outside. Also, there was enough extra skin so that the procedure to correct the liver would not need to be done in stages as previously anticipated.

I wanted to know how this could be. My doctor shrugged and looked happily baffled. "I can't say for sure," he admitted. "Maybe the organs were going in and out." In my heart, I knew how the other two organs ended up in Victor's body; it was God's handiwork.

The surgery was a success, but we were warned there would likely be a roller coaster of setbacks and recovery. There were, but each time there was a setback, it seemed as though prayer brought Victor back out sooner and stronger than anyone expected. Twenty-three days after Victor was born, we brought home a healthy baby boy.

Not a day goes by now that we do not thank God for our miracle baby. We have not only been given a son, but we have also been given the gift of a renewed faith in the Lord.

—Maureen (Mo) Merritt Bergman

Maureen (Mo) Merritt Bergman, husband Alan, and son Victor live in Dearborn Heights, Michigan. Victor is now a happy, healthy, and amazing two-year-old. His parents thank God every day for their blessing.

God's Answer

Ten days overdue with my third baby, I felt like I had been pregnant forever. I also felt bigger than a barn. My baby was estimated to weigh more than ten pounds, was posterior (sunny side up) and acynclitic (the head was lodged the wrong way in the pelvis.) The plan of action was that I would be induced in four days.

My inclination was to be scared, but my caregivers assured me that the situation was nothing to worry about and that everything would be fine. "But what if they are wrong?" I wondered. I decided to pray.

"Dear God," I prayed. "You know all things. Is this right for me? Should I be induced?" No answer came. I kept praying and waiting for a sign. By morning, stress burdened my heart. I still had no answer. Before waking my other children, I prayed again, this time asking God: "Should I skip the induction and get a C-section instead?" In my mind came the crystal clear command: "Go!"

As if life depended on it, I packed my bags and rushed the kids over to my mother-in-law's house. My husband, Peter, and I then hurried to the hospital. I was sure that the staff looked upon me as an overemotional pregnant woman who had gotten herself all stressed out. But since I was in tears and because my first baby had been a C-section, my request was granted. In a matter of minutes, I was on the operating table.

Laying on the hard, cold table and prepped for surgery, doubt crept into my mind. "Am I just a chicken? Am I taking the easy way out? Was it really God who told me to do this, or was it my stressed-out imagination?" I put myself in God's hands. "Please Lord, take care of me and my baby," I prayed.

After the incision, my womb became visible. The surgeon immediately saw there was a huge problem. At the sight of my previous C-section scar, the uterine wall was translucent and as thin as plastic wrap. It could rupture at any moment. The surgeon said the membrane would not likely have lasted the day, much less survive the rigors of an induced labor with its intense contraction.

When the incision was made into the uterine wall, a river of thick, black merconium poured from my womb. The baby was clearly under stress and needed to be born immediately.

In the euphoric aftermath of having delivered a healthy baby boy, the nurses and surgeon proclaimed me a very lucky woman. They raved that my decision to have an immediate C-section had saved both my life and my baby's life.

"It was not my decision," I told them, "but the grace of God that saved us." I named our little boy Matthew, which means God's Gift.

—Cathy Tressider

Cathy Tressider is a 32-year-old homemaker and mother of three. Born and raised in Queens, New York, she moved to Raleigh, North Carolina, in December of 2000. She says she took her faith for granted and never truly prayed until the birth of her first child—Jonathon—in August, 1997. She took one look at his angelic face and had no doubt there really is a God.

I Know He Hears Me

"Oh, you think you are so holy!" my daughter, Monica, screamed into the phone before hanging up on me. I shakily put down my own phone and made a futile attempt to wipe away the tears that flowed freely. My heart broke, not just from the verbal lashing but from the realization that my daughter had not only rejected her Catholic faith, but had rejected me also. Monica was a successful lawyer who thought of me as too old-fashioned and uneducated to understand the world she lived in. My attempts to get her to realize that living with a man outside of marriage was wrong brought forth only anger and resentment towards me.

I was trying to plan for my son Michael's upcoming wedding at that time. He and my daughter had remained in California after I married my second husband, Tony, and moved to North Dakota with our two young sons, Ryan and Anton.

My divorce had ended a very troubled marriage. Although I had received an annulment from the Church, there would always be part of me plagued with guilt that my first two children suffered from the effects of a broken home. Still, I had always provided for them both spiritually and materially. I made sure they attended Catholic school and practiced their Catholic faith at home. But once they left for college it was as if all of their Catholic upbringing never existed.

It was exciting for Tony and me to move to his home state of North Dakota and realize my childhood dream of opening an authentic Mexican restaurant, but a piece of me remained in California with my other children. During my previous visit to my daughter's home, I felt like a hypocrite. I felt dirty. She was living with a man without the benefit of the sacrament of marriage. For Michael's wedding, I would be bringing Ryan and Anton with me. The feeling that it would be wrong for me to stay with her nagged at me. Yet, I did not want to cause friction between us.

I discussed the situation with Father Wayne Sattler, a trusted priest from my parish. "Celia, you cannot take your two beautiful boys into that situation," he counseled. "I don't care what it costs; you need to ask your daughter to find you a hotel room close to the church or the reception."

I knew Father Wayne was right. I went before the Blessed Sacrament and prayed to Jesus for the strength to tell Monica what was in my heart.

I began the conversation with my daughter in a strong voice, trying not to betray my fear. "Monica, we don't agree on a lot of issues, but it is my job as your mother to let you know that your lifestyle is sinful. I cannot stay with you when I come for the wedding."

The angry exchange was brief, but the wound it inflicted was deep. I knew I had done the right thing, but I could not escape my feeling of failure as a mother. All I could do now was to pray that somehow God would heal our relationship and provide a place for us to stay before the July wedding.

On Easter Sunday, I answered a phone call from Monica. "Mom?" she asked laughing. "What was it that you prayed for?" She explained that her friend, Mary, was planning to vacation in England during the same time that I would be in California. Mary wanted me to stay at her house so it would not be left vacant while she was gone.

My heart leaped for joy and my tears were now out of happiness. "Thank you, Lord, for answering my pleas," I immediately prayed. Monica's heart had softened, and she even seemed to be just a little bit in awe at how things worked out.

Although Our Lord had worked things out so there would be no family feud at my son's wedding, my prayers for Monica continued. I could not rest while she was still living with a man to whom she was not married. Two months after the wedding, Monica called me in tears. She had discovered that her boyfriend was dating other women.

"You hang on," I comforted her. "My prayers are with you. God will send you the right man."

Six months later she began dating Mark, a fellow lawyer. After just a few dates, Mark brought Monica home to meet his mother, Judy Salz. "Monica, you are the answer to my prayers," she told her when she discovered that Monica was Catholic.

When I met Judy after Mark and Monica announced their engagement, we developed an immediate bond. Both of us had been praying for a good Catholic spouse for our children. Mark and Monica often laughed about their two mothers. They would argue in a joking way as to whose mother was holier.

Monica and Mark did not live together before they married in a Catholic ceremony. They gave me my first grandbaby, Emily Francis, on November 8, 2003, a year after their wedding. Now, my daughter, who once vowed that she would never send her children to a Catholic school if she ever had any, insists that her children will not go anywhere else.

God surely hears the prayers of a mother. Monica now embraces her Catholic faith and realizes that God's teachings are never outdated.

Once you are a mother, your prayers are never ending. And so it is with me. But God has given me assurance that He does hear my prayers, loud and clear.

—Celia Sattler

Celia Sattler and her husband, Tony, own and operate Los Amigos, an authentic Mexican restaurant in Bismarck, North Dakota. Her son, Michael, is a strategic customer manager and computer engineer in California. Anton received a degree in biology and Ryan is at University of Nebraska-Lincoln studying accounting.

The 21-Year Wait

When I played baby dolls as a little girl, I never doubted that one day it would be for real. But shortly after my marriage to Bob, I stopped thinking about having children. Instead, I asked myself, "What have I done?"

Married at eighteen to a 23-year-old alcoholic, my life became a nightmare. I spent many nights home alone since I was not old enough to accompany him to the bar. Our friends were partiers, and in this environment, our marriage quickly fell apart. Our frequently violent relationship became on and off again. After four years, I finally left Bob for the last time.

I found someone else to give me attention and Bob found comfort in alcohol. One day, he stopped by and we had another big argument. He left promising that he would kill himself. His words almost became the truth; Bob went home and shot himself in the chest. A couple of friends found him and put him in the back seat of their car. They came pounding at my apartment door. They were afraid to drive to the hospital because the driver had lost his license for drunk driving.

Panicked, I jumped in the car and sped the short distance to the hospital. I stayed long enough to hear the doctor's prognosis: "I would not give you a plug nickel for his life. He won't make it through the night."

Guilt seared into my shocked disbelief. I went out and got high. Later, I called the hospital and found that Bob had been given a room. It looked like he might make it after all. I rushed to the hospital to see him. He told me that while he lay on the table in the emergency room, he prayed to God to take away his alcoholism. Later, he asked for a

Bible. For perhaps the first time in his life, Bob began to read—really read—God's Word. He was fully aware that if not for the grace of God, he would be dead by his own hand. Bob did not imagine that heaven would have been his resting place, either. Now, he vowed, whatever time he had left would be lived for God. I learned later that after Bob shot himself, before he passed out he prayed, "Oh God, don't let it end this way."

Doctors determined that he would need a minimum of two weeks more to recover in the hospital. On day three, he was taken for X-rays; the nurses could not get any phlegm up, which is crucial for a chest injury such as his. The X-rays revealed he had mended beyond scientific explanation. Two days later, Bob was released, totally healed.

Bob was a new man, but I did not trust it to last. He had disappointed me with broken promises too many times. So, I kept my own apartment. When the weeks passed and I saw the new Bob was still there, I wondered if I really could trust him. We began dating. Initially, most of our dates involved trips to church. Through Bob and church, I, too, began to change. Out of the rubble of my past sprouted a new life in Christ. And Bob was there at my side. Bob and I never drank or used drugs again.

We fell in love all over again. Now our marriage had three persons in it: Bob, me, and God, who was at the center. Once we had a secure Christian union we began desiring children.

After a year of hoping in vain for a baby, we consulted a fertility specialist. Endless appointments—sometimes as frequent as twice a week—left no stone unturned. I sensed with all my being that I was to be a mother. Bob, too, had a sense that God was promising us a baby.

The heartbreaking news of failure month after month was more than I could endure. I carried the deep pain of barrenness daily, but it became especially overwhelming at Mother's Day. At church that Sunday, a special tribute was given to moms, asking them to stand and be blessed. The pain crushed me. I ran out of the service and cried for the rest of the day. I eventually stopped going to church on Mother's Day and Father's Day. So many things were hard on me emotionally, particularly baby showers and any women's gatherings (at which they all talked about their kids.)

Finally, after a year and a half of seeing a fertility specialist, I was pronounced sterile.

"Lord, what is going on?" I cried. "I believed you promised me a child? You restored our marriage and now we are ready to accept a child. I believe in my heart that you have promised us a child!" Often, during a sleepless night, I turned to Scripture. Slowly, the old feeling that God was promising us a child returned. I often read the words of Hannah in the book of Samuel: "For this child I prayed; and the Lord has granted me my petition which I made to him. Therefore, I have lent him to the Lord; as long as he lives, he is lent to the Lord" (1 Samuel 1:27).

"Surely," I thought, "one day I will have a child to be thankful for and dedicate to God. This assurance also grew in Bob. "But how and when?" I wondered. We looked into adoption but we both had a strong sense that it was not God's will for us. "How about foster care?" I suggested to Bob. "Maybe this is God's way for us to be parents."

For eleven years, Bob and I were foster parents. One boy in particular won our hearts. We would have spared no expense to make him our own had he been available for adoption. But instead, after six years with us, he left. My heart shattered.

Bob and I had so much love to give but no child to call our own. We wanted to desire only what God wanted for us. More than anything else in this world, we yearned for a child. "Lord, why is there no one for us?" I cried out. "Why have we felt so strongly that you have a child for us?"

For so many years, friends and even pastors counseled me to accept the fact that it was not God's will that I would bear a child. I could never do that because of the stubborn feeling that refused to leave me—there would be a child for me.

Shortly after I turned 39, a number of symptoms indicated to me that I might be pregnant. Still, I didn't dare to hope. It was more logical to think that menopause was starting or something more serious. Since a relative had just been diagnosed with cancer, I thought it best to see a doctor when the symptoms persisted for three months. In the recesses of my mind, the thought of a pregnancy still flickered. After all, with God all things are possible. When the nurse called later in the day to tell me that I had tested positive for pregnancy, I was stunned. The words echoed in my brain: You are pregnant after 21 years of marriage!

"Could it really be?" I wondered. "Me? Pregnant?" I shakily dialed Bob's work number. "Bob, I'm pregnant!" I screamed.

At that point, our conversation did not consist of any words. We excitedly giggled at each other. The realization that Bob would become a father for the first time after 21 years of marriage was overwhelming. He took the rest of the day off work so we could celebrate.

Hannah—which means "grace of God"—was born on February 4, 1997. God's grace and mercy was definitely bestowed to us through her. We have dedicated her to the Lord and never, ever stop thanking Him for this indescribable blessing. We are in awe at our little daughter's Spirit-filled enthusiasm for God. Those 21 years were worth waiting for Hannah, our child of promise. Yes, we can trust God. In Mark 9:23 Jesus said, "All things are possible to him who believes."

—Carrie Olson

Carrie Olson thanks God everyday for the privilege of home schooling her daughter and instilling her with godly values. Carrie and her husband, Bob, live in Mandan, North Dakota, and recently celebrated their 28th wedding anniversary.

Mary's Magnificat

My soul magnifies the Lord,
and my spirit rejoices in God my Savior,
for He has regarded the low estate of His handmaiden.

For behold, henceforth all generations will call me blessed;
for He who is mighty has done great things for me,
and holy is His name.
And His mercy is on those who fear Him from generation
to generation.

He has shown strength with His arm,
He has scattered the proud in the imagination
of their hearts,
He has put down the mighty from their thrones,
and exalted those of low degree;
He has filled the hungry with good things,
and the rich He has sent empty away.

He has helped his servant Israel,
in remembrance of His mercy,
as He spoke to our fathers,
to Abraham and to His posterity for ever.

—Luke 1:46-55

Angel to the Rescue

One foggy morning, I heard my son's truck leave and I began to hustle. I was a slow starter that chilly morning and knew my husband would be waiting—not so patiently—for me to begin our own route.

We have an unusual family business: garbage hauling. We called it Circle Sanitation in honor of our family circle. My son, Dan, had been very instrumental in getting the business off its feet. Later on, my other son, Randy, also joined us in this family business. Now, twenty-five years later, even some of the grandchildren help out.

During the early years, I often filled in working on the trucks. On this particular morning, I hadn't gone but a few steps from the house when I froze in terror. The strongest sense of danger I had ever experienced paralyzed me like a statue. I could not move. My mind and heart raced. I had a strong sense that my son, Dan, was in danger.

I felt panicked and helpless. "What could I do?" I thought. My beloved Grandmother Frances suddenly came to mind. She was part of a large population of devout German Catholics who immigrated to North Dakota via Russia. Her iron-strong Catholicism was the center of our close-knit family. Her words came to me. "In times of trouble, you can send your guardian angel." Frantically I prayed, to my angel: "Go to Dan. Help him!"

Moments later, I was able to take a step. Bewildered, I slowly walked outside the house to the shop. The whole incident baffled me. I decided I had better not tell my husband since I did not really understand what had just happened.

My husband, Ray, and I hopped into the truck and drove to our destination. "This fog is really bad," Ray commented as we passed a car in the ditch.

Once again Grandma's influence came through as I recited my mini-prayer, "Jesus, Mary, Joseph, please help them."

Gradually, the scary premonition faded as the work day got underway. At the end of the day, we all parked our trucks in the shop and gathered to talk. Dan then related his early morning experience. While he was driving toward his route on the four-lane highway, wondering when the fog might lift, he was suddenly overcome with a strong urge to pull into the other lane. Since there seemed no logical reason why he should pull over, he resisted. Wondering where the feeling was coming from, he looked around for any signs of trouble. There were none, but he could not shake the strong feeling to pull over. Dan finally gave in and pulled over. No sooner had he done that than a vehicle came driving down the wrong side of the road. It sped by him in the lane he had just vacated.

I asked him, approximately, what time this had happened. The time of his dilemma and mine coincided. Was it a coincidence? I don't think so. I think the angel, called on at the prompting of my Grandma's influence, protected my son that day.

—Paulie Ruby

Paulie Ruby and her husband, Ray, have been married for forty years. They raised their two sons in rural Minot, North Dakota, and are very proud of all their sixteen grandchildren.

A Good Friday Blessing

I had intended to spend Good Friday of 2003 quietly meditating at home after the service of the Lord's Passion. My thoughts centered on the depths of God's love for me to have suffered such a terrible, ignominious death, nailed to a cross. A meditation like this always overwhelms me, especially on Good Fridays. My mind kept echoing the refrain to that old gospel hymn: "Were you there when they crucified my Lord? Were you there when they nailed Him to the tree?"

Suddenly the ringing of the phone disrupted my thoughts and prayers. It was my daughter, Robin, on the line. She was crying. Immediately my heart sank with fear. "Momma, please help me!" she cried. "I am so sick and I was trying to put the dogs in the basement before going to the doctor."

Robin gasped out the story as best as she could. She had actually fallen into the basement because she stumbled over one of the dogs. The door shut behind her and locked her in. Luckily, her purse with her cell phone had been over her shoulder when she fell into the basement.

Robin has a propensity for strep infections and she tends to get very ill very fast. She also had been dealing with a thyroid imbalance that the doctors could not get under control. Strep infections for those who have it regularly and who have a lower immune system can cause death in a matter of very few hours. Without proper treatment, strep can shut down the entire body system in some people. Sometimes, it is too late for antibiotics treatment.

I knew that time was of the essence. Since she lives twenty minutes away, I wasted no time leaving the house and jumping into my car. I drove as fast as the speed limit allowed, but each block seemed a mile long. I prayed all the way for angels to open the door and escort her quickly to the doctor's. I was so afraid I would arrive too late and the time involved to break into the house would further delay getting her treatment. She had sounded so ill, I truly feared for her life.

Looking at the clock on my dashboard just made me worry more. I needed to calm down and give it to Jesus' care, so I began to pray:

"Lord, on this holy day of days, by the wounds of Your most sacred nail-scarred hands and feet, please send Your angels to surround my daughter. Cover her with Your most precious blood and open the basement door. Lord, help her get safely to the doctor. Keep her safe for me, dear Jesus."

When I arrived there was a note on her garage door saying she had managed to pry the basement door open and had left for the hospital. She had found a nail lying on the stairwell ledge to pry the lock with. Later, she called to say she was feeling much better. She had suffered a thyroid reaction with fever and dizziness. The doctor was finally able to get her on the correct medication because she was having this episode while in his office. It finally proved to be the exact dose she needed after months of trial and error by her specialist.

My Good Friday meditation on the nails that crucified our Lord became especially meaningful to me. Without the nails that pierced Jesus' hands and feet there would be no saving grace. I praise Him, too, for that precious nail that He provided for my daughter—without that nail, she may not have been saved.

—Christine Trollinger

Chrsitine Trollinger's biography appears after Please Hold Him For Me *in Chapter 4.*

Parent's Prayer

They are only little once, Lord.
Grant me the wisdom and patience
To follow in Your footsteps and
Prepare them for what is to come.
They are only little once, Lord.
Make me take the time to play pretend,
To read or tell a story, to cuddle.
Don't let me for one minute
Think anything is more important
Than the school play, the recital,
The big game, fishing, or the quiet walk
Hand in hand.
All too soon, Lord, they will grow
Away and there is no turning back.
Let me have my memories with no regrets.
Please help me to be a good parent, Lord.
When I must discipline, let me do it in love,
Let me be firm, but fair;
Let me correct and explain with patience.
They are growing away, Lord.
While I have the chance, let me do my best for them.
For the rest of our lives, please Lord,
Let me be their very best friend.

—Mary L. Robbins

The Angel's Nudge

"Three down and one to go. Oh, but this one I don't want to put down!" I thought to myself, as I gazed into the angelic face of my infant son, Brendan. It was naptime, and my older children—Sean, four, Laura, three, and Patrick, almost two—were soundly sleeping upstairs. Getting them all to sleep at the same time wasn't easy, so this was a rare moment I had alone with Brendan. At seven months, his attention was usually on what his siblings were doing. I continued to rock him just a few more minutes as he nestled snugly in my arms, but I knew if I stayed in the rocker another moment we would both be asleep, and I had vacuuming to get done. It was an unusually warm March day, and I had plans to do some major cleaning while my little ones napped.

Brendan looked up at me with his sleepy pale blue eyes as I laid him in his crib by the living room window. Sunlight bounced off the ringlets of golden blond hair that encircled his head, and I lingered for one last look, before rushing out of the room to start cleaning. "He'll be asleep soon," I thought, as I headed into the dining room to start vacuuming. I was racing the clock to get as much done as I could before the other children finished their naps. With four little ones, not much cleaning can take place while they are awake.

Just a few brief moments into my grand attempt to conquer the vacuuming, I stopped and turned it off. Not sure why I did it, I paused and then reached to turn it back on. "No stopping," I thought, "I've just gotten started." Just then the phone rang. Unhappy that my cleaning was once again being interrupted, I ran to the kitchen to answer the phone. "Hello," I said, hoping this would be a quick call, and I could return to what I needed to be doing. "Hello," the voice on the other end said, "Are you Beth Matthews?" "Yes," I replied. Then she asked, "Are you the person in charge of weddings at the church?" Somewhat surprised I said, "No," and gave her the name of the person she was probably looking for. *Why didn't she call the church first?* I thought as I hung up the phone.

Suddenly, I felt a strong need to check on Brendan. *While I'm in here, I'll take a peek at him,* I thought to myself. I have always loved to watch my babies sleep and to kiss their little heads. It had only been a few minutes since I put him down, but I was sure he was asleep. *One quick look, and then I'll get back to work,* I thought.

As I walked from the kitchen, I could see he was lying still in his crib. I smiled, and whispered to myself, "He's sound asleep." As I neared the crib, my smile turned to an expression of horror. Yes, Brendan was motionless, but not with sleep. His lips were purple, and he was not breathing. As a cardiac nurse, I had done CPR many times, but never on a child. I had no time to think. As I grabbed him I screamed, "No, God, please, not my baby!" The next few moments seemed like an eternity as my hands moved the way they had been trained. My heart cried out to God to save the life of my baby. Suddenly, a dime flew from his mouth to the floor, and he began to cry. The color returned to his beautiful face as I collapsed into the rocking chair.

All energy drained from me as I realized the difference one seemingly incidental decision had made. Brendan could have left our family that day. With my baby nestled safely in my arms again I began to cry tears of sadness at what could have happened if I had continued vacuuming, tears of love for the precious little person I held in my arms, and tears of thanksgiving to God for the angels He sent to stop me from doing what I wanted to do and brought me back to exactly where I needed to be.

—Elizabeth Matthews

Elizabeth Matthews and her husband, Mark, are home schooling parents of ten children. Elizabeth is the co-founder of Chelsea Shire Communications, a speaking and communications apostolate. She is a freelance writer, a frequent conference speaker, and the author of Precious Treasure *and* A Place for Me, *both of which are based on the life of her autistic son, Patrick, and written to help others see God's blessing in all suffering and trials. To learn more, please visit www.chelseashire.com*

Thank You for My Little Ones

Thank You, Lord, for the dirty walls smudged with sticky fingerprints and marked with crayons. The walls would be spotless if it weren't for the chubby little fingers; the same fingers that, learning to reach for You, gently trace my face with love. Lord, thank You for my little ones.

Thank You, Lord, for the stack of dirty dishes and the kitchen counters covered with traces of peanut butter and jelly. They would be clean if it weren't for the beautiful little mouths that can't seem to kiss me enough. Lord, thank You for my little ones.

Thank You, Lord, for the piles of laundry stained in grape juice, grass, and mashed banana. There would be little to wash if it weren't for the precious little bodies that I get to hold next to mine. Lord, thank You for my little ones.

Thank You, Lord, for the lost shoes hidden in the mess of books, toys, and treasures under the bed. They would not need to be found if it weren't for the soft, little feet I've held in my hands and tickled time and again. Lord, thank You for my little ones.

Thank You, Lord, for the tracks of footprints throughout the house. My carpet would be spotless if it weren't for the strong, little legs that run to greet me when I walk through the door. Lord, thank You for my little ones.

Thank You, Lord, for each tipped glass of milk that makes a mess on the table and floor. There would be no spills if it weren't for the tender arms that wrap around my neck in hugs that never want to end. Lord, thank You for my little ones.

Thank You, Lord, for the unmade beds and the blankets thrown here and there. They would be neatly made if it weren't for the sleepy little eyes that light up when they see me in the morning. Lord, thank You for my little ones.

Thank You, Lord, for the endless noise, the crying, whining, and screaming at play. There would be silence if it weren't for the sweet little voices that whisper in my ear, "Mommy, I love you." Lord, thank You for my little ones.

Thank You, Lord, for the suffering, the pain, and the sorrow. There would be no need for Band-Aids, or tissue to wipe away tears, if it weren't for the souls You've placed in my care for today. A time may come when You must take them away, and my lips won't move, but my heart will say, "Lord, thank You for my little ones."

—Elizabeth Matthews

Elizabeth Matthews' biography appears after the preceding story in this chapter, The Angel's Nudge.

Witness to a Miracle

"Push!" the nurse encouraged me. "She's almost out!" After one last big push, my fourth child, Amanda, entered the world on October 25, 1991. I breathed a sigh of relief. The worst was over. Now, I could hold my baby girl.

I waited as the nurse and doctor cut the cord and suctioned her mouth. Then I watched the nurse gently rub her belly. "Breathe, little girl, breathe," she pleaded. I froze and looked down at my infant daughter. She was turning blue. My doctor pushed the nurse aside and tried unsuccessfully to get Amanda to breathe.

"Get another doctor," he demanded. My husband, Mike, and I grasped one another's hand and began praying: "Our Father who art in heaven..." In less than a minute, a second doctor arrived.

"She needs oxygen, now," the second doctor commanded. "We need to get her to the nursery immediately!" The whole scene took only five minutes, but it was an eternity to me. Each second without a breath brought her closer to death.

In the surreal stillness of our room, Mike and I waited and prayed. My faith had always been strong, but never had it been tested like this. "After nine months of sustaining my baby's life, could it be that God would take her from me?" I wondered. After about fifteen minutes, my doctor came in to tell us he was baffled as to why she could not breathe on her own. A medical team from Hershey Medical Center in nearby Hershey, Pennsylvania, was coming over. We were reassured that everything possible would be done for Amanda.

Mike and I were fearful, but thanks to our strong faith, we were not powerless. We trusted in the power and mercy of

God and prayed with all we had. Mike called family, friends and the priest at our church, St. Gertrude. Amanda had been born at 8 a.m., and by noon word of our situation had spread throughout the community like wildfire. Hundreds of prayers were reaching God, pleading for a healing.

Amanda needed to be taken to Hershey for further testing. She was brought to my room for a few minutes before her departure. I looked down upon her soft pink skin and beautiful, thick, dark hair—the same color as mine. I gently held her tiny hand and stroked her fingers. "Mommy's here, Amanda," I whispered softly. "Everything is going to be OK." Then, I said good-bye, knowing that it could mean forever.

At Hershey, it was determined that Amanda had diaphragmatic hernia. A hole in her diaphragm had allowed her intestines, spleen and pancreas to overtake the left side of her chest. Her left lung was not developed, so her right lung, which was crowded by the other organs, had to do all the work. Her doctor believed she was strong enough to withstand corrective surgery the very next day.

Although we were told Amanda's problem could be fixed, there were no guarantees. Half of these babies do not survive and, if they do, there are usually multiple ongoing problems. Another baby with the identical condition had been at Hershey for two months and was still struggling. Again, our faith sustained us. Whether Amanda would be healed or taken to heaven, we would trust in God.

I checked myself out of the hospital that evening. I could not bear my roommate's complaints about the challenges of a new baby. My empty arms yearned to hold my own precious little one. It was too painful to be around someone so blind to her incredible blessing. At least I could go home to be with my other three young children.

The next morning, Mike and I watched from the hospital corridor when Amanda was wheeled out of surgery and into her room, where she would be hooked up to a ventilator. It was at this point that we both broke down. Mike put his arm around me as we both sobbed uncontrollably.

Once we got ourselves under control, we cautiously entered Amanda's room. She was so very small and helpless, and surrounded by tubes and machines. The doctor smiled gently and said, "Everything went better than we could have expected. She's not out of the woods yet, but she is doing very well."

Much to the surgeon's surprise, after her intestines were pulled into her abdominal cavity, Amanda's heart and esophagus slipped into place on their own. Recovery was still expected to take a very long time. We were told that for her left lung to fully develop, it could take months to years. But Amanda continued to amaze everyone. We brought a healthy baby home just two weeks after her surgery. God had truly answered our prayers and healed her beyond anyone's expectation.

I know that not everyone who prays for a healing receives a "yes" for an answer. But I do believe that God has a purpose for everything He does. In my case, Amanda's ordeal has deepened my faith and increased my appreciation of the blessing of motherhood a thousand fold. The little things that once irritated me—the trials of motherhood, such as potty training and spilled juice—do not bother me now. Even today, eleven years later, I still experience parenting as a complete blessing.

Amanda's life also touched many others. For years, people came up to us and shared how the experience deepened their own faith. They prayed more and harder than they would have on their own. They asked God to heal our baby girl, and when He did, they were in awe that they had been a witness to a miracle.

—Rita Pastal

Rita and Michael Pastal have been married for eighteen years. They have eight children, six girls and two boys, and are members of St. Cecilia's Parish in Lebanon, Pennsylvania. For the past four years, Rita has worked part-time as a medical transcriptionist at the Lebanon V.A. Hospital.

Chapter Eight
A Mother's Blessing

Meeting My Daughter

Christmas break from college was always great, but it was especially enjoyable during my senior year. With graduation so close, I had much to look forward to. I basked in the holiday cheer with my parents and five siblings. By January, however, there was something else on my mind: motherhood. My boyfriend, Jim, and I had dated for four years. Only recently had we become serious. We had given in to temptation, just once. That was all it took.

When the pregnancy test confirmed what I suspected, I immediately told Jim. He expressed his love and wanted to marry me. But we had never previously even talked of marriage. "No," I said, "This is no way to begin a marriage."

I confided in my twin sister, Margot. We were roommates at the University of Kentucky and had always been close. I knew she understood and felt my pain. "What are you going to do?" she asked.

"Jim and I discussed marriage, but I do not want to make a life commitment based on a pregnancy," I explained. "I could keep my baby, but what kind of a life could I give a child right now? We decided to place our child up for adoption."

It was the '70s and abortion had recently been made legal. I could have instantly and discretely changed my situation. But as a committed Catholic, abortion was not an option. We knew it was not our place to interfere with God's plan for our baby.

Telling my parents was extremely difficult. They were so very disappointed and asked that I not tell others about my situation. Out of respect for them, I agreed. During my visit home at spring break, I was still able to conceal my pregnancy. I did not return home again until after the baby's birth on September 4, 1976.

For the nine months that I carried my developing child, the little kicks reminded me that there really was a little life growing within me. I prayed often for my baby and took care of myself knowing that the baby needed to be healthy to get a good start in life. Catholic Charities allowed me to select the parents; a couple with twin boys. Being a twin had always meant so much to me. Now, that experience would be a part of my child's life, too.

Margot was at my side during the miracle of my little girl's birth. I named her Margot, after my twin sister. Although I never wavered in my decision, that did not prevent the pain in separating from my own flesh and blood. Jim was in the waiting room because, back then, only a husband had the right to be in the delivery room. It was an emotional time for him, too. He tearfully asked me to marry him again. Even in the throes of love for both my baby and Jim, I held firm to our decision. The sacrament of marriage was intended to last a lifetime. It was a commitment I was not ready to make.

I was not allowed to hold my daughter in my arms, but I held her in my heart. Margot and I peeked into the nursery at her; she was beautiful. Jim and I wrote our daughter a letter and also purchased a 14k gold necklace with a cross for her new parents to give her someday. Although my own mother wanted to keep her first grandchild's birth a secret, she, too, felt the pain of separation. She wrote her own letter on the day the baby was born: "...Be a very good girl, now, and I will see you one day in heaven. Always know that you will have a special place in my heart and in my prayers...'

I had already begun graduate school at the University of Kentucky and missed only a couple days for the delivery. I transferred to Arizona State University the following semester and earned a master's in special education. Jim and I had a bond and love that survived several jobs, schooling, and a long-distance romance. We married in October of 1979 and had three more children together: Erica, Lindsay, and Clay.

I experienced boundless joy at the births of our other children, but there was always a part of me that belonged to my first daughter. Although I thought of her often, God gave me a great sense of peace knowing that we had chosen life for our child and placed her with a loving, Catholic family.

During the '80s, there was a growing movement for adopted children to seek out their birth parents. Jim and I fully expected that our daughter would find us one day. When her eighteenth birthday came and went, and then her nineteenth and on into the twenties, I sometimes wondered what happened. Why didn't she ever contact us?

Then a year and a half ago, I came home from leading a parish youth group meeting to find Jim on the phone. He immediately motioned for me to pick up the other phone. Our daughter, Margot, had finally called! My hand shook as I picked up the receiver. "Hello, this is little Margot," she nervously said in a voice identical to my other daughters. She had decided it was time to contact her birth parents. First, she also had to overcome her fears of rejection and have the courage to trust that God would guide her.

My little Margot had been renamed Susan. She was home on break before returning to her teaching job in

Ireland. We talked for over two hours. Susan expressed her desire to meet us. As excited as we were to hear from our daughter, we knew accepting her into our lives would not be easy. Only my sister and parents knew about her.

My decision all those years ago was based on what I thought was best for my daughter. Now, if she wanted to be a part of our life, I wanted that too. It was a Wednesday night when she called. The following Saturday, she made the one-hour drive to our house. Our two daughters were away at college and our son was out for the evening.

Butterflies filled my stomach when I saw the beautiful young lady stepping out of the car that had pulled up to our house. Jim and I nervously looked at each other. Susan walked to the door with a little green box full of baby photographs, report cards, school pictures, and our letters. She smiled nervously as we opened the door. As she walked through the door the first words out of her mouth were, "Thank you for giving me life." We hugged our little girl, all grown up now. As I stood back and gazed at her, my heart fluttered. She was wearing the little gold cross we had bought for her so long ago. Her mother had told her to keep the necklace for a special occasion. This was it.

She had all the mannerisms of our other daughters and had features from both Jim and me. We spent six hours catching up on the life of our first-born. Tears streamed down my face as I gazed upon the pictures and report cards of my daughter. I was deeply touched to learn that Susan had become a special education teacher just like me.

We all knew that this was the beginning of a new relationship for us. It was not an easy road, but we had to step beyond our own fears and again do what was best for our daughter. We broke the news to our children, family and friends. Everyone, especially our own children, readily welcomed Susan into our family.

The Monday following our meeting, Susan sent us an e-mail saying, "At church on Sunday, I could have knelt there and said thanks to God all day. He really does work wonders. It has been quite an amazing weekend."

Not only did Susan become a treasured member of our own family, but also our family became a part of hers. Carol, Susan's adoptive mother, e-mailed us shortly after our first meeting with Susan. "I have always wanted to communicate with you over the years to let you know what a beautiful, sensitive, and gifted child you gave us to love and cherish. Now I can tell you myself and thank you from the bottom of my heart. We know Susan is now complete with all of you in her life."

That summer our families attended a conference at Catholic Familyland in Ohio. At one point Carol took me aside and said, "At a time in your life when you could not care for Susan you gave her to us when we really needed her. Now, at this time in Susan's life, she really needs you and your family, and we want to share her with you."

We have all become extended family to each other and often gather together for holidays. In the end, none of us has lost anything. We have all gained so much.

—Marsha Stocker

Marsha Stocker was born in St. Charles, Missouri, and now lives in Lexington, Kentucky. Marsha works as a special education teacher and her husband, Jim, is a police officer. They have three children: Erica, Lindsay, and Clay.

Miracles Can Happen

The hour had come.

My wife was up at 6 a.m. and at the hospital at 7 a.m. Our daughter, Joan Avin, had been admitted the evening before with our first grandchild nestled in her womb. Due to some complications, she was being "induced" a full week before her scheduled due date.

So, on the morning of April 28, the family was officially on alert. By 9 p.m. that night, the doctors had decided the process itself was not working very well. They proposed a Cesarean section. Our daughter and her husband, Rob, agreed. When there was no news by 11 p.m., we grew worried. My wife, who had given birth to seven children— two of whom were by Caesarean section—was normally done with the procedure well within an hour. We sought information from the desk on the fifth floor of Lankenau Hospital. They had none to give. By 11:30 p.m. we were convinced that there was a problem, perhaps a serious one. We began a rosary.

During the meditations I thought back to the events of the past year within our family. We had lost one of our children under very tragic circumstances. My brother had lost his wife and daughter—my godchild—under equally tragic circumstances. We had lost our mother to end-stage Alzheimer's. Yet in the midst of this sorrow came the joy of new, precious, sacred life. And it was a joy most unexpected.

Rob and Joan had struggled mightily, without success, to conceive in their first years of marriage. Doctors advised artificial insemination. The couple said no. Then their neighbors, Jim and Felicia Coffey, told them the story of Gianna Beretta Molla.

Gianna Molla was a wife, mother, and physician who lived and worked in Italy from 1922 to 1962. When complications arose with her fourth pregnancy, her doctors advised her to abort the child so that they could remove a uterine tumor. They told her it was quite likely she would die giving birth otherwise. Gianna Molla said no. She knew that her child was a gift from God and could not be aborted under any circumstances. "No," she said, "deliver the child. The rest we will leave to God." Physicians did as they were instructed. Gianna Molla gave birth to her daughter, Gianna Emmanuela Molla, on April 21, 1962. Seven days later, Gianna died.

Her heroism gave rise to a popular following—first in Italy, then in Western Europe, spreading ultimately to the United States.

Young couples in particular began petitioning for her intercession, asking that they might conceive and safely deliver children. A growing number of couples reported having their prayers answered. Ultimately, all of this caught the attention of the Vatican. A canonization process was initiated on November 6, 1972. Gianna Beretta Molla was beatified by Pope John Paul II on April 24, 1994, and canonized a saint on May 16, 2004.

The Coffeys gave Joan and Rob two Gianna prayer cards—one for their nightstand, and another for their refrigerator. Night and day, literally, the young couple prayed to Gianna.

One night, a number of months ago, the Coffeys knocked on the door of Joan and Rob's home. They bought with them a first-class relic—a glove—of Gianna Beretta Molla. They asked if they could lay the relic on Joan's abdomen and pray with the couple, beseeching Gianna's intercession that Rob and Joan might conceive and safely deliver a child. The two couples prayed and trusted.

As our family prayed in the hospital, we knew the first part of the prayer had been answered. We were now praying that the child, and her mother, would be safe.

Shortly before midnight, a rather large figure emerged from the shadows of the hallway. He was grinning, quite literally, from ear to ear. It was our son-in-law. He announced: "She made it. She's here. Alive and well. Eight pounds, fourteen ounces. She's all girl."

My wife and several of our children immediately asked if they could see mother and daughter. Our son-in-law said, "Sure, follow me." We walked past a station of nurses who looked like they wanted to flag our little posse but, in their great kindness, resisted the urge. In moments, we beheld a small miracle. The child was bright pink with dark hair and eel blue eyes. She also had a very strong set of lungs... like her mother.

Our daughter said, "Her name is Mary Kate Michelle Avin." The name was, if you'll excuse the expression, pregnant with meaning. Her great-grandmother's name is Mary and she was now lying on her deathbed just five miles away. Kate is the name of a sister that had stood with Joan through some of the most difficult moments in her life. And Michelle was the name of our lost child, Joan's sister, for whom we all continued to mourn.

But the greatest surprise was to come. I asked the time of delivery. "10:39 p.m.," our son-in-law said.

I said, "You mean this child was delivered before midnight? Why did it take over an hour to tell us?"

"Well, there were a few complications," Rob said. "We were told about them by the doctors some months ago; we just didn't share the information with you. The baby had a two-cord vessel in the umbilical cord. Normally there are three. There were concerns that she might be severely underweight or autistic, even retarded. That she came out perfect is a small miracle.

Then our daughter spoke. "Do you know what day it is, Dad?" she asked.

"No," I said. To be honest, I didn't have the faintest idea at this point what day of the week it was.

Joan said, "She was born before midnight, Dad, on April 28th—the feast day of Blessed Gianna Beretta Molla."

—Brian J. Gail

Brian J. Gail is a husband and father of seven children – and one miraculous grandchild. He is the founder and CEO of GailForce Inc., a strategic marketing communications firm headquartered outside of Philadelphia.

Ten Minutes

No, Mommy! I don't want to go!"

David, my five-year-old, was expressing himself very vocally after I told him it was time to leave the swimming pool. "Come on, honey," I pleaded. "Let's get our things."

I scooped up his littlest brother, Matthew, not even one yet, and balanced him in one arm as I gathered plastic buckets and float toys in the other arm. My two-year-old daughter, Caroline, was already in the stroller, and four-year-old Michael was standing obediently next to it, holding all of the towels. Amidst David's protests, we slowly made our way into the changing area of the pool's restroom, balancing our belongings as we trudged. It was really a lot of work to take the little ones to the pool, but they enjoyed it so much. Changing into dry clothes, gathering the wet things, and curbing the hunger they inevitably felt after so much activity made the endeavor challenging every time.

After the slow process of peeling off wet suits and putting on dry clothes, of diaper changing, and once more gathering things, we were finally in the car with everyone buckled up. The float toys were loaded. The stroller was folded and in its rightful place in the back of the mini-van. Ritz crackers had been distributed. Phew! Now, what could I make for dinner that was quick and easy? I was pondering that thought as I climbed into the driver's seat. In ten minutes we'd be home.

As I started the engine I heard crying from the back of the van.

"Who's crying?" I asked, turning around to see for myself. It was David. "What's wrong, honey?"

"My bathing suit! I left it in the bathroom!" He was whimpering softly.

Could I have missed his suit? Did I see it when I put the others in the bag, which was now tucked deeply in the trunk?

"It's probably in the bag," I said, "We'll check when we get home."

"No! I *know* I left it there! I put it on the handle. I know I did!" The volume in his voice was increasing.

It was possible the suit was still in the dressing room, hanging on the handle. But, it had just taken me ten minutes to load everyone up. If I went back, it would be another ten minutes of unloading four small children, walking carefully over the slippery surface and walking back. It was approaching 6 p.m. and I wanted to get home.

"I'll tell you what, sweetie," I said, "We'll come back tomorrow. The lifeguards will find it and put it in the lost-and-found box. I'll call them when the pool opens and they will save it for us."

This absolutely did not satisfy him.

"Nooooooo!" he wailed, "Oh, Mommy! I want my bathing suit! I have to get it! I don't want to lose it! Please, please, please! I want my bathing suit!" He was sobbing as though someone had poked a hole right through his heart, like he had lost a very dear friend. While my oldest son was always fairly dramatic, this behavior was over the top, even for him.

By now, baby Matthew was starting to fuss, too, and Michael had joined in to plead David's case. Soon, the whole vanload of children was begging me to return to retrieve the forgotten pair of swim shorts.

"This isn't worth it," I thought to myself, but then I said aloud, "OK. Let's go get it."

I silently chided myself for giving in to my children's whining. What was the big deal, anyway? There was absolutely no chance the suit wouldn't be there in the morning. I knew the lifeguards personally. They would have been happy to set the suit aside for us. Normally, I would have insisted that everything would be fine and continued on my way home. But for some reason I felt pulled to give in. "Just do it," a little voice nudged, and so I did.

As expected, it took about ten minutes to retrieve the suit, which *was* exactly where David had said. He clutched the wet fabric all the way out to the car. And soon, everyone was happily munching crackers again, and the baby started to doze. OK, I told myself. I was only slowed down by ten minutes.

I drove down the long drive and onto the county road that would take us home. At the end of the road I turned onto another county road, and then again. We were almost there. My goodness, the evening sun was bright, I noted. Since we were traveling west, it was directly in my eyes. I pulled down the visor and adjusted my sitting position so I could see without a glare. "Now, what is in the freezer?" I was thinking. Right at that point I noticed the traffic markedly slowed. This was a county road that never had traffic jams. What was going on? The cars in front of me were slowing more and more. Finally, they stopped. "What on earth?" I thought as we inched forward. Finally, we came to a traffic policeman, waving the cars to a detour. As I approached him I rolled down my window.

"Is there a problem?" I asked.

"Accident." he replied, "About ten minutes ago."

"Ten minutes ago?" I repeated. Immediately I knew the significance of that time frame.

"Yeah," he replied, "A bad one. Keep to your left. You'll be directed where to go."

Ten minutes. Ten minutes.

Have you ever had an epiphany? An earth-shattering realization that affected you deeply but might only have seemed coincidental to someone else? This is how I felt. Somehow I *knew* that if I had not gone back for that bathing suit, we would have been in that accident. The timing would have put us exactly on the road where the accident happened at exactly the time it happened. Ten minutes. As we always do when we hear sirens, I began to lead my children in some Hail Mary's for the accident victim. What had happened? I could not push the thought out of my mind. It stayed with me all night.

The next morning the newspaper filled in the details. A man had been coming home from work, traveling west on the county road as we had been. The sun had been glaring in his eyes, as it had in mine. Then, a drunk driver had crossed the yellow line and hit him head on. There was nothing he could do. The difference between his fate and mine was ten minutes. I continued reading. The man lingered for a short while, asking for his wife and children. It was amazing, I read, that he wasn't killed on the spot. He was able to say "good-bye" to them. A priest blessed him, and then he died.

Did the prayers of my children help that man live long enough to receive hugs from his family and blessings from his priest? Did my son's guardian angel or God Himself prompt my son to uncharacteristically fuss over a wet bathing suit so as to stall our coming upon that fateful intersection? I will never know. I do not know why God spared us and not that man that day. Perhaps He still has work for us to do. Divine Providence makes no mistakes. However, I can't help but think of how close we came to his fate. That could have been *my* family saying goodbye. That could have been *me.* An ordinary family just like mine lost their father and husband that day.

Today, years later, the place of the accident still bears a small wooden cross engraved with the man's name. Periodically, someone will change the flowers. Since it is so close to my home, I pass it frequently. Every time I drive by I pray for that man and his family, and I thank God for that twist of fate that kept me and my children safe from harm. I can't help but think that some day in heaven we will meet. I feel confident that he will recognize us as the family that continues to pray for him and his family.

I still ponder this thought—how many moments like this do we have in our everyday lives—little moments of grace in which God provides protection and guidance if only we are perceptive enough to pay attention? Being at a place a second too soon or a second too late can change the entire course of our lives. God gives us gifts of grace daily. We only need to look for it. His gift of grace to me on that summer evening so many years ago was simply a little bit of time—ten minutes to be exact.

—Theresa Thomas

Theresa Thomas, who has been homeschooling for eleven years, lives in northern Indiana with her husband, David, and their eight children. She is still thankful for every ten minutes she has.

Keep On Giving

The laughter was almost unbearable as I inhaled the smoke of the downdraft from the freshly lit fireplace. The colors of the leaves were brilliant against the murky sky on this brisk and blustery fall morning. Despite the powerful setting of this beautiful day, tremendous waves of paralysis dulled my senses of feeling alive and tears of hopelessness kept strolling down my pale face. The unyielding demands of motherhood had tested my fortitude to the extreme lately. I felt pulled and dragged in every direction until I felt I couldn't possibly give anymore.

Perhaps one of the heightened sufferings in this life is the cross of loneliness, exacerbated by being in the presence of those you love most on this earth. This day was no exception. Their playful antics seemed captured in a movie scene from which I felt far removed. The sounds of belly laughter reached me as each of my children was left breathless from their daddy's tickling.

"Me next!" "No, me!" rang in my ears as the children took turns jumping into their father's arms. In those echoing few moments, I believed no one even noticed my existence just a few yards away. When someone turned toward me, I strategically closed my eyes and swooped my coffee mug beneath my lips as if enjoying one more lingering sip. Their giddiness only seemed to fuel my feelings of inadequacy. I felt unloved, unappreciated, and so washed out as a wife and mother this particular morning that crying was a necessary relief. My family carried on without a care in the world and oblivious to my pain, or so I thought.

Suddenly my seven-year-old, Noah, burst in front of me, and looking up at me with those ineffable big blue eyes he solemnly muttered, "Mommy, are you crying?" Without answering his question, I wiped my last tear and said with desperation, "Noah, do you know how much Mommy loves you?"

"No Mommy, how much?" he responded innocently.

"If we were stranded on an island and there was *one* berry that meant survival for you or me, I would give you that berry."

He peered through me with complete understanding and without reservation he sweetly asserted, "Mommy, do you know how much I love you?"

"No, Noah, how much?"

"I would give you that berry right back!"

Just when I was feeling so unappreciated his words made my spirit soar. I was filled with knowing that my sacrifices are noticed and are not in vain. Many times, when I felt least able to go on, I have felt God's immense love poured out on me through my children in wet sloppy kisses or a sweet unpredictable embrace. God gives us the heavenly grace to dig even deeper, which then graces us with the sustenance to give even more.

—Deborah Harding

Deborah Harding is a full-time housewife and busy mother of three. She resides with her husband, David, and their children in Ashburnham, Massachusetts. She is the founder and owner of The Children's Prayer Station, a family based apostolate which builds adjustable prayer kneelers for children. Deborah is a CCD instructor, a leader of Our Lady's Family Cenacle, a conference speaker, and was a contributing writer to Amazing Grace for Those Who Suffer.

An Easter Miracle

It was a cold and dreary February day as I was rushed to the hospital by ambulance. Six months earlier I was diagnosed with blocked fallopian tubes. My husband and I had wanted a child, and I had searched for a medical answer. Elective surgery was my last hope. Six months later I was elated to know I was pregnant. But now with the whir of the sirens and rush of the hospital attendants everything became a blur.

The ill-fated signs were apparent the day before, but I was convinced that I would save my baby with bed rest. My disappointment and heartbreak were harder to bear than even the hemorrhaging and knife-stabbing pain I was enduring. The ectopic pregnancy led to the removal of one fallopian tube while the other blocked tube was left intact. The doctors informed me that I could never conceive a child.

In 1976, the scientific remedies for infertility were becoming more advanced. Some of these remedies—such as *in vitro* fertilization—are contrary to the teachings of the Church. So, being a Catholic, I left the issue to God—or so I thought. As time went on and there were no more tests or surgeries to be done, my hopes diminished. Instinctively, my husband and I started on the adoption path, putting our names, hopes, and dreams on any list we could find. After months of agonizing disappointments we had exhausted our resources and dwindled my hopes of ever becoming a mother.

Then one day in early September, I felt the signs of pregnancy. I tried not to fall into false hope but I still harbored one small spark. Despite the facts before me I made an appointment to see my obstetrician. After a negative pregnancy test the doctor concluded I was having a false pregnancy. I returned home empty, forlorn, and heartbroken.

"God, I just want my own child," I cried uncontrollably. "Why can't I have a child? Why won't you answer me?" I felt abandoned.

That night, drained of my tears, I drifted off to sleep and had a dream. Jesus was dressed in a white, cassock-like robe adorned with a red surplice. It was night and I had an aerial view of the lights of a city and stars all around. I was face-to-face with Jesus. I told Him: "Oh, Jesus, I'm so glad you're here!" I was overcome with joy and anxiety when I asked, "Jesus, am I having a child? Am I pregnant?" He nodded his head, "Yes." I asked, "Will I have a boy?" Again, He nodded yes. At the same time I could understand what He was saying—not with words, but His expression seemed to convey disappointment over the doubt I had. He seemed to say, "What little faith you have in me." Instantly, I was humbled and sorry. I understood that all I really had to do was ask. It was something I had not done.

One week later I returned to the obstetrician. He was mystified to find I was ten weeks pregnant. My son was born during Easter week. The doctor said, "Somebody up there likes you. This is a miracle!" On April 6, 1977, Chad James Doran was born, four days before Easter. As I cradled my Easter miracle in my arms, I looked up and silently said, "Thank You, Jesus."

—Margie Doran

Margie Doran gleans her stories from her Catholic upbringing and life experience. Her poetry and articles have been widely published, and she has been a guest poet on "Poet's Corner," a radio program produced by Fairleigh Dickinson University. A mother and grandmother, she is the author of the children's book Sunflower Seranade, *and has lectured on creative writing and poetry in elementary schools throughout New Jersey. Margie teaches CCD and is chairwoman of her parish's Respect Life organization.*

A Blessing, No Matter What

Watching my nine-year-old son, Luke, glide by our home on roller blades, I stop and smile. Although doctors once predicted a life of severe disability—if he lived at all—I prayed for and believed the opposite. And sure enough, he has been healthy and active since the day he was born. Regardless of the outcome, I knew Luke would be a blessing from God, no matter what.

When I found out that I was pregnant with Luke I was thrilled that I was expecting again; now I would have three children to love. My four-year-old daughter, Jamie, was just as excited. "We're going to have a baby!" she shrieked. But a checkup in my fourth month showed a problem; the placenta had slipped into my cervix. "You could lose this baby," the doctor told me.

My heart sank. *No, not again*, I thought. My first pregnancy had ended in a miscarriage. And even though I had lost the baby early in the pregnancy, I had grieved. Now, as then, my baby was already part of me.

The doctor continued and said that in spite of this dangerous situation, the baby boy seemed fine. It would be hard to follow doctor's orders of bed rest, but I was willing to do anything for our little baby. The days spent waiting were agonizing. *Hang in there, Luke*, I would think, calling our baby by the name my husband, Jerry, and I had chosen.

Several weeks later at the next doctor's visit, I squeezed Jerry's hand as we waited for the results of my second ultrasound. *Please let everything be OK,* I prayed. But the doctor looked grave as he studied the screen. Following his gaze, I saw a mass at the back of the baby's head.

"What's wrong?" I asked, fearing the worst.

The doctor explained that there appeared to be a tumor growing at the base of Luke's skull—an irreversible and often fatal condition. Even if our baby lived, the tumor's pressure on his brain would cause severe brain damage and paralysis. "There's nothing we can do," he said. He told us we should consider terminating the pregnancy.

I had been willing to do anything to save our baby, but I was totally unprepared for this last piece of news. "This can't be happening," I thought as we drove home. I spent the next few days in tears. Would I be able to give this baby the special care he needed? And would I still be able to give Jamie and my son, Adam, the love and attention they needed, too? Every day, I prayed for answers, yet, none were forthcoming.

One morning, Jamie climbed into my lap with a worried look on her face.

"Why are you sad, Mommy?" she asked.

"Honey, the doctors think baby Luke is very sick," I told her gently.

"Don't worry, Mommy" Jamie said. "God will help us take care of him."

Tears came to my eyes at Jamie's trusting faith. I wanted that same sureness but could not stop myself from wondering, *Will I have the strength to cope? Can I handle what's to come?*

When our priest spoke that Sunday about the beauty and love of motherhood, it was more than I could bear. I fled the church, sobbing uncontrollably. My mind was flooded with doubts and fears and I was tempted to go home, not to return to Mass. Then, out of nowhere, I was consumed by this thought: *God would not abandon me.* Within moments I had regained a sense of peace that drew me back into church. I knelt and prayed that I would be given the strength to carry out God's will. I knew that the Creator of my baby already knew every inch of my baby's being and that He would not abandon me.

I began praying to St. Anne on a daily basis. My grandmother had received a healing after visiting St. Anne of de Beaupre in Quebec many years earlier. Of course I hoped and prayed for a miracle, but my faith in God went beyond that. For even if there wasn't a miracle in store for us, I knew God would give us what it would take to accept His blessing.

Although I knew it was irrational, I had a strong sense that Luke was going to be fine. I wanted to visit the St. Anne shrine not so much to ask for a miracle but as a testimony of my faith in God. This attitude was perceived by Jerry as a state of denial on my part. So when I asked him if he could take me to the shrine in Quebec, I knew I was asking a lot.

Jerry agreed, with apprehension. But after the trip, he, too, had received an indescribable sense of peace that he could accept whatever God gave us. The future was uncertain, but we were both on the same page: hopeful, but willing to accept God's will no matter what.

At the next doctor's visit, I informed my doctor that I was keeping our baby. He stared at me in disbelief. "That baby will never have a normal life!" he warned. I felt a fierce, protective love toward our unborn baby, no matter what life held in store for him.

"He'll have a family that loves him and wants him," I said with determination. "And he'll have the best life we can give him." The next day, I switched doctors. Kevin Deighton, M.D., had delivered our son, Adam. He listened to me with great sympathy.

"It doesn't look good right now," he said. "But all we can do is take one day at a time and hope for the best." With each flutter of life within me, I whispered a prayer of thanks. I pictured little Luke growing and each little kick filled me with hope.

I began keeping a diary of my thoughts, hopes, and prayers for Luke. I encouraged Jerry and Jamie to share what was in their hearts, too. Jamie drew a picture of a baby, and with my help wrote: "I was too little to help out when Adam was born. But now I'm four and will be a big helper when you get here." Jerry added: "Our love for you is very real and we will be the best parents we can."

You are our present from God, I wrote. *He wanted us to have you exactly the way He packaged you.* As my due date drew nearer, only the final pages remained blank.

Finally, in the delivery room, with Jerry at my side, Luke entered the world. I heard his first hearty yell and burst into tears. Then a nurse placed him in Jerry's arms.

Looking into the soft, newborn face of our tiny son, I cried "He looks perfect!" Jerry and I looked closely at Luke, searching for any imperfections, but saw nothing. Tests were run, but aside from a slight harmless swelling in his neck Luke was proclaimed a perfectly healthy baby!

Luke has grown into an active, outgoing boy. He loves sports, easily makes friends, and tries relentlessly to make his two younger brothers laugh. He has always been in great health, thanks be to God!

Some may say that the ultrasounds may have been erroneous and that Luke's life was never at risk. All I know is that my faith has grown through such an experience and my trust was strengthened in God. It no longer matters to me if the doctors were right or wrong, but that God never abandoned me through such a difficult time—no matter what.

—Kathy Smith

Kathy Smith and her husband, Jerry, have been married for fifteen years and home school their children. Kathy says that her pregnancy with Luke was a milestone in their lives, leading them to a deeper love for God and their Catholic Faith. Their sixth child was born in April, 2004.

Hug of Faith

Lifting my head from my pillow one morning, a sharp pain shot through my neck. "OUCH," I groaned. "I must have slept wrong last night." It was a stiff neck, the likes of which I had never experienced. With two young boys, Richard, twelve, and Michael, eight, I knew I needed to get on with my day—stiff neck or not.

Although I took a couple painkillers to help reduce the discomfort, the stiffness remained all day. It only seemed to get worse. By dinnertime, when my husband, Steve, came home from work, I told him I planned to see a doctor the next day. "There must be something else going on besides a bad night's sleep," I concluded. "I've never felt such pain from a stiff neck."

By bedtime, I had to opt out of our usual routine with the kids. After Richard and Michael had their pajamas on, they expected me to come to their bedroom for nighttime prayers. "Steve, I just can't do it tonight," I said. "My neck hurts too much. Will you please go and say prayers with them?"

The boys gingerly kissed me good night and reluctantly skipped the usual hugs. It would just hurt too much. "I hope you feel better," Michael comforted me, looking into my face.

"Thanks. I'm sure I will," I reassured him.

When Steve returned from saying goodnight to the boys, he told me they had prayed for my neck. "That's nice, honey," I said, somewhat distracted by the pain. A few minutes later Michael was out of his room and in the hall, looking into the room.

"Mom," he announced, "I prayed for you to be healed."

"I know, honey," I said. "Thank you." He turned to leave but then paused and turned back.

"Is your neck feeling better?" he asked.

My neck was not one bit better. I looked into my son's trusting eyes and considered my throbbing pain. How could I answer no? I could not disappoint such a strong faith.

"Yes," I lied. "It feels a little bit better."

His face lit up with a smile. But then he started running toward me. Horrified, I realized that he was going to hug me. *Oh no!* I thought in a panic. *Don't let me cry out and disappoint him*, I prayed.

I braced myself for a hug that was sure to hurt. But as Michael wrapped his arms around me, all pain vanished. Shocked, I stood up and moved my neck around. The pain was gone; every last trace of it. "Michael, my neck really is better!" I cried. "It's completely healed!" I was in awe.

That night Michael was a very happy little boy and I was his very enlightened mother. I thought I was the one who had to give Michael his faith. I learned it was not me but God who would ultimately handle that job. When Jesus told us that faith the size of a mustard seed could move mountains, my son believed Him. His sure faith moved the pain right out of my neck.

—Mary Frovarp

Mary Frovarp and her husband, Steve, live in Hazen, North Dakota. Their sons, Richard and Michael, are now attending college.

What I Want to Be
From a Daughter to Her Mother

How can you thank someone so dear?
How can you show your love?
She is someone who can calm any fear
With her hands like a gentle dove.
How can you thank someone for your life?
How can you show what you feel?
She mastered the role of a perfect wife
With an unmatchable zeal.
How can you thank someone so kind?
How can you show that you care?
She's someone who proves that love is blind
With willing forgiveness to share.
There are no words to show
A gratitude so great.
How can I make her know
That I admire her every trait?
I'll simply love her every day,
And hope that she will see
That I'm following in her way,
Because she's what I want to be.

—Carly Cavins

Incomparable Joy

Before I was married, I was worried that becoming pregnant would be difficult because my menstrual cycles were sporadic and infrequent. My husband, Jeff, told me he was marrying me for me and not because of future children. That was comforting, but as the years passed, we both felt a longing for children. We considered adoption, but on our minuscule salary at the time, adoption fees were far beyond us. After seven years of marriage, I went to a fertility doctor and after being prescribed the drug Clomid I was pregnant within two months. We were thrilled beyond belief and were blessed with a little girl we named Carly.

I thought certainly getting pregnant would be easy now. Just take Clomid and boom—I'd be pregnant. It didn't turn out that way. We tried for several more years to conceive and looked into adoption again, but neither route succeeded. To keep our sanity, we put the "having another child issue" to rest.

For Carly's tenth birthday we bought her a beautiful cat. We all loved him so much that we bought another one that looked just like him. This breed of cat is very affectionate, and the new kitten wanted to be held all the time. He would drape himself around my shoulders as I did dishes and meowed like a baby whenever I put him down. Finally, I made a sling for the cat and carried him around like an infant.

Jeff came home from work to find me toting our "son." Seeing my maternal instincts in action, he said, "I know what you need. You need another cat!" He was being loving and sincere, but I snapped at him.

"I don't want another cat! I don't want to raise cats! I want to raise a baby *human!*"

Jeff's eyes glazed over. "We put all that behind us! You know how much we tried!"

I knew we had put the issue to rest in our heads, but in my emotions it was there bigger than ever. "I don't want to spend my energy loving cats. I want to love children that will last for eternity. I want to invest in children. We have a home with plenty of room…Why don't we adopt?"

The idea of starting diapers and sleepless nights again after so many years was a jolt. But Jeff could see how much I wanted more children, so he agreed. "We'll tell everyone we know that we're interested in adopting and see what happens," he suggested.

I was thrilled and began filling out forms and checking into adoption options. Not long after our decision, a friend who had recently adopted called.

"I know a young woman who is pregnant and looking for a Catholic family. She is due in two months. Would you like to contact her?"

I had heard so many stories about private adoptions falling through that I didn't let myself get too excited, but we arranged to talk to the young woman by phone. As we waited for her call, Jeff asked one more time if I was sure I wanted to go through with this. My eyes filled up with tears. I knew I wanted to hold that little bundle and kiss him and watch him grow until he was ready to face the world as an adult. I wanted to fill him with love and give him all I had. "I just want to love," I sniffled.

We listened to the sweet, curious voice of the young mother on the phone. She asked us several questions about how we would raise the baby she was carrying. (She told us the ultrasound showed it was girl.) Her voice grew very excited when I told her we would teach the child to play the violin like we had our eleven-year-old daughter, Carly. "I play the violin," she told us. The conversation held many interesting correlations between her and us. We knew we were a good fit.

We arranged for the birth mother to fly to Alabama the week before she was to deliver. She stayed at the home of my friend. As we went to the house to meet her in person, I became nervous to meet the woman who carried our child. We sat at the dinner table observing one another. She was so much taller than I, left-handed like me, and had sparkling brown eyes. "What will you name her?" she asked.

Jeff and I had decided on her name a few days before. "Jacqueline Joy," we replied.

Tears sprang to her eyes and she said through a big smile, "That's my middle name! My parents waited so long to have me that they were filled with joy when I was born."

"That's how we feel about Jacqueline Joy!" we said, sharing smiles and tears.

On her due date, the doctor decided to induce her. Jeff and I wished her our best, while my friend came to be her birthing coach. Jeff had to return to work to do his live television show, so Carly and I waited in the waiting room. I could hardly believe that night I would have a new baby girl. Around 5 p.m. my friend came out to announce that the baby and birth mother were doing fine.

When Jaki was thirty minutes old, Carly and I got to go in to see her. She was squalling at the top of her lungs and her long limbs were flailing in every direction. I couldn't wait to hold her. The nurse corralled her flapping arms and legs and bundled her into a blanket. The hospital kindly allowed me to stay in a private room until Jaki was ready to be discharged. Jeff arrived as soon as his show was done, delighted to hold his now sleeping daughter. We were so thrilled to have her.

During the next few days the birth mother would request for Jaki to be brought to her room, so I would wait and wonder if the birth mother was changing her mind. She had five days to decide. I imagined the agony she was going through, holding a little part of her that she was giving up so the baby would have a stable family. It had to be heart wrenching. She was as sad as we were happy. Her only joy was in knowing we would love her and raise her to love God. Our sadness was in knowing the grief she would suffer at parting with her baby and the task ahead for her to piece her life together.

We brought Jaki home and began the sleepless nights and countless diapers, just the way we wanted it. The cats were indignant that this little bundle took their place. They must have thought we had set up the crib just for them.

Full-time mothering had been in full swing for eighteen months when we received a call from a lawyer who had counseled us just before Jaki's adoption. "Are you still wanting to adopt? We found your name in our files and you fit the profile for a baby girl who will be born in about six weeks." Another baby seemed to be dropping from heaven right into our laps.

I called Jeff who was lunching with a friend. "Do you want another daughter?" I asked.

"What?" he stammered. I explained to him the few details I had about the birth mother and baby. We immediately decided to say yes. She seemed to be walking right into our hearts.

In six week's time we rearranged the house to move our preteen to a room downstairs and moved toddler Jaki into her own room so the new baby could have the crib. We received the anticipated call from the lawyer when Antonia Teresa was born and hurried to the hospital to see her. She was a chubby, restful little cherub, peacefully sleeping in her nursery crib. All of us took turns holding her. Carly and Jaki were delighted with their new sister. I stayed in the nursery for long shifts until Toni was released from the hospital two days later.

Adoption has been such a tremendous blessing to my husband and me. It brings a smile to my face (and often tears of joy) whenever I reflect on how Jaki and Toni came into our lives. Now as the girls grow, we see how wonderful it is to have two so close in age. They are great companions. True sisters. Their noise, music, laughter, and personalities have filled our lives with incomparable joy.

—Emily Cavins

For Love of Mom

Chris Zorich has had a storybook football career. Coming from a Chicago ghetto, he became an All-American at Notre Dame, where he led a national championship team. Then he earned a roster spot in the National Football League with the Chicago Bears, his hometown team. Though now retired, he is still admired by fans nationwide for his ferocious play.

But Zorich is even more remarkable for his off-the-field accomplishments. For it's outside football that he is a true All-American. Zorich—who prays daily at a Catholic church—faithfully delivers food baskets to the poor, spends hours with orphaned and abused children, and sponsors a scholarship at Notre Dame for needy students as well.

To really understand this young man, though, you have to know that during his career he visited his mother's grave before each Bears game in Chicago. The bond between mother and son was extraordinarily close. His background indicates the reasons why.

Zorich was raised by his mother, Zora, in a tiny apartment in a housing project in one of Chicago's worst neighborhoods. Zora, the daughter of Yugoslavian immigrants, was a single parent. Chris's father left his mother after she told him she was pregnant, and she was forced to fend for herself and her son.

Disabled by diabetes, Zora survived on $250 a month. She and Chris dined on macaroni and cheese night after night. When the cupboard was bare, young Chris hopped on a bus and carried rice and powdered milk home from the public-aid office. Or he stood in line at the local church's food pantry.

Being poor was tough. But being poor and different was nearly intolerable. A biracial child, Chris was taunted with insults both by the blacks in his neighborhood and the whites he met elsewhere.

Not surprisingly, the neighborhood was a cruel place for most kids. But Chris was no angel either. He estimates that he was involved in 100 childhood fights; one of his pastimes was hurling rocks and bricks at passing police cars.

Chris' world was mean and nasty, except for his mom, who was loving and forgiving. She also set limits. Once, when he was eleven, Chris insisted on going outside, though the streetlights were on and his personal curfew had begun.

Frustrated at his rebellion, Zora lightly slapped him on the arm. Then she began crying. Chris joined in. The two spent the rest of the evening talking and watching old movies on television. At that point, Chris realized that home was the one place where he was safe and loved.

Zora let her son know that God loved him, too, and they sometimes prayed together. Zora also taught Chris that the color of his skin was unimportant. "My mother never talked about race," says Zorich. "All she said was, 'You're my son. I love you.'"

But Zora was under no illusions about the lure of the streets. One day, she sat down with Chris at the kitchen table and warned him outright. "Listen," she said, "You have a choice. Do you want to go with the gangs and the drugs? Or do you want to make something of yourself?"

The one thing Chris desperately wanted in life was to make his mom proud. Someday, he promised himself then, he would be a success and move her out of the neighborhood. No way would he let her down.

Chris had joined the football team at Chicago Vocational High School as a freshman. Early on, he was not particularly talented; he did not even especially like the game. But it kept him out of trouble.

Head coach John Potocki had noticed Zorich in the school hallway and encouraged him to join the team. "There was something deep inside pushing him," says Potocki. "You could feel it. He was bursting with energy."

CVS was a famous football school. The legendary Dick Butkus played there before achieving fame with the Chicago Bears. Despite shoddy facilities, the school was a place where a teen athlete could dream about glory.

Zorich soon latched on to football as his and his mom's escape from their hard life. True, he was only marginally talented. But if hard work counted, then he had a chance. Day after day, he honed his skills. He grew stronger and faster. By the time Zorich was a senior, a Notre Dame recruiter came to one of his games. Zorich made two extraordinary plays that won over the recruiter.

When Zorich first heard Notre Dame was interested in him, he was confused. Wasn't that some place in France with a hunchback? But by the time he set foot on campus, he was well aware that Notre Dame was the mecca of college football. It was the place of Rockne, the four Horsemen, Touchdown Jesus, national titles. Zorich was so revved up he hardly slept his first two weeks on campus.

College broadened Zorich. The rough edges of the scrappy street fighter were smoothed out. He learned to play the piano. He fed the ducks on campus. He fell in love with the poetry of Robert Frost. Yet, his favorite passage from Frost indicated that he still was the same person, determined to make his mom proud:

The woods are lovely, dark and deep.
But I have promises to keep,
And miles to go before I sleep,
And miles to go before I sleep.

Notre Dame expanded his horizons in another way. Like other Notre Dame players, Zorich attended Masses in the dormitories and lit candles in the Grotto before the big games. He listened intently as head coach Lou Holtz weaved in quotes from the Bible in his pep talks. The faith at Notre Dame was practically part of the curriculum.

On the field, Zorich became a star, a fierce defensive lineman who dominated play. When he was a senior, *Sports Illustrated* said he should win the Heisman Trophy as college football's best player. The magazine also called him the toughest player in college football.

Throughout college, Zorich remained as close as ever to his mom. They spoke on the phone nearly every day, sometimes for hours. She came to the games in South Bend and chatted with Coach Holtz and mothers of other players. She was in her glory. Zora, of course, was also relieved that her son had left behind the gangs and drugs. Not all of her son's peers had been so fortunate. One day, she told Chris how the police had found someone he knew, brutally murdered.

After Zorich played his last college game in January of 1991, he returned home. His mom had watched the game on television the day before. Zorich had called her, told her that he loved her, and that he would see her the next day. But when he arrived home, he looked through a window and saw his mother lying on the floor. Zorich, the strongest man on the Notre Dame squad, broke down the door.

His mother had died of a heart attack. The grief Chris felt then was by far more painful than any football injury. Through the years, she had shielded him from harm. Now he was helpless to save her. He had lived his life for her. Now she was gone.

But before long, Zorich realized in one sense nothing had changed. His mission still was to be the best person he could be.

"My goal is to see her laugh and smile again," he says. "Everything about my mom was good. If I can live like she did, I know I'll see her again."

Although football pundits questioned the Bears' drafting of Zorich as high as they did, he proved the critics wrong. On the starting lineup, Chris averaged 100+ tackles per season, placing him among the league's best defensive lineman. John Madden, the zesty TV football commentator, put Zorich on his All-Madden Team, an honor reserved for the game's blue-collar heroes. Chris retired in 1997 from the NFL to pursue a law degree at Notre Dame Law School in order to further his ability to help those in need. In 2000, he married Camille Henderson, a native Chicagoan. In May of 2002, Chris received his law degree and currently works for a Chicago law firm. He continues to be active in charitable and community organizations.

Zorich never forgot his mission. He started the Christopher Zorich Foundation in 1993 to honor his mother. The Foundation's programs offer diverse community support. In the off-season, Chris would spend six hours a day on charitable efforts. Rather than sit in the office, he preferred to deliver corsages to women's shelters and bags of groceries to the needy. His charity neatly recalled his own hardships. The flowers, for example, were a reminder of his impoverished boyhood when he innocently picked dandelions and other weeds to present to his mom.

Robert Frost wrote about taking the less-traveled road. Zorich took such a road, a path that began in poverty and fisticuffs and blossomed into prayer and promises. It is a road that always passes his mom's grave, a reminder to him that time is short and good deeds beckon.

—Jay Copp

Jay Copp is a part-time freelance writer and a full-time communications manager for a non-profit organization. He lives near Chicago with his wife, Laura, and three young sons.

*The mother is the most precious possession
of the nation, so precious that society
advances its highest well-being when it
protects the functions of the mother.*

—Ellen Key

A Christmas Delivery

This year, Santa, could you make a car for my mom?
If you can't make her a car, could you make her a
raincoat? My mom has to walk a lot to take my sister to
the doctor. She also walks me to school every day and
when it rains, she gets very wet. Please help, if you can.

As customer relations coordinator for the Postal Service in Tampa, I take on the project each year to assure that every letter addressed to Santa at the North Pole is answered. But some letters require a little special attention, like this one we received one December, from seven-year-old Nicole Colon of Carrollwood.

We knew we had to try to help, but how? Then letter carrier Jim Cantrell heard about the letter. "Phyllis Lancaster, a customer on my route, is selling a 1985 Honda Accord," he said. "Maybe she'd sell it at a reduced price."

We contacted Phyllis who, moved by the letter, said, "Take the car."

Amazed by her generosity, Jim thanked her. He then stopped by Dale's Auto Parts, where Linda Marsonek, the owner, said, "We'll donate the labor, if you'll cover the parts," after reading Nicole's letter.

The employees at the Carrollwood Post Office took up a collection to pay for the parts and the Glass Doctor replaced the cracked windshield.

When I called Nicole's mother, Madeleine, to tell her about the car, she was stunned, "I knew she had written to Santa, but I never thought…"

My heart overflowed with sympathy as she explained that without a car, each time Nicole's baby sister had to visit the doctor, Madeleine had to walk six miles. Plus, she was walking two miles twice a day to drop Nicole off at school!

No wonder Nicole had written her letter!

We agreed to keep the car a surprise from Nicole. On Christmas Eve, as Nicole stepped outside of her friend's house with her mother, her eyes grew wide when she saw the sight. A car in the driveway, covered with a big red bow, a backseat full of toys and fifteen postal employees on the front lawn! "See Mommy!" Nicole said. "Wishes *can* come true!"

As everyone was hugging that afternoon, I realized how right she was. This one small request, from a little girl for her mother, had transformed our postal employees into a very special group of Santa's elves!

—Bridget Robertson

Bridget Robertson is a twenty-year employee of the United States Postal Service and currently serving as the customer relations coordinator in Tampa, Florida. She is very involved with numerous non-profit organizations and foundations in the Tampa area, serving on several boards. She has been married to her husband Dale for fourteen years, and has four cats and two birds.

Billy: A Family Story

Billy Lutter tumbled to the wooden floor of his home. His parents picked him up and tried again to help him walk. It was no use. This was 1939, and doctors had been telling the Lutters to institutionalize five-year-old Billy for some time, a common recommendation then for children with physical and mental disabilities. Billy's parents, a steelworker and a homemaker, struggled with the decision to send Billy away.

"This was back in the Depression," says Fred Lutter, Billy's older brother by two years. "Things were tough all around. It was a very tearful situation." Their hearts breaking, the Lutters drove Billy from their home outside Chicago to a state facility 200 miles away. They visited regularly for a year. But administrators, worried that such meetings might upset the other residents, advised them to stop coming.

"My brother realized who his parents were," Fred says. "To be left like that was very traumatic. I felt very sad to see my parents in such turmoil."

The years rolled by. Billy's siblings got married and had their own children. Everybody thought about Billy, but his name was not spoken. Billy's parents grew old and, as they aged, grew infirm. They had done what they thought was best for Billy, but his absence had left a gaping, raw wound for the family.

The Lutters' sad story inadvertently took a happier turn thirty-five years later. It began when Julie Hess signed up her six-year-old daughter Jenny, who had Down Syndrome, for a religious-education program for the disabled. Sadly,

Jenny never had a chance to take a class. She died shortly afterward.

Julie Hess nevertheless went on to volunteer with the program that she had hoped her daughter might enjoy. By 1987, she had become a full-time employee of the Archdiocese of Chicago's Special Religious Education Division.

One of Julie's favorite students was an easygoing older man with a white mustache and gray hair. His records labeled him mildly retarded. He suffered from cerebral palsy and needed a walker to get around. His hearing was bad, but he knew a bit of sign language.

Despite his circumstances, Bill had a special spark. Though he could only say a handful of words, he was a good communicator. And he radiated cheerfulness. Bill was especially religious. He wore a cross around his neck and enjoyed being in church. He took part enthusiastically in the sacraments.

"He's very prayerful," Julie says. "He has a deep sense of the sacred. God is a presence in his life, bringing him peace and a reason to hope."

Bill grew very animated when Julie talked about family, so she decided to find at least one member of his family. But the group home told her that Bill had no family. Even still, Julie was determined. As the years passed, she took up Bill's cause with renewed passion. Finally, in 1993, an administrator gave Julie a name and phone number. The suburban number was for Kathy Dever, Bill's sister.

Only brother Fred was old enough to have memories of Billy. His sisters, Kathy and Bonnie, knew next to nothing. "My brother said he was a vegetable," Kathy says, "and that it was best that we didn't see him. You have to understand the times. People ask us, 'How could your parents give him up?' There was no schooling like there is today. No way would they do the same thing today. But things are different today."

As time went by, Fred thought more and more about Billy. What was he like? Was it possible to bring him back to the family? It was the fear of the unknown, not knowing what to expect, that kept Fred from initiating contact.

It was decided that Fred would meet with Billy first. On the day of the meetings, Fred brought a photo of their mother. Bill studied the photo. Julie Hess realized the challenge. "Bill understands family," she says. "But how do we get him to understand this is his mother?"

Julie put the photo on Bill's chest and pointed at him. "His face suddenly changed and lit up like a light bulb," Julie recalls. "He nodded and got excited."

The next challenge was to help Bill understand that Fred was his brother. Julie put the photo by Bill and signed "mother" and placed the photo by Fred and signed "mother." An amazed look rushed over his face.

"Bud," Bill said.

Fred nearly fell off the chair. "That's what he called me when he was little," Fred said.

That night, Fred called his sister Kathy. "I just met my brother," Fred sobbed.

Bill's sisters visited two weeks later and then it was time for Bill to meet his mother. It happened on Mother's Day in the church basement, where they embraced for the first time in fifty years.

Until she died three years later, mother and son were inseparable, at least emotionally. "They saw each other, held hands and never let go, at least figuratively," says Hess. "She was so happy when they were together." Fred says that Bill filled a big hole in their mother's life. "She felt so relieved to have her family back again," he adds.

Bill now spends his weekends and holidays with his family. He has bonded with his great-nephews and great-nieces. "He loves kids," says Kathy.

Not long ago, Bill visited Fred in Florida, where the elder brother has retired. Being near the clouds on the plane ride stirred his religious feelings. "He pointed at the clouds and made the sign of the cross," Kathy says. "He thought we were up by Jesus."

The Lutter family has since moved Bill into a more pleasant group home in a suburb closer to his sisters. "This has changed his life entirely," Julie says. "He held on to the memories of his family for his whole life, and now they've become real."

—Jay Copp

Editors' Note: You may recognize this story from the previous book in the series, Amazing Grace for the Catholic Heart. *Although we received many more entries for this book than we needed, we felt compelled to include this poignant story of a mother and son.*

Jay Copp's biography appears after For Love of Mom *earlier in this chapter.*

Casting My Cares on the Lord

A number of years ago my husband was out of work for an extended period of time. We had two children and would soon have no food. The little unemployment money coming in was just enough to pay the rent, and we would have just five to ten dollars a week for groceries. It was enough for some potatoes, cornmeal, and bacon for seasoning.

Luckily, I had an Irish grandmother who had lived through famine and destitution. She taught me how to forage for greens when I was a small child. And so, while my neighbor was poisoning his dandelions, I was out watering mine. My children learned to call it "God's garden" as we gathered prickly pear fruit—cactus flowers—and greens for cooking. We were never healthier, but we were familiar with hunger, too.

At the beginning of this difficult time, we had the most stubborn cat you would ever want to meet. He would hunt, but he was also adamant about eating only one kind of cat food. I'd had him for twelve years and did not mind the money so much when the cat foot company ran a special rebate of ten cents per label. Suddenly his food was less expensive than any other brand at the time. For months I kept throwing those labels into a drawer.

Fluffy, as he was named, developed an illness and passed away just about two months into the very lean times. It was the last straw, and I sat down and cried like a baby. He was always there to listen and purr understandingly when I did not want to worry my husband with just how bad things were. I had forgotten that Jesus was with me, experiencing every pain I felt.

Looking back on this time and many other occasions, however, I can say that Christ never once left my side. Faith and fear cannot coexist, but in my blindness I had skipped right past fear and into despair. I simply could see no way out. It was not until I was cleaning out a drawer in the kitchen that a moment of faith arrived. The drawer used to contain food, but now I found cat food labels—thirteen dollars and forty cents worth of labels!

I was ecstatic! I was sure God had heard my prayers and sent a small answer. I was overwhelmed with thanksgiving. My children came in from the yard to sing love songs of worship to the One who had the power to help in even the most desperate times. But my heart sank again when I read the directions for redeeming the labels. A sales slip was required for each purchase. First I prayed. Then I wrote a letter explaining that I had bought all the food from the same store and for the same amount. I included the one receipt I could find, even though it was several months old. I also gave a few details of our circumstances and mailed it.

Life returned to normal for a few weeks and my faith began to sag. I had been so sure that God was helping us, but then nothing happened. It was like lifting weights. First the struggle, then the relief, only to begin the struggle again. A few weeks later, with a sense of great repetitive effort, I dragged myself to the mailbox. Among the usual junk mail I found a letter of some kind and walked all the way home without opening it because I was afraid it was another bill.

I sat at my kitchen table staring at it for a while before I opened it. It was a letter from the cat food company explaining that the funds for every label had to be accounted for and many people had sent in labels with no return address on them. Since the company could not redeem those rebate requests, it was including them in my refund amount.

My heart pounded as I saw a check for eighty-seven dollars and ten cents!

This time I remembered to thank God first. I did not ask for another thing because I had been reading the Bible and found a verse that said, "Cast all your anxieties on Him, for He cares about you" (1 Peter 5:7). All along, God had been trying to teach me to leave my cares with Him and let Him care for them instead of worrying about them. All I had to do was love Him—even though I had very little faith and was exceedingly human.

My children came in the house, and I told them we were going to the market. When we reached the store, I told my daughter to put everything in the cart that we really needed and that I would find the rest. I also admonished her not to pick up items we did not really need.

When we arrived at the checkout counter, I could see my daughter's anxiety as the shopping basket was emptied. The total came to eighty-seven dollars and eight cents. We had two pennies left over. Immediately my three-year-old son started asking for some gum. In that split second I saw what a true Father provided. Everything we needed was there, as well as something so important to His little children.

When I got back into the car, I started to cry. My daughter asked, "Mom, what's wrong? We have everything we needed." When I looked at her I realized that I was seeing my whole family through our Father's eyes. We were all His little ones and so beloved that He sacrificed more than I could even contemplate to prove it to us.

"No, we didn't." I replied. "I didn't have enough faith, so God had to help me see who really takes care of us."

When I got home, I was greeted by my husband, who had tears in his eyes when he saw the groceries. He was holding the phone in his hand. A call had just come offering him a job at a restaurant. Eventually he became the manager. But that is another story, one of many others that happened when I was at the end of my faith and could hold on no longer. What I learned during those times was to let go of my frail end of the rope and let God hold me. He was there all along, just waiting to catch me. You see, the only place a child of God can fall is into the Father's hands.

—Adrian McKee

Adrian McKee has two grown children and five grandchildren. She lives in the San Bernardino Mountains of Southern California. She is a sculptor, painter, and writer.

Five Miracles in One Day

"I can't do this anymore," I told my husband, Kevin. After three years of painful fertility treatments with no results, enough was enough. The strong medication and the extreme hormone surges brought physical pain and put me on an emotional roller coaster. I did not want to live like that anymore.

Even before I married, I knew conceiving a child would be difficult. When I was a teenager, I was diagnosed with polycystic ovarian disease. My health was fine, but my chances of ever getting pregnant were slim.

Kevin and I shared a deep desire to raise children, but we both agreed it did not matter if they were our own flesh and blood. We prayed to God for children and asked Him to lead us to the ones that needed us. Kevin and I felt drawn to foster care. Our caseworker understood that our ultimate dream was to adopt, so when she learned of twins that were free for adoption, she called us immediately.

Five-year-old twins, Brittany and Brandon, came to live with us on July 3, 1997. I was a little scared at the enormity of my instant responsibility, but still, my heart sang, "I'm a mom, I'm a mom!" Our prayers had been answered.

But within the week, we received crushing news. The caseworker had been mistaken. The plan was to eventually reunite the twins with their birth mother. It was my responsibility to make the hour and a half drive into Buffalo once a week for a two-hour visitation with their birth mother. I wanted to be a mother to these kids, but I would do whatever was best for them. I had asked God to send me children that needed me, and whatever the outcome,

Brittany and Brandon needed the love and care I could give them.

Within three weeks of coming to our home, Brittany asked, "Is it OK if I call you Mom?" It was what I yearned for.

"Yes, I would like that," I told her. By the next week, Brandon also began calling us Mom and Dad. I loved them more and more each day but my heart had to hold back; they were not mine to keep. The hope that I could one day be their mother for real grew deep within me.

Four months after they came to live with us, we celebrated Thanksgiving. As we went around the table explaining what we were all thankful for, my heart melted when it got to the twins. "I'm thankful for my mom and dad," Brittany announced smiling at us.

"Me, too," chimed in Brandon.

Six months after the children had been placed with us, their birth mother stopped showing up for visits. She also had never enrolled in the court-mandated treatment necessary for her to regain custody of her children. "If this continues, she could have her rights terminated and then they would be free for adoption," the caseworker told us.

When the year was up, we met with the birth mother and the caseworker. The mother decided she would relinquish her rights if she knew we would adopt them. My heart soared. I did not have to hold back my love any longer. I could truly be the twins' mom—forever.

All that was left was paperwork and a final court proceeding; then the kids would be ours. Returning home, we excitedly told the twins that their wish to be "Murphys forever" would come true. That was in July of 1998. In September, I received a phone call from the caseworker that cut through my heart. "I have some bad news," she began.

"The birth mother has an aunt who has come forward and is pursuing adopting the twins."

"No!" I cried. "They barely even know her! Somehow you have to stop this!" I ran outside to be with my children. I hugged them close and cried. "I love you both so much," I told them. "Your mother's aunt wants to adopt you, but I'm not going to let her."

We held each other tight. "We don't even know her," they cried. "We don't want to go to her!"

Kevin and I retained a lawyer and were ready to fight with all we had. But the law at that time decided heavily in favor of any biological family members. Our case did not look good. The thought of losing my children was unbearable. They had made me realize how much I loved being a mom. "Please God," I prayed. "Don't let me lose my children." I could not imagine being childless again. And yet, I had to face that very likely possibility.

In October, I returned to my fertility specialist. Even though I knew it was a long shot, I decided to try one more time to have a child of my own. But by November I was again experiencing terrible problems with the treatment to increase ovulation. One day I felt so sick, Kevin stayed home from work. When I called my doctor, he told me to come into his office that morning. Shortly after I hung up with the doctor, our lawyer called. "I need to see you and Kevin," he said. Both offices were in Buffalo, so we arranged to see them one right after the other that morning.

Our lawyer had unbelievable news: "The aunt has stated she will withdraw her petition on the condition that you two agree to adopt the children." We were ecstatic. In spite of still feeling ill, my spirits soared. God had answered our prayers. The children would really be ours! No one would ever take them from us. I cried tears of joy.

When we continued on to the doctor's office I was so happy that I did not even mind the prospect of failing to conceive again. The doctor had me do some blood work and then went over the results with me. "I have some great news," he announced. "You're pregnant." Before the unbelievable news could sink in, he continued: "But there is a slight problem. It's probably twins."

"No, I'm adopting twins," I laughed.

"No, you are pregnant with twins," he laughed in return. "Your hormone levels are so high, it must be twins."

Initially, there were medical complications that threatened to end the pregnancy. I had prayed so hard to keep Brittany and Brandon, I feared that now I would lose my other babies. "Please God," I pleaded, "let me have them all."

Within the month, my situation improved and the pregnancy progressed. At six weeks, I went in for an ultrasound. "There are three heartbeats!" the doctor announced. I could not wait to call Kevin at work.

"How does three sound?" I asked him.

"You mean the twins and one more baby?" he asked.

"No, I mean the twins and triplets." We were both too excited to be scared. Before I knew I was pregnant, I had prayed a prayer to conceive to Our Blessed Mother. I had prayed it three times in a row. It is a family joke now that it is a good thing I did not pray it seven times.

Kevin and I had the name Kiley picked out for one of the babies. We wanted to include the twins in our family situation so we asked them each to help us name one of the babies. Brittany picked out the name Emilee for one of her new little sisters and Brandon selected the name Matthew for his little brother. The triplets were born on April 27, 1999. Nearly a year later the triplets were with us when the judge banged down her gavel to symbolize the adoption proceedings were complete. Brandon beamed and announced: "Now we're forever Murphys!"

And now, I am forever thanking God for giving me five miracles all in one day. Being a mom to my five little Murphys is a greater blessing than I ever could have imagined.

—Jody Murphy

Jody Murphy and her husband, Kevin, have been married for twelve years. Jody is from Olean, New York, and is the youngest of nine children. After the twins were placed with them, Kevin and Jody bought the large house Jody had grown up in, only to discover that they would be raising their growing family in it. The twins are now eleven and the triplets, four.